Medicine, Education, and the Arts in Contemporary Native America

Medicine, Education, and the Arts in Contemporary Native America

Strong Women, Resilient Nations

Edited by Clifford E. Trafzer,
Donna L. Akers, and Amanda K. Wixon

LEXINGTON BOOKS
Lanham • Boulder • New York • London

Published by Lexington Books
An imprint of The Rowman & Littlefield Publishing Group, Inc.
4501 Forbes Boulevard, Suite 200, Lanham, Maryland 20706
www.rowman.com

86-90 Paul Street, London EC2A 4NE

British Library Cataloguing in Publication Information Available

Library of Congress Cataloging-in-Publication Data

Names: Trafzer, Clifford E., editor. | Akers, Donna L., editor. | Wixon, Amanda K., editor.
Title: Medicine, education, and the arts in contemporary Native America : strong women, resilient nations / edited by Clifford E. Trafzer, Donna L. Akers, and Amanda K. Wixon.
Description: Lanham : Lexington Books, [2022] | Includes bibliographical references and index. | Summary: "This book highlights indigenous American women throughout modern American history, countering past stereotypes by offering twenty original scholarly chapters featuring historical and biographical analyses of Native American women who excelled in education, health, medicine, and the arts"— Provided by publisher.
Identifiers: LCCN 2021056340 (print) | LCCN 2021056341 (ebook) | ISBN 9781666907025 (cloth) | ISBN 9781666907049 (paper) | ISBN 9781666907032 (ebook)
Subjects: LCSH: Indian women—United States—Biography. | Indians of North America—United States—Biography.
Classification: LCC E98.W8 M44 2022 (print) | LCC E98.W8 (ebook) | DDC 305.48/897—dc23/eng/20211129
LC record available at https://lccn.loc.gov/2021056340
LC ebook record available at https://lccn.loc.gov/2021056341

Dedication

We Thank the Ancestors and Our Teachers

We Remember Missing and Murdered Native American
and First Nations Women

For Éléonore Tecumseh Sioui and Rita Coosewoon

For Aishki, Mary, Genevieve, Sarah, and Michael

Contents

Preface

For many years, much of our research as authors and editors has focused on the history, culture, and spiritual beliefs of Native Americans. We have also investigated various aspect of women's history, particularly among Indigenous tribes where women have played significant roles since the creation of the Native Universe. Some of that research has depended on the generosity of tribal elders willing to share their knowledge, experience, wisdom, and stories.

In Native worldviews, women are the life-givers and have special spiritual powers that are essential to the well-being and continuation of the tribe. Recognizing the central role of women reflects the importance in tribal life of harmony and balance which rejects Western world views of gender hierarchy and male domination. Among the many important aspects of Native women's lives, the preservation of tribal oral traditions has been instrumental in conveying knowledge and wisdom from one generation to the next. These rich traditions provide a deeper understanding of Native cultures and history, and an essential Indigenous perspective that counters much erroneous information in the libraries, archives, and special collections used by many scholars as authoritative accounts. The value of oral traditions, passed from generation to generation, is inestimable in not only correcting the historical record authored by non-Native people, but also in preserving important cultural and social knowledge often overlooked by the military, government officials, missionaries, and male writers as "unimportant." In this volume, we pass on the generous contributions of Native women, who share with us their memories, their stories, and their wisdom. These keepers of tribal history and traditions greatly enrich our understanding of Native peoples, their values, their lives, and their worldviews.

Serrano elder Martha Manuel Chacon and Pauline Ormego Murillo once explained that they preferred to share their tribe's history and culture with scholars than have them make incorrect assumptions about their tribe's past. Since the beginning of time, Native American women have kept tribal and familial histories. They have been the foundation and strength of Native nations. They remain the strength of the Native nations today, serving their people in so many diverse ways and giving of themselves and their time to benefit others, including non-Natives interested in learning more about Indigenous people and cultures.

When Donna Akers was a small girl, her Grandmother would gather the children on the porch on hot summer evenings in Oklahoma to tell them about their heritage as Choctaw people. Her Grandmother asked the children to hold hands, close their eyes, and go on a journey back in time with her to the Great Mother Mound, *Nanih Waiya*, in the old Choctaw Nation across the Great Father River in what is today called Mississippi. As they traveled, the children "saw" and "heard" the cries of the Long People Clan lamenting the forced removal implemented by the Long Knives who wanted their land. They traveled with Grandmother along the Trail Where They Cried in their terrifying journey by foot over hundreds of miles, many of them in summer dresses and barefoot in the middle of winter storms. For weeks, they traveled through the Louisiana swamps in chest-deep water, where children and mothers drowned when, exhausted and starving, they slipped quietly under the water. In many successive summer nights in Oklahoma, these Choctaw children touched hands with their ancestors, the sacred places, and essential knowledge. They learned how Choctaws struggled, yet overcame, persisted, and emerged from overwhelming odds, battered and scarred but determined to survive. These and many other lessons are passed down in today's Native families through their rememberings, conveying wisdom and hope through oral traditions.

In 2019, Wendat elder and professor Georges Sioui published *Eatenonha: Native Roots of Democracy*, which pointed out that women and those that identify as women are truly mothers of the nation. He argues that women, past and present, hold a central place within the Native Universe since every person is born from a mother's womb just as humans are born of the earth's womb. Sioux argues that women are the first creators and thus meant to be the nurturers of human societies. His arguments are supported by Professor Kathryn Magee Labelle in her book, *Daughters of Aataentsic: Life Stories from Seven Generations*, which offers community-based research and the voices and contributions of seven generations of Wendat women leaders who remain in leadership positions today.

The editors have assembled twenty chapters focused on the lives and contributions of twenty Indigenous women of North American who offer examples of leadership in various fields of life, including the arts, education, medicine, and cultural preservation. Many of the women featured in this volume contributed (and some continue to contribute) in multiple areas, but all of them made their mark as leaders in diverse areas of life. The editors understand that since ancient times, thousands of Native American women have contributed to their tribes in local, national, and international spheres, but only a few are offered here as examples. Hopefully, this volume will elicit greater interest in women's history among the First Nations of the Native Universe, encouraging greater scholarship on Indigenous women around the world.

Several people and institutions have contributed to the research found in this work. The editors wish to thank all the authors who contributed their work in the creation of this book. Many of the authors are from institutions where college and university librarians helped them obtain documents used in their chapters. The Rivera Library of the University of California, Riverside, especially Special Collections, was of particular help in this research project. Clifford E. Trafzer and Amanda K. Wixon wish to thank Steven Mandeville-Gamble, Cherry Williams, and Karen Raines for their assistance. We also offer our gratitude to Kim Wilcox, Daryle Williams, and Michele Salzman for their continuing support of our research. Trafzer wishes to thank the Rupert Costo Endowment and the Senate of the University of California, Riverside, for research support for the creation of this book. He expresses his gratitude to Lee Ann, Tess, Hayley, Tara, Louise, Donna, and Sally for providing time to work on this project. He also wishes to thank Michael Austin, Allison Rogers, Alesha Serene Jaennette, Monte Kugel, and Allison Hedge Coke for their support of this book.

Donna L. Akers wishes to thank the Chahta ancestors and people, whose wisdom and traditions have enriched and nourished her life, and to especially express gratitude to Aishki, Mary, Genevieve, Sarah, and Michael for providing love and support over the years.

Amanda K. Wixon thanks her people and her family for their continued support of her academic work.

Introduction

Woven into the fabric of every Indigenous Nation are ancient female cultural heroes and sacred spiritual women who brought essential food like corn to the People, in addition to fundamental teachings about the world and everything in it. Beloved women among the Cherokees and the warrior women of the Southwestern and California Native peoples emerge in the oral traditions to provide guidance and wisdom, teaching generation after generation of Indigenous peoples about courage, persistence, adaptation, patience, and kindness. Sacred spirit women like White Buffalo Calf Woman of the Lakota, the Algonquin/Objibwe's Nokomis, and many others brought essential knowledge to Indigenous peoples, providing beautiful, sacred teachings to successive generations through the oral traditions. Their stories speak to the strength of Native women, conveying the sacred beliefs in balance, harmony, and generosity, and providing fundamental lessons in existing in wholeness and peace with all the creatures of the earth, the plants, trees, rivers, and land—ancient wisdom that may help save our planet.

These oral traditions provide significant cultural accounts that tell us much about the people, their place on earth, and their relationship with all things, animate and inanimate, seen and unseen. They also provide an understanding of the place of women in Native societies, the fluid gender roles and independence of women in many Indigenous communities throughout time, which confounded and astonished invading Europeans (and later, Americans) and their religious missionaries who understood women to be inferior, dependent beings, ruled by men and straight jacketed by narrowly prescribed cultural beliefs. By contrast, Native women worked in balance with males, ordering their universe through beliefs of a world in which humans, plant, animals, and spirits each had needs and hopes and dreams that bound each to all others, not in the Western foundational beliefs in hierarchies but in a circular, kinship-based way of being.

To Indigenous peoples, all the various beings of the world existed in kinship to one another, with responsibility to one another. In Native stories and oral traditions, we see that women played important, central roles in their tribes, in a way of living and being that provided the basic tenets for peaceful co-existence, sustainable ecosystems, and lives lived in balance and harmony. In the following stories related by esteemed women of the nations, we hear echoes of the oral traditions and contemporary understandings of the power and place of women within specific Native communities.

In her new book, *Daughters of Aataentsic: Life Stories from Seven Generations*, Katharine McGee Labelle demonstrates the continuance of leadership among Wendat/Wyandot/Wyandotte women today and the importance of listening to and learning from contemporary Native women. Since the beginning of time, every descendant of the people has been one of the children of *Aataentsic*, the Woman Who Fell From the Sky. She is the mother of all her people. With mud from the ocean water surrounding Big Turtle's back, *Aataentsic* put the earth into motion and set the example for others to follow. Through her creative powers and constructive actions, she taught women to be industrious, caring, thoughtful, and active in ways that benefit others. Like other Native creators, she showed the way for others to follow, which became the case in many ancient cultures and is found in Native accounts of their origins. In many of these stories, women took center stage and offered a pathway to be followed by future women.

Nuwuvi people honor a female sacred ancestor who put their world into motion. The people commonly known today as Southern Paiute believe that a creator woman in the form of a worm fell from the sky. She fell to earth when the world contained only a primordial soup or water with life-giving elements, the building blocks of life. As a result of her descent into earth's ocean, she took many female forms and is known to the people as *Hutsipamamau'u* or Ocean Woman. She created her first helpers, including Coyote and Cougar, and she used the skin and oils from the inside of her thighs to sprinkle on the ocean. *Hutsipamamau'u* then began creating a massive landform by laying her body on the elements from her body that were floating on the surface of the ocean. Bending, stretching, and contorting her body in every direction, she formed geographic and geologic formations of the earth.

Ocean Woman spread out the landform, making mountains and valleys, deserts, and forests. She made the clouds and brought forth rain, sleet, snow, and ice to the mountain tops, which flowed down from the mountains and helped further shape the earth, a creative process that continues today. *Hutsipamamau'u* was and is the living force that moves the earth today through earthquakes, tsunamis, volcanoes, and natural shifts in the earth. Ocean Woman is alive in the Spring Mountains of Southern Nevada and throughout her homeland where spiritual power resides in the form of puha or spiritual power the people access to help them continue creative endeavors. Her image can be seen by viewing the mountains from the east. She remains active throughout the Western hemisphere. After Ocean Woman put the earth into motion, she took many forms, including that of Louse, described in the oral narratives as a beautiful maiden who attracted the attention of Coyote.

As *Hutsipamamau'u* trotted along on a journey going west of *Nivaganti* or Charleston Peak, her breechcloth flipped up and down, exposing her genitals. Coyote grew eager to make love with *Hutsipamamau'u*, and attempted to woo her into bed as she journeyed to the Pacific Ocean to visit her mother. Ocean Woman agreed to help Coyote swim to an island in the Pacific Ocean by carrying him into the water. Louse dumped her suitor, attempting to drown him. But Coyote changed into a water spider and skirted over the ocean waves to the island where he met Louse's mother. She was busily weaving a basket.

Coyote rested from his journey and when Louse arrived, she joined Coyote and made love. From their union, Louse produced many eggs, which her mother placed into the basket that she sealed with pine pitch. The elder gave the basket full of eggs to Coyote to take to his brother, Wolf. She told Coyote not to open the basket, but once he was on the mainland, he disobeyed her instructions. From the womb of the basket, human beings emerged, traveling in every direction to populate the Native Universe. Crushed and bleeding humans remained in the bottom of the basket, so Coyote took them to Wolf who used breath medicine to revive them. These people became the first *Nuwuvi* or Southern Paiute people, children of Coyote and Ocean Woman.

Nde and *Diné* people (Apache and Navajo) have rich oral accounts of Changing Woman, one of the key cultural heroes of both peoples. They believe Changing Woman is alive today and becomes spiritually connected to every young girl who undergoes ceremonial puberty rites. Changing Woman taught the first Earth Surface People (humans) how to act correctly. Changing woman had sex with Sun and gave birth to Slayer of Monsters. Apache say four days later, she had sex with Water-Old-Man and gave birth to Born-of-Water-Old-Man. For Apache and Navajo, these boys were the first people and heroes. They rid the earth of many evils, described by Navajo people as monsters. Changing Woman gave Apache and Navajo people female puberty rites or *Na ih es*. Navajos call their ceremony *Kinaalda*, a four-day ceremony that is the gift of Changing Woman to young girls to have a long life beneficial to the people. Changing Woman is alive today and never died. During the puberty ceremony, the girl becomes Changing Woman.

The Cahuilla of Southern California say they are the children of *Menil*, the moon maiden. *Menil* was a *Nukatem*, a first being who once lived on earth. *Menil* taught her children to be kind and helpful to others. She taught them the culture of Cahuilla people, how to act correctly, how to seek good health, to respect women, and to do each other no harm. Sadly, *Menil* suffered an ugly assault and left the earth and became the moon. Other women appear in ancient oral narratives to teach people proper behavior, including the seven sacred council fires of the Lakota. According to one account, as two young men set out to hunt, they met a beautiful young woman dressed in white. One man had sexual thoughts about the women and reached out for her. A huge cloud surrounded him and turned him into a pile of bones. The woman told the other Lakota man to return to his camp to tell everyone she was coming. The woman brought the people the gift of a sacred pipe and taught them how to use it as a living prayer. She taught the people the value of buffalo, and she told the women they were from Mother Earth and had as much value as men. As she left the camp, she rolled on the earth four times, turning into White Buffalo Calf Woman who is revered to this day.

Ancient Indigenous stories place women at the center of creation. Through their intelligent and creative power as well as their interest in teaching and nurturing their people, women have always held important roles within communities and contributed to the survival of the people. Indigenous women remain at the center of creation. As Lummi elder Theresa Thomas Mike has explained, creation is a process that takes varying amounts of time. Reaching a goal is not always immediate. She teaches that as humans, our job is to pursue creation and be patient. This book is a product of Theresa Mike's philosophy. It has taken some years to research, write, and produce this volume. The editors wish to thank Lexington Books of Rowman & Littlefield for their expertise in creating this book, especially Eric Kuntzman, Kasey Beduhn, Alexandra Rallo, Jasper Mislak, and Crystal Branson.

During the twentieth century women continued to exert the resilience, accomplishments, and creative energies throughout the Native Universe. The lives of Indigenous women counter silences and stereotypes perpetrated since the European invasion of the Western Hemisphere.

Unfortunately, few scholars took seriously the lives of Native women until the late twentieth century when Donna Akers, Tsianina Lomawaima, Joy Harjo, Brenda Child, Paula Gunn Allen, Louise Erdrich, Devon Mihesuah, Suzan Harjo, Lucy Covington, Wilma Mankiller, Jeanette Armstrong, Leslie Silko, and a host of others—too numerous to name—challenged the old paradigms through their writings, illuminating the significance of Native American women in the modern world. These women and many others from reservations and Indigenous communities informed the non-Native world about the significance of Native women.

The present volume offers stories about eight notable Native women internationally known for their work in the Arts, including Maria Martinez, the talented potter from Pueblo San Ildefonso, New Mexico. Maria perfected black-on-black pottery prized throughout the world for its graceful beauty. From her small village along the Río Grande, Maria's art spread world-wide fueled by glowing reviews. In addition to selling her pottery, Maria's work was shown in galleries and museums world-wide. An artist far less known during her lifetime during the late nineteenth and early twentieth centuries was an Interior Salish woman named Christine Quintasket.

The Okanagan writer used the pen name *Humishuma* or Mourning Dove lived primarily in Washington, British Columbia, Idaho, and Montana. Like many Native Americans of the era, she worked in the agricultural fields of the inland Pacific Northwest. Mourning Dove produced one of the first novels written by a Native American woman. Her novel *Cogewea, the Half-Blood: A Depiction of the Great Montana Cattle Range* did not receive national or international attention until the 1990s with the republication of the novel and her autobiographical work, *Mourning Dove: A Salishan Autobiography.* Professor Jay Miller skillfully edited Mourning Dove's manuscript in 1990s. It is a treasure of personal and cultural information about Indigenous people of the Columbia Plateau.

During her lifetime, Pomo basket maker Elsie Allen received notoriety around the world for the quality of her baskets and for her insistence that the precious baskets of her family would not be burned at the time of the maker's death. Allen was a gentle but forceful woman who loved and protected basketry materials in Northern California. She became a premier teacher of basketry. Her works are prized worldwide. Maria Tallchief became another internationally famous Native American woman through the art of ballet. Born and raised among her Osage people, Maria and her sister, Marjorie, became world renown ballerinas at a time when Russian dancers received most recognition. Maria Tallchief danced for Ballet Russe where she met choreographer George Balanchine who developed the School of American Ballet and organized the American Ballet Company in New York City. Maria married Balanchine and her fame rose after dancing *Firebird.* Although Maria received international fame, she always returned to her home in Oklahoma and her Osage people.

Paula Gunn Allen was born in New Mexico with roots in many cultures, including Laguna Pueblo. She was an extraordinary writer of prose, poetry, fiction, and non-fiction. Allen earned the master's and doctoral degrees. As a student, she learned she had a unique flare for writing. She held teaching positions as a professor of literature and Native American Studies at the University of California, Los Angeles and Berkeley, San Diego State University, San Francisco State University, and others. Her free spirit led her into activism as a feminist and LGBT writer and fighter of human rights. Allen emphasized the significance of women in Native American societies, which remains a significant element of the canon today.

Joy Harjo was born in Tulsa, Oklahoma, and is Muscogee Creek and Cherokee. She is best known for her poetry, but she is an accomplished jazz and blues musician as well as an accomplished songwriter, filmmaker, painter, and writer of children's literature. The winner of many awards, Harjo has worked in many aspects of the arts, making her presentations sing with joy and understanding as one means of countering the past and present violence perpetrated against Indigenous peoples.

Anishinaabe novelist, poet, and short story writer Louise Erdrich is one of the most prolific Native American writers of the late twentieth and early twenty-first centuries. She has won many book awards, including the National Book Critics Circle Award for her first novel, *Love Medicine*, which was the first in a series of books that included *Beet Queen, Tracks, and Bingo Palace*. Each of these early books received national attention for a talented writer providing stories that educate others about Native Americans of the past and present. Erdrich breaks many stereotypes and offers readers some understanding of Indigenous families, kinships, and spiritual healing. She has provided honest and revealing information about American Indian boarding schools and the long-term consequences of the schools. She has written novels for children and adults, including *Birchbark House*. In 2020, Louise Erdrich won the Pulitzer Prize in literature for her book, *The Night Watchman*. Although known for her novels, she considers herself a poet and storyteller.

Buffy Sainte-Marie is a singer, songwriter, and innovative artist of music, acting, and education. Born on the Piapot Reserve in Canada, Buffy was adopted and grew up in Wakefield, Massachusetts. As a young woman, she reconnected with relatives on her reserve where those relatives named her Medicine Bird Singing. She attended the University of Massachusetts. Her life in music began in 1964 with the release of her album, *It's My Way*. That same year *Billboard Magazine* gave her career a great lift describing her talent to the music world. Donovan sang her anti-war song, "The Universal Soldier," and Sainte-Marie used her resources to begin the Nihewan Foundation to provide scholarships and other financial aid for Native students to attend college. In the early 1960s, Buffy began her activism supporting the American Indian civil rights movement, which has continued throughout her life.

Sainte-Marie remains an innovative artist and mentor to many young Native people seeking to advance in the arts.

Seven of the women featured in this volume contributed to their people and society at large through their efforts in education, preservation, and conservation of culture, landscape, history, and civil rights. Vivienne Jake grew up among her *Nuwuvi* or Southern Paiute people. She spoke her language and her elders taught her the old ways of her people, including respect for the lands given to the people by their creator, *Hutsipamamau'a* or Ocean Woman. Elders taught her to protect tribal homelands and protect the flora, fauna, and sacred sites. She grew up singing Salt Songs used during *Yagap* ceremonies to send their loved ones to the spirit world. Concerned that fewer people sang Salt Songs, she became the spark that initiated the Salt Song Project designed to preserve and protect these ancient songs. Although Vivienne walked on in 2016, her legacy is present each time Salt Song singers meet to sing loved ones into the Milky Way.

On the Northwest Plateau of eastern Washington and Oregon, another voice emerged destined to preserve and protect Indigenous homelands, plants, animals, and places. Mary Jim was born on the lower Snake River in the early twentieth century where her people had resided since the time of creation. Mary grew up riding horseback across the plateau to hunt, gather, and fish like her elders before her. During the wars with the United States, Mary's family was among the leadership of warrior men and women. Mary carried that fighting spirit into the twentieth century, giving it to her daughter, Carrie Jim Schuster, and granddaughter, Ione Iron Jones. The Snake River-Palouse refused to move to reservations, remaining on Snake River until the 1960s when state police, county sheriffs, and others forced Mary, Carrie, and the family and off lands given them by the Creator. The family was removed to the Yakama Reservation where they lived with elder friends and relatives. Mary spent her life fighting for her home, which was flooded by Ice Harbor Dam. She was a talented artist, and her oral histories provided the basis for *The Snake River-Palouse* and *River Song*.

Katherine Siva Saubel was a Cahuilla scholar, teacher, and preservationist. Born in Southern California, Katherine Siva's family lived in Coyote Canyon near present-day Anza Borrego State Park, but she spent her childhood and school days in Palm Springs, living Desert Cahuilla. At a ceremony conducted at the Big House on that reservation, Katherine and her friend, Jessie Mike, saw a handsome man that Katherine announced would one day be her husband. She married Mariano Saubel and moved to his home on the Morongo Reservation. Katherine blossomed as a scholar of Cahuilla culture, coauthored *Temalpakh: Cahuilla Indian Knowledge and Usage of Plants*, and cofounded the Malki Museum. Saubel served on the Native American Heritage Commission protecting ancestral remains and sacred places. She received many awards and was named to the Women's Hall of Fame.

Following in the footsteps of Katherine Siva Saubel, Lorene Sisquoc has spent her life as an educator and preservationist. Sisquoc is Fort Sill Apache and Cahuilla. Her ancestral lands are in Arizona, New Mexico, and Oklahoma, but she has spent most of her life near Cahuilla people in Southern California. In the early twentieth century, Sisquoc's grandmother, Ida Gooday (who was born a prisoner of war at Fort Sill, Oklahoma), moved to Riverside, California, where she taught at Sherman Institute, the country's largest off-reservation American Indian boarding school. Sisquoc's mother, Tonita Gooday-Largo, also worked at Sherman. Lorene grew up on the campus of Sherman, and she has spent her career as Curator of the Sherman Indian School Museum and a teacher of Native American culture, history, and art. Sisquoc has coedited two books on Sherman's history and coauthored another, *Shadows of Sherman Institute: A Photographic History of the Indian School on Magnolia Avenue*.

Tlingit activist Elizabeth Wanamaker Peratrovich spent her life fighting for Native Alaskan civil rights and equal opportunity for Indigenous people throughout the Western Hemisphere. Born in 1911, Elizabeth and her husband Roy worked tirelessly to change laws in Alaska that permitted outright discrimination against the first peoples of the region. Working privately and through organizations, Peratrovich educated lawmakers and convinced the Alaskan Territorial Legislature to pass the Anti-Discrimination Act that became law in February 1945. Of course the law did not end discrimination against Native Alaskans, but it paved the way for the modern civil rights movement of modern Native people. Just as Peratrovich educated others about Indigenous civil rights, Tohono O'odham linguist Ofelia Zepeda has spent her life preserving Native American languages and teaching others how to do the same among Indigenous tribes of North America. Trained as a linguist, Zepeda is interested in preserving and teaching languages, and since the 1980s, she has been in the forefront of the reclamation of Indigenous languages through the oral and written tradition. A MacArthur Fellow, Zepeda has greatly expanded the teaching of Native languages by teaching tribal scholars and academics how to preserve and perpetuate language learning. She teaches at the University of Arizona, and she is an exceptional poet, professor, and preservationist whose work continues today.

Roberta Conner is the magnetic and innovative Director of the Tamástslikt Culural Institute on the Umatilla Indian Reservation in eastern Oregon. She helped create Tamástslikt, which is an active, living, learning. and vibrant learning center that is part museum and cultural center as well as a site of song, dance, art, ceremony, lectures, and center of learning through the oral and written traditions of the people. Born in Pendleton, Oregon, Conner grew up on her reservation and attended the University of Oregon. After working for United Indians of All Tribes Foundation and the United States Small Business Administration, she returned home to work for and with the Confederated Tribes of the Umatilla Indian Reservation. She is an educator, preservationist, and advocate for language reclamation. She has served on the National Council of the Lewis and Clark Bicentennial Board of Directors and Chair of the Board directing the Smithsonian Institution's National Museum of the American Indian. Conner is a leader in sustainability for her people and Indigenous people of North America. She is highly intelligent and eager to help anyone interested in learning about the first peoples of the Great Columbia Plateau of Oregon, Washington, and Idaho.

The last five women featured in the volume focused their lives on health and medicine, including *Diné* activist Annie Dodge Wauneka. Born and raised on the Navajo Reservation, Annie was the daughter of a chief and first tribal chair Henry Chee Dodge and his third wife. Like many Navajo children, Annie cared for the family's sheep herds and learned the relationship of the *Diné* to their wonderous Southwestern landscape. She grew up speaking *Diné Bizzad* and English, which served her well as a translator and educator. During the influenza pandemic of 1918–1919, Annie nursed her fellow students at the Fort Defiance Boarding School, which ignited her interest in serving the people by fighting disease and death through health education. She married George Wauneka, nurtured her family, and entered tribal politics. She is best known as the Legendary Mother of the Navajo Nation for her community-based health work to stamp out tuberculosis among her people. She taught her people about invisible enemies such as bacteria and viruses that *Diné* people could not see but knew existed. Through her teachings, the people learned how to identify and prevent tuberculosis, which declined on the reservation and brought some balance and beauty to the people.

Tuberculosis and other infectious disease ravaged Native communities during the late nineteenth and early twentieth centuries. Women had long served their communities as nurses, doctors, and spiritual healers, including Susan La Flesche who was born on the Omaha Reservation in Nebraska. She grew up in a family that believed in the benefit of American civilization and education. After receiving formal education as a young person, Susan returned to the reservation to teach at a mission school. Susan wanted further education and matriculated into Hampton Normal and Agricultural Institute in Virginia. With financial support and encouragement of reformers of American Indian Affairs, La Flesche attended the Women's Medical College of Pennsylvania, graduating in 1889 and becoming the first Native American woman to earn a medical degree. La Flesche fought tuberculosis infecting Native people on a national, regional, and national level, working tirelessly to improve the health and conditions on reservations. She died in 1915, but she set an example for many Native American women to seek medical degrees and health-related education for the benefit of Indigenous people of North America, including Lori Alvord, Terry Maresca, and Beverly Patchell.

Born in Tacoma, Washington, Lori Alvord grew up at Crownpoint, New Mexico, on the eastern edge of the Navajo Reservation. Like most Navajo people, she did not grow up privileged in any way but received her education on the reservation. She learned her culture and language that centered on the power of the earth and Holy People, which are spirits that keep the people *hózhó* in balance. A graduate of Stanford School of Medicine, she became a talented surgeon but she learned to be a quality healer through the ancient teachings of her people, particularly medicine men and women on her reservation. Dr. Alvord combines traditional Navajo medicine ways with Western medicine. She is dedicated to the health and well-being of all people, and she continues to support better health conditions among Indigenous people of North America, especially those living on the Navajo Reservation.

Dr. Terry Maresca is a member of the Kahnawake Band of Mohawk and grew up learning from her elders who emphasized the importance of family, friendships, fresh foods, and a mindset of positive thinking and being. Maresca uses the knowledge given to her in her work as a physician, medical educator, and community-based advocate for Native Americans. She is the Director of the Native American Center for Excellence at the University of Washington School of Medicine, but she also works closely with the Seattle Indian Health Board, which serves many Native people, as well as the Puyallup Tribe. Like Dr. Alvord, Dr. Terry Maresca employs Native American spiritual beliefs and methods with Western medicine, seeking to help others find health and balance in their lives. Like other Indigenous people, Maresca believes that food, diet, games, music, art, ceremony, and song are all part of good medicine and the path to better health.

Dr. Beverly Patchell holds a PhD in nursing and is a community-based health care provider. A member of the Cherokee Nation of Oklahoma, Patchell grew up along the road from Tahlequah to Six Killer Lake in northeast Oklahoma. This is a hilly and beautifully wooded area where her family resettled years ago after the Trail of Tears. Like Maresca and Alvord, Patchell first learned community-based Native medicine from her elders, including Jim Henderson and Croslin Smith. In addition, Kenneth and Rita Coosewoon, Comanche healers, mentored Beverly in the art of Indigenous medicine ways, especially sweat lodge. In addition to her formal training as a nurse, she has deep knowledge of Native American healing ways and medicines, which she employs daily in her work. She has worked in youth programs for the Cherokee Nations and is the former Director of the University of Oklahoma's prestigious Native American Nursing Program. Today she works in community-based health in Minnesota.

The women featured in this volume are only a sample of the thousands of Native American women who worked during the twentieth century to serve their people and the larger world around them. Many Indigenous women succeeded in work and accomplishment in the last century. Indigenous woman of the past contributed significantly to the power, place, and significance of women today. They set the stage for the younger generation to do more for the people through many opportunities. Perhaps Secretary of Interior Deb Halaand of Laguna Pueblo explained it best when she stated that contemporary Indigenous people cannot overstate the importance of Native elders, especially women. They have focused on caring for and advancing their extended families, tribes, and nations. They fought assimilation and discrimination. They reclaimed their Native language, education, medicine, and the arts. They carried forward stories, memories, and strength of character. Women of the past brought cultural knowledge into the future, which many young people have carried into the twenty-first century. Contemporary Native American women received their first knowledge from their mothers, grandmothers, and aunties who instilled in young people the resilience so apparent today. Native American women have always been the strength of the nations, and they continue that role within every Indigenous community in modern society.

Chapter One

American Artist, Pueblo Potter

Maria Antonia Montoya Martinez (?–1980)

Emily Molesworth-Teipe

Looking out from the *Pajarito* Plateau of northern New Mexico, gazing out in any direction all one sees is brown. Everything is brown: the land, the houses, the pottery, the potter's hands. In this environment, at *San Ildefonso Pueblo*, home of the *Tewa* tribe,[1] a young woman, Maria Montoya (Martinez) revitalized Native American pottery and created a renaissance in Native American Art at the turn of the twentieth century. Both the soil of the region and Maria's heritage played a critical role in the style of pottery she devised and the revival of Native American Art that she created. Using only the raw materials available to her, Maria crafted museum quality pottery.

San Ildefonso Pueblo has been inhabited at least since 1300 A.D. and consists of a small cluster of simple adobe houses situated eight miles east of *Los Alamos* and about twenty miles northwest of *Santa Fe*, New Mexico. Located on the east bank of the *Río Grande*, the village is near a large volcanic outcropping known as the Black Mesa.

By the end of the nineteenth century, pottery making in the Southwestern pueblos had become almost obsolete. Among the tribes, the use of cheap manufactured tinware and ceramic pieces had replaced handmade pottery. However, in 1908, Dr. Edgar Lee Hewett, Director of the Museum of New Mexico sparked interest in native culture when he began an archaeological dig at *Tyuonyi* and *Frijoles* Canyon, near *San Ildefonso*, a region that the *Anasazi,*[2] the ancient ancestors of the Southwestern pueblos had once occupied. Prior to Hewett's excavation, scholars assumed that the *Tewa* and other pueblo people of northern New Mexico had inhabited the area since 1500 A.D. at about the same time the Spanish began exploring and colonizing the country. What Hewett found corrected long held beliefs about the pueblo's origins when his team unearthed examples of ancient pottery pieces in Frijoles canyon. By dating the pottery, this stunning discovery indicated that native people had lived along the *Río Grande* as early as 1000 A.D. or perhaps earlier.

Born into this ancient culture, Maria Antonia Montoya's exact birth date is unknown, but the closest reckoning is that she was born sometime between 1881 and 1887. Her mother Reyes Pena and her father Thomas Montoya named her *PoVeKa*, the *Tewa* word for Pond Lily. She was the second child born to the Montoyas who would have five daughters. To support the family, Maria's father worked as a farmer, a herdsman, and a carpenter. At the age of nine, Maria nearly died of smallpox but through her mother's intervention, she made a miraculous recovery. Her mother and aunt burned green cedar boughs to smoke the sickroom and prayed to *Santo Nino*, the patron saint of children promising that if Maria lived, they would make a pilgrimage to *El Sanctuario*, a healing chapel nearby.[3] Growing up in the pueblo, nurtured on tribal custom, Maria learned to love her community and to respect the God-given gifts of the earth. She expressed this core belief when she said, "We all come from the clay of the earth, and we will return to the clay of the earth, so it is up to us to be happy and continue the harmony of mind and heart."[4]

In the Native American custom of making pottery, clay is not thrown on a wheel but is formed by hand using the coiling technique. Before retrieving the clay from the ground, a labor intensive act in itself, the potter sprinkles cornmeal on the ground and gives thanks to Mother Earth for providing the material. Next equal parts of clay and volcanic ash are mixed with water and left to set for a few days. The potter begins forming the clay by using a *puki*, a hardened bowl-shaped mold to make a base to support the pot, plate, or vessel, as it is built. The typical method is to roll coils of red clay between moistened hands to fashion a long cylinder that is circled around a base until the coil is blended creating the sides of the vessel. Once the desired height for the pot is achieved the sides are smoothed and shaped into curves using pieces of gourd called, *kajepes*. The *San Ildefonso* potters do not glaze their pottery. It is finished by applying slip, a watery clay and then burnishing and polishing the piece with a stone. Neither is the pottery fired in a kiln, instead after pots and dishes are polished, they are baked in a wood fire at a temperature of about 1200 degrees Fahrenheit.

By the late nineteenth century, only a few pueblo women continued to make pottery in the traditional way. Fortunately, Maria's family had preserved and continued the custom of handmade pottery. Thus, her lifelong passion for pottery began as a child, when after finishing her chores, she was allowed to observe her *Tía* Nicolasa Pena making pots. The first pottery Maria made with her small hands was a set of miniature dishes for her dollhouse. She and her sisters even built their own playhouse out of clay. As a little girl making small pots and dishes, Maria gained the rudimentary potter's skill of the *Tewa* style.

Maria attended the government grammar school at *San Ildefonso* until 1896 completing third grade. At about the age of 10 or 12 years old, the Pueblo's tribal council chose Maria and her sister Desideria to go to Santa Fe, New Mexico, to matriculate at St. Catherine's Indian School but after attending one year there she became very homesick and returned to *San Ildefonso*. In her adolescent years she achieved some economic independence by mastering the traditional craft of pueblo pottery, specializing in the coil-built bowls and water jars known as *ollas.*

Consequently, Maria had already established herself as a native potter when she married Julian Martinez in 1904. For their honeymoon, the couple traveled to St. Louis, Missouri, where they demonstrated pottery making and performed the traditional *Tewa* dances at the 1904 World's Fair.[5] In keeping with tribal custom where women traditionally formed the pots and the men painted them with native motifs, Maria would shape, and polish pots and Julian would decorate them. They made small-scale pieces painted in multiple earth-toned colors (polychrome) and sold them as souvenirs to visiting tourists. However, despite the artistic endeavors and intensive labor of potters such as Maria and Julian and given the downright unconscionable dealing of sellers and collectors, the ancient art of pottery making in the pueblos faced extinction. That is, until Dr. Edgar Hewett's team made their discoveries.

In 1908 when Hewett brought anthropologists Dr. Kenneth M. Chapman, Jesse Nusbaum, and John P. Harrington to the dig, the team turned up several types of pottery: the typical black on red, black on cream (plain ware), and polychrome pieces. They also unearthed pottery unlike any ever found in the Southwest, specifically, jet black shards. Fortuitously, Julian hired to dig at the excavation and Maria cooking for the team were on hand to witness the discovery.

Enthralled by this unusual find, Dr. Hewett asked the workers to recommend the best potter in the village to make facsimiles of the artifacts. They suggested Maria Martinez, their cook who was without question one of the few skilled potters and renowned for making the roundest, thinnest pots.[6] She agreed to duplicate some full-scale examples of the ancient polychrome but had no idea how to make the jet black pottery. During this experimental stage, Maria hid the first pieces she and Julian fired regarding them as poor examples of the type found. When by chance, Hewett found them stored away, elated with the results, he bought all of the pieces from Maria and asked her to make more. News of the discovery traveled quickly, and Santa Fe dealers also offered to buy Maria's creations.

Based on the artifacts unearthed at *San Ildefonso*, Dr. Hewett created an exhibit at the Museum of New Mexico in Santa Fe and invited Maria and Julian to work there and to learn more about ancient pottery and for Maria to demonstrate pottery making at the Palace of the Governors. Many of her original pieces are still housed at the Museum of New Mexico and ironically, those pieces that Maria and Julian made to serve merely as *copies* of the treasured artifacts are among the *most* valuable *objets d'art* in today's market. Maria and Julian's success which began as a collaboration with museums, curators, and promoters of public art would last a lifetime.[7]

Any discussion of Maria's life, or her contribution to the arts in America, would be incomplete without mention of the vital role her husband Julian played in their creative endeavor. While employed at the Museum in Santa Fe, Julian studied the murals of *Anasazi* rock art found on cave and canyon walls and filled notebooks with these design sketches. Though he rarely painted the same pattern twice on pottery, the *avanyu (*a mythical horned water beast*)* and the *mimbres* (an ancient Native American feather motif) were exceptions and characteristic favorites. Julian also created his trademark technique by painting the pieces with clay slip (which contained some iron) just before firing to produce the subtle silvery black-on-black matte designs. He also became an accomplished artist in watercolor painting and other media and many of his masterpieces hang in museums of Native American art throughout the United States. The couple gained recognition early on as officials invited them time after time to demonstrate their art at events such as the Panama-California Exposition in San Diego in 1915.

Julian, determined to find a firing method that would yield flawless pottery every time, knew of the black ware made at the *Santa Clara* pueblo. That pottery was embellished with carved or pressed-in designs and not painted. What made Maria and Julian's black on black pottery so unique and unmatched lies not only in the tireless burnishing that yielded the high gloss surface but also the exacting skill—the very hands of Maria and Julian—which formed, painted, and fired the pottery. Although Maria manually shaped each piece, when finished each vessel's opening formed a perfect circle.

Over several years using the most rudimentary tools and equipment, Julian would develop a firing technique for the much sought after black pottery. In this environment, which is harsh and unyielding, where trees are a precious resource, utilizing what is available is critical to the end result. Nearly a century later, Julian's process is unchanged and still used today. Observing a firing at *San Ildefonso*, one notices that no modern equipment or machinery is used, and it is impressive how ingenious and frugal the potters are at recycling discarded items for re-use. Before a firing time is chosen weather conditions must be ideal with no wind, so that the smoke can evenly infiltrate the pieces. Before firing, the ritual cornmeal is spread on the firepit and a prayer of thanks is offered to the Great Spirit.

The firing platform consists of discarded 46 oz. juice cans to serve as table legs on which a large metal grid made from old iron stove grids is laid in place. Then a wooden stand is built to hold the pots. All of the pottery is stacked carefully to avoid marring any surfaces and to ensure that each piece is away from direct flames yet evenly exposed to the smoke. Over the pots old metal army mess trays and discarded license plates are placed to shield the pots. At each corner, a space is left open to act as an air draft. Then on top of the stack more license plates are added, folded to form a tent-like roof. After cedar or juniper wood is inserted beneath the dome structure and large cakes of dried cow dung are placed over all the metal plates, the pottery is ready for firing. Under the grille, the wood is doused with kerosene and ignited to produce a fast-burning fire which will reach a temperature of about 1200 degrees Fahrenheit. Toward the end of the burn, usually about one hour, the fire is smothered with fine particles of manure to produce a heavy carbon smoke which penetrates throughout all the pottery and renders the dense black color.

This open-fire burning probably dates back to the prehistoric period when the early people dug pits in the ground in which to bake their pottery. Maria and Julian improved upon the ancient method by adding metal insulation and lifting the grille off the ground, a process which produces a fire with better circulation and allows the pots to fire at a more even temperature. One of the outstanding features of *San Ildefonso* clay is its volcanic properties, which gives it greater endurance under fire. Pots made with other clay materials or burned in a kiln frequently crack or explode.

A key to Maria and Julian's achievement lay not only in their artistry but also in their ability to balance the Indian way alongside modern innovation. Maria knew how to market her pottery observing at exhibits and fairs that, "white people seemed to like the plain polished bowls."[8] So, they concentrated their production on plain polished ware. Julian's firing technique allowed them to produce quality pottery, more of it and in less time and then to sell it at a higher price than other pueblos did, all sound manufacturing practices.[9] At first having perfected making the black ware pottery, they covertly protected the process from competitors but this was not the pueblo way and by 1920, Maria and Julian in the interests of their community began teaching the black-on-black technique to their family to enable everyone to earn a living.[10]

The Martinez success showed results by 1924 when profits from selling pottery reached $200 per month and yielded at year's end an income of $2,000. While this seems a mere pittance, it amounted to about 70 percent of all of *San Ildefonso's* annual profits from agricultural production. Maria and

Julian were earning as much in a year as a professional archivist or curator did in Santa Fe; put another way, by today's standards the couple made $5400 in monthly sales. They charged more for their pottery than other pueblos, increased production by partitioning labor within the family, dispatched sales by mail order and sold pottery in the Santa Fe market on a commission basis, unlike potters of other pueblos who had to sell through a trader.[11] With their first profits, they made what were for them extravagant purchases: a sewing machine, a gas stove, and an addition to their home. The extra space was to be used as a store where they could sell pottery directly to visitors. These innovations resulted in an industry that would make *San Ildefonso* a center for Native American crafts transpired at the perfect juncture, i.e., the completion of the *Otowi* bridge in 1924 across the *Río Grande* connecting their pueblo to the outside world. This occurred just as the growing popularity and affordability of the automobile brought thousands of American tourists to the pueblos of New Mexico and Arizona.[12]

As Maria used fresh approaches to market her pueblo's art, she also instinctively knew what to retain of Indian tradition. At the Chicago World's Fair, for example, when asked to try a potter's wheel and the gas and electric kiln, she adamantly refused explaining that it was not the Indian way as using modern adaptations would offend those who came to the fair expecting to see pottery made in the pure Indian way.[13]

However, contrary to the pueblo belief that a potter should not sign their work because it represents the efforts of many, Maria early on signed her pottery as "Marie," or "Marie and Julian," or by the *Tewa* name, "*Poh ve ka*," or "*Maria Poveka*."[14] Some of her work went unsigned. To the consternation of art dealers and collectors, a signed or unsigned piece did not signify whether it was a Maria original (which could bring dealers top dollar). Maria's somewhat unorthodox approach succeeded as she explained that it was all *San Ildefonso* pottery, made to the same standards and overall a uniform style. What seemed like a risky move proved Maria's instincts were right. By creating distinctive black ware pottery as a *brand* identified with the *pueblo,* she bypassed the merchandizers rule of selling art exclusively as a single artist's original piece. Not only did Maria and Julian maintain the tradition of their art within a modern market, their skill, persistence, and hard work revived the ancient black pottery into a *San Ildefonso* hallmark of gallery and museum quality which enabled the pueblo to thrive.

Considering the labor-intensive demands life at *San Ildefonso* placed on Maria, it is remarkable that she managed to devote any time to pottery making at all. Pueblo life is harsh and modern conveniences are almost nonexistent. Pottery is usually not made during the severe winter and the days and seasons throughout the year are taken up with food preparation, caring for the children, the endless household duties and the round of pueblo ceremonial dances as well as the kiva councils.[15] Maria and Julian had a large family to support and extended family to care for as well.[16] Over the decades, because the communities survival would depend more and more on the men finding work outside of the pueblo, the duty of maintaining home and family fell more to the women, and in the case of the Martinez clan especially to Maria. Yet faced with many responsibilities, she managed to set aside every possible moment to devote to her passion—pottery making.

In 1932, officials of the State Indian School at Santa Fe called upon Maria to teach the native students her art of pottery making. There was one drawback however—formal instruction is not the pueblo way. Knowledge, skills, and culture are passed down from one generation to the next through observation and the repetition of activities. In this manner children learn the ritual dances through active participation. Thus, in the way that Maria had learned to make pottery by observing her *Tia* Nicolasa, so too, she told the officials, "I come and work and they can watch."[17]

Pueblo people tend to be withdrawn and shy around outsiders but for their generation, Tewa artists Maria and Julian Martinez were outgoing innovators. They were the first couple at *San Ildefonso* to own an automobile, a 1924 black Dodge sedan. It proved a real asset for conveying the sick for medical care, shopping for groceries, and hauling their pottery to market. Maria described how Julian "painted the car with black decoration all around just like the pots." The car's unusual exterior, served as mobile advertising catching everyone's attention whenever they drove into Santa Fe.[18]

Their work frequently took them away from the pueblo and into a *Settlers* world as ambassadors for their culture. Traveling extensively in 1916, they went to San Diego and stayed for a year as part of a Native American exposition where Dr. Hewett's staff built a model Indian village including adobes and a kiva. As many tribes of the Southwest gathered there, Maria met Geronimo with whom she conversed in Spanish. After Julian and Maria exhibited their work at the Chicago World's Fair in 1934 they were invited to demonstrate their pottery making at nearly every world's fair in the intervening years. Their appearances showcased *San Ildefonso* pottery and identified Maria Martinez as the potter, at a time when most pueblo artists did not sign their work.

Maria Martínez gained international fame for her work as prestigious institutions recognized her artistic contributions. People came to *San Ildefonso* from all over the world to meet her and she went to meet other famous people and to receive awards. Both Japanese master potter *Shoji Hamada* and Hong Kong potter Bernard Leach, visited to observe her skill. In 1934 she became the first woman to receive the bronze medal for Indian Achievement by the

Indian Fire Council.[19] In 1939 John D. Rockefeller, Jr., a patron of her work, asked her to lay the cornerstone for the Rockefeller Center in New York City. Four universities including the University of New Mexico and the University of Colorado conferred honorary doctoral degrees on her.

When Julian Martínez fell victim to alcoholism and died in 1943, it is reputed that Maria grieved so deeply, that she did not make any pots for four years. Still accolades for her work continued to pour in. The American Institute of Architects gave her the prestigious 1954 Craftsmanship Medallion and the French *Palmes Académiques* recognized her contribution to the world community of art.[20] The Minnesota Museum of Art awarded her the Symbol of Man Award in 1969 and she became the first recipient when the New Mexico Arts Commission instituted the First Annual Governor's Award in 1974. Eleanor Roosevelt and Maria shared a mutual admiration; when they met the First Lady encouraged Maria to, "keep the Indian way, send your children to school but keep your own way."[21]

After Julian's death, the growing popularity of Maria's pottery and economic necessity pressured the family to step up production. Their youngest son Tony took over the artistic painting and eldest son Adam supervised the firings and made pottery alongside his mother. When her health failed and her eyesight weakened, she retired from making pottery in 1978.

In her advanced years Maria reflected on her exceptional life: "When they built the Golden Gate Bridge in San Francisco, I was there. . . . I go to New York to place the cornerstone for that Rockefeller Center. . . . The last time I was in Washington, D.C. I was staying with [First Lady] Mrs. Johnson."[22] She met in her lifetime four United States presidents: Herbert Hoover, Franklin D. Roosevelt, Dwight D. Eisenhower, and Lyndon B. Johnson. Intuitively, Maria knew that her work and her art would endure and often advised her great-granddaughter Barbara Gonzales, an accomplished potter, "Don't forget what you see, don't forget what you hear, remember what I did, for what we are doing will be important."[23]

For nearly one hundred years, until her death in 1980, Maria's life at *San Ildefonso* centered on family, pottery making, and the *Tewa* tradition; these took precedence over everything else. Almost single-handedly in her lifetime she had rescued and restored the fading skill of pueblo pottery making and left an astonishing legacy to *San Ildefonso*, to America, and to the world community—five generations of trained Martinez potters to ensure that pottery making would sustain their community. Maria's generous sharing of her craft transformed *San Ildefonso* from a poor, remote village into a Native American arts center of international repute. The artistry of Maria Martinez elevated pueblo pottery—from what had become mere Indian curios to sublime art—recognized and acclaimed throughout the world. In the exhibit, *Touched by Fire: The Art, Life and Legacy of Maria Martinez*, John Torres distinguished Maria as "a true master of her art" who along with her collaborators, "established many of the striking and recognizable traditions of contemporary pueblo pottery." Her unique work "ultimately led to the acceptance of pottery-making as a form of art."[24]

NOTES

1. The Tewa people are a Native American pueblo culture; pueblo, being the name the Spanish ascribed to Indigenous people of the Southwest, their permanent village settlements and the flat roofed homes they built of stone or adobe. The Tewa live in northern New Mexico along the *Río Grande* and consist of six groups: Nambe Pueblo, Pojoaque Pueblo, San Ildefonso Pueblo, San Juan Pueblo, Santa Clara Pueblo, and Tesuque Pueblo.

2. *Anasazi* is a Navajo term meaning ancient enemies. They were a Native American group whose cliff dwellings in the four corners region of the United States comprising northern Arizona, northwestern New Mexico, Southern Utah, and Southwestern Colorado existed from about 200 to 1300 A. D.

3. El Sancutario de Chimayo in the village of Chimayo 25 miles north of Santa Fe, New Mexico, is a small chapel built about 1816 which has served as a site of pilgrimage and healing and is referred to as the Lourdes of America; its sanctuary contains a pit in the floor with sacred dirt, which pilgrims may take home with them for its reputed healing properties.

4. Cavan "Eagle Trail" Gonzalez, great-grandson of Maria Martinez quoted his grandmother in *Maria Montoya Martinez, Notable New Mexican,* PBS-TV production, New Mexico PBS, 2018.

5. The Louisiana Purchase Exposition commonly referred to as the World's Fair commemorated the centennial of the purchase of the Louisiana Territory in 1803. Held in St. Louis, Missouri, from April to December 1804, and reflecting the era, it boasted themes of race and empire and highlighted popular culture and consumerism. Some 60 countries, and all the U.S. states displayed exhibits for 20 million attendees.

6. When Anthropologist Carl Guthe observed and timed Maria making pots, he noted she was "the swiftest and most dexterous potter at *San Ildefonso*" and operated her own assembly line. By turning out a pot every 18 minutes, sometimes working on several at a time, she could produce more pots and each was of the highest quality. Carl E. Guthe, *Pueblo Pottery Making: A Study at the Village of San Ildefonso* (New Haven: Yale University Press,1925), 12–13, 40.

7. Some of the museums that exhibit the pottery of Maria Martinez today include: The Millicent Rogers Museum in Taos, New Mexico—one of the most comprehensive and extraordinary collections of pottery by Maria and Julian Martinez. Her family conserved much of Maria's finest pottery to be shown to the public and retained as a permanent collection of the museum. The Museum of New Mexico in Santa Fe—in the Santa Fe Plaza, Palace of the Governors—houses much of Maria's work and that

of other *San Ildefonso* potters. Dr. Edgar Lee Hewett conserved many of Maria's early pieces for the permanent collection at MNMSF. The Maxwell Museum of the University of New Mexico holds pieces of Maria and Julian Martinez pottery within a larger exhibit of Native American art dating to the prehistoric period. The National Museum of the American Indian, a recent addition at the Smithsonian Institution in Washington, D.C., opened in 2004 on the National Mall and is the first national museum dedicated to Native American culture and lists items of Maria Martinez pottery. The Museum of Anthropology and the Nora Eccles Harrison Museum of Art, Utah State University, Logan, Utah, merged and completed in 2005 this Southwest Indian Art collection, which includes ceramics and pottery of Pueblo artists and showcases Maria Martinez pottery.

8. Alice Lee Marriott, *Maria the Potter of San Ildefonso* (Norman: University of Oklahoma Press 1948), 120.

9. Cody Hartley, "Maria Martinez, Industrial Designer," in *The Journal of the Society for Industrial Archeology* 34, no.1/2 IA in ART (2008), 76.

10. Hartley, "Maria Martinez," 78.

11. Hartley, "Maria Martinez," 78.

12. Hartley, "Maria Martinez," 77.

13. Hartley, "Maria Martinez," 77.

14. Pots signed Marie/Santana show the collaboration of Maria, her son Adam and his wife, Santana, and were made from approximately 1947 to 1954.

15. The kiva is a partially underground chamber used for ceremonies among the Pueblo villages in the southwestern United States. Outsiders are never allowed in the kiva. It is primarily used for men's rituals but women and children may also enter for political councils or informal gatherings. A kiva contains decorative murals and a small hole in the floor's center symbolizes the place of origin of the tribe. Kivas built in a round form in contrast to the otherwise square or rectangular Pueblo buildings recall the circular pit houses of the prehistoric basket-weaving culture from which these tribes descend.

16. Maria had one daughter who died in infancy. Only her eldest son, Adam, survived her. Her sister, Clara, came under her care when their mother Reyes died in childbirth shortly after Clara was born.

17. Quoted in Susan Peterson, *The Living Tradition of Maria Martinez* (Tokyo: Kodansha International, 1981), 83.

18. Peterson, *The Living Tradition of Maria Martinez*, 85.

19. The Indian Fire Council or the Grand Council Fire of American Indians, founded in 1923, is dedicated to a more authentic portrayal of Native Americans historically and within our contemporary culture. The council awards individuals who honor Indian leadership. They also legally represent Native Americans in cases of discrimination in law, education, housing, and in the workplace.

20. The oldest order bestowed by the French government for achievement in the arts, education, or science. It was established by the Emperor Napoleon in 1808 to recognize esteemed faculty at the University of Paris.

21. Peterson, *The Living Tradition of Maria Martinez*, 110–111.

22. Peterson, *The Living Tradition of Maria Martinez*, 110–111.

23. Barbara Gonzales as featured and quoted in *Maria Martinez, Notable New Mexican,* PBS-TV, KNMT.org New Mexico Public television, 2018.

24. *Touched by Fire, the Art, Life and Legacy of Maria Martinez.* An exhibition at the Museum of Indian Arts and Culture, Santa Fe, New Mexico, displayed from March 2002 to January 2003; conceived and curated by John Torres, Tony Chavarria, and Douglas Patinka.

BIBLIOGRAPHY

Anderson, Peter. *Maria Martinez, Pueblo Potter.* Chicago: C.P. Press, 1992.

Ankerberg, John F. and Richard Spivey. *The Legacy of Maria Poveka Martinez.* Santa Fe: Museum of New Mexico Press, 1995.

Gonzalez, Doreen. *Maria Martinez, Tewa Potter*. New York: Silver Burdett Press, 2000.

Guthe, Carl E. *Pueblo Pottery Making: A Study at the Village of San Ildefonso.* New Haven: Yale University Press, 1925: 12–13, 40.

Hartley, Cody. "Maria Martinez, Industrial Designer," *The Journal of the Society for Industrial Archeology* 34, no.1/2 IA in ART (2008): 73–86.

Hyde, Hazel. *Maria Making Pottery: The Story of the Famous New Mexico Potter.* Santa Fe: Sunstone Press, 1991.

Kriescher, Elsie. *Maria Montoya Martinez, Master Potter.* New Orleans: Pelican Publishing, 1995.

Lamar, Howard R., ed. *American West.* New Haven: Yale University Press, 1998.

Maria Martinez, Notable New Mexican, Video, PBS-TV, KNMT.org New Mexico Public television, 2018.

Marriott, Alice Lee. *Maria, the Potter of San Ildefonso.* Norman: University of Oklahoma Press, 1948.

Morris, Juddi. *Tending the Fire: The Story of Maria Martinez.* Scottsdale: Rising Moon Publishers, 2009.

Peterson, Susan. *The Living Tradition of Maria Martinez.* Tokyo: Kodansha International, 1981.

Ward, Alfreda M. Maloof. *Recollections from My Time in the Indian Service, 1935–1942. Maria Makes Pottery.* Klamath River, CA: Living Gold Press, 1997.

FURTHER READING

Anderson, Peter. *Maria Martinez, Pueblo Potter.* Chicago: C.P. Press, 1992.

Ankerberg, John F. and Richard Spivey. *The Legacy of Maria Poveka Martinez.* Santa Fe: Museum of New Mexico Press, 1995.

Gonzalez, Doreen. *Maria Martinez, Tewa Potter*. New York: Silver Burdett Press, 2000.

Guthe, Carl E. *Pueblo Pottery Making, a Study at the Village of San Ildefonso.* New Haven: Yale University Press, 1925: 12–13, 40.

Hartley, Cody. "Maria Martinez, Industrial Designer," *The Journal of the Society for Industrial Archeology* 34, no.1/2 IA in ART (2008): 73–86.

Hyde, Hazel. *Maria Making Pottery: The Story of the Famous New Mexico Potter.* Santa Fe: Sunstone Press, 1991.

Kriescher, Elsie. *Maria Montoya Martinez, Master Potter.* New Orleans: Pelican Publishing, 1995.

Marriott, Alice Lee. *Maria, the Potter of San Ildefonso.* Norman: University of Oklahoma Press 1948.

Morris, Juddi. *Tending the Fire: The Story of Maria Martinez.* Scottsdale: Rising Moon Publishers, 2009.

Peterson, Susan. *The Living Tradition of Maria Martinez.* Tokyo: Kodansha International, 1981.

Chapter Two

A Bridge between Worlds

Mourning Dove (c. 1888–d. 1936)

Amanda K. Wixon

In 1888, during the Moon of the Leaves (April), Christine Quintasket was born in a canoe on the Kootenay River near Bonner's Ferry, Idaho. The Kootenay steersman, named Swansen, paddled hard across the river to where her newborn clothes lay packed, but Christine came into the world before they reached the bank. Thus, her first clothing was a man's flannel shirt provided by the Kootenay canoe man, her mother, and grandmother to the camp across the river.[1] Christine's unusual entrance into the world set the pattern for her life—one of constant movement and labor. Although frustrating and difficult, her labors eventually bore fruit, allowing Christine to publicly express her greatest joy – being born an Indian. Through her writing and activism, she became known as Mourning Dove, one of the first Native American woman to publish her work.

Mourning Dove's father, Joseph Quintasket (Okanagan/Scottish), was born in the Lake Okanagan community of *En-hwx-kwas-t'nun*, in British Columbia. Joseph's grandmother was *Pah-tah-heet sa*, a famous Nicola medicine woman. Orphaned at a young age, Joseph grew up without a formal school education, learning broken English and some French. Over his lifetime, he worked running packtrains, as a tribal policeman and later, as a farmer. Mourning Dove's mother, Lucy *Stui-kin*, was a full blood of Lakes and Colville ancestry. Lucy's mother, *Soma-how-atqhu* (She Got Her Power From Water), was the youngest daughter of Head Chief *See-whelhken* of the People of the Falls of Colville. *Soma-how-atqhu*, Mourning Dove's grandmother, visited the family often, and Mourning Dove loved her deeply.[2]

Mourning Dove was the eldest of seven children and she generally lived happily, enjoying the attention of her parents and extended family. She fondly remembered living in a tipi (*swool-hu*), riding her ponies, and traveling freely between camps with her family during the summer. As a girl, she met a sad and lonely elderly woman named *Teequalt*. Mourning Dove's mother invited Teequalt into their home and she stayed with the family until her death. *Teequalt* told Mourning Dove about the old ways and the time before the whites came, before smallpox. In her later years, *Teequalt* was Mourning Dove's tutor and mentor, supervising the young girl's spiritual, moral, and traditional training. The elder also taught Mourning Dove how to harness Love Medicine, which became a new skill of Mourning Dove.[3] Although her family was respected in traditional society, Mourning Dove knew they did not have the resources valued by the dominant white society.

In 1895, Mourning Dove entered Goodwin Mission School for Indians, in Ward, Washington. Like most Indian schools of this period, administrators sought to eradicate Native cultures and languages. At school, the staff punished Mourning Dove for speaking Salishan, her first language. After a few months, she became ill and left school. In 1897, Father LaRouge, a local Jesuit priest, persuaded Lucy, a devoted Catholic, to send her daughter back to Goodwin Mission School. Mourning Dove stayed at Goodwin Mission School for two years. Unlike her first school experience, she was now anxious to learn English. Mourning Dove also reported never seeing the white students that boarded next door. She felt as if settlers and Native people lived in different worlds. In 1899, the federal government cut funding for Indian religious schools according to the Browning Rule of 1896, which stipulated that federal government schools must be filled before Indian students enrolled in church-oriented institutions. In 1900, Mourning Dove, along with other Native students from Goodwin Mission School, transferred to the Indian school at the Fort Spokane Agency.

In 1902, while at school, Mourning Dove's mother died. Mourning Dove returned home to help her family manage the household. After her father remarried in 1904, she enrolled at Fort Shaw School in Montana, near her maternal grandparents. While in Montana, in 1908, Mourning Dove witnessed the roundup of the last free-ranging bison herd. The roundup affected her greatly, and she later wrote about the event in her first novel. In 1909, she married a classmate named Hector McLeod (Flathead). After a few years, Mourning Dove separated from Hector, due to his abuse and violent tendencies.[4]

In 1912, Mourning Dove moved to Portland, Oregon. She began to work on a novel, taking the pen name Morning Dove. Years later, after seeing a mounted bird labeled as a "mourning dove" at a museum, she changed the spelling. As a writer, Mourning Dove or *Humishuma* was discouraged by her first attempt at a novel. To improve her skills as a writer, she enrolled at a business school in Calgary. From 1913 to 1915, she learned typing, shorthand, bookkeeping and basic writing skills, earning high grades. During her time at business school, Mourning Dove continued to write about her experiences in journals. According to one article, she began to imagine herself as a voice for her people, which would help Native people and white people understand each other better.

In 1916, Mourning Dove met Lucullus Virgil McWhorter, a Yakima rancher and advocate for Indian rights. His impression of Mourning Dove was very positive, and he encouraged her as an activist and a writer. In a letter to Mourning Dove, McWhorter deemed her responsible for preserving Salish traditions. The pair corresponded until she died. In a newspaper interview in 1916, Mourning Dove explained her intention to fight negative stereotypes of American Indians. She stated that Indians have feelings just like white people, which is the character of Native people. During the interview, she also identified education as a key element in the future of her people.[5]

In 1917, Mourning Dove began to teach at the Inkameep (*Nk'mip*) Indian Reserve in Oliver, British Columbia. Her sister had married the brother of the reserve chief, and Mourning Dove also lent her writing skills to local Native leaders. In 1919, she married Fred Galler (Colville). Although the couple occasionally fought and separated, they remained together, working as migrant laborers in hop fields and apple orchards. Living on the Colville Reservation, Mourning Dove switched her focus from fiction to folklore, collecting traditional interior Salish stories. Meanwhile, McWhorter edited her novel, adding new material and elevating her prose while searching for a publisher. Scholars have criticized McWhorter for changing her prose, but the correspondence between Mourning Dove and the rancher shows how much Mourning Dove appreciated his intervention into her prose and use of the written language.[6]

After various setbacks, Mourning Dove's novel, *Cogewea, the Half Blood: A Depiction of the Great Montana Cattle Range,* was finally published in 1927.[7] Although the book is somewhat inconsistent in writing styles and language, and encumbered with McWhorter's own research, Mourning Dove's work is highly significant. As one of the first known published work by a Native American woman, it represents a unique collaboration between two writers of different genders and cultures. With the publication of *Cogewea,* Mourning Dove created an opportunity for non-Natives to understand Native history, culture, and lifeways by blending cultural knowledge and her own family history with Western style of writing. In her work, Mourning Dove made aspects of Native life accessible to white readers for the first time. In 1930, with McWhorter and a new editor, Heister Dean Guie, Mourning Dove published *Coyote Stories* (1930), a re-telling of the stories she had collected from Salish elders. Originally conceived as a children's book, the trio agreed to omit stories containing incest, transvestic, and infanticide. Indeed, many of the stories included in the book were unrecognizable to Salish elders, a conscious effort on the part of Mourning Dove to suppress a negative image. By promoting her work as fiction, she felt relieved of the need for accuracy. More importantly, Mourning Dove rooted her work in the oral traditions of her people, and preserved Native cultural knowledge and practices for the benefit of future generations.[8]

Throughout her life, Mourning Dove advocated for awareness and Native rights through public speaking engagements. In 1930, she spoke to the Campfire Girls during their Indian Year. The same year, she addressed the Omak Commercial Club about fishing rights. In 1935, she spoke to the Brewster Women's Christian Temperance Union. Mourning Dove also promoted Native crafts and traditions in the Wild Sunflower Club. As a charter member of the Eagle Feather Club, a group devoted to social welfare and betterment for Indians, Mourning Dove fought for girls with legal troubles to be released into her custody.

Mourning Dove's activism was not limited to non-Native organizations. She was politically active for her tribe, insisting the Biles-Coleman Company in East Omak hire Indian workers in exchange for locating a lumber mill on reservation land. She also spoke in favor of reducing the number of agency workers. In 1935, Mourning Dove was elected to the Colville council, the first woman to hold the position.

For much of her adult life, Mourning Dove's health suffered. She was childless but spent years taking care of other children in housekeeping positions. She labored long hours as a migrant worker, writing on scraps of paper and loose sheets in her spare time. Her mental health also suffered, which she attributed to her nervous disposition. In July 1936, she became disoriented. Her family took her to the state hospital at Medical Lake, near Spokane, Washington, where she passed away. According to the coroner, she suffered from depression and exhaustion. Mourning Dove was approximately 50 years old.

Mourning Dove believed herself to be a dreamer of her own life and that of her people. In doing so, she always thought back to the teachings of her parents and tribal elders to be truthful and honest. Her elders offered the foundation of her education and the way to success in life. Mourning Dove's desire to bridge the past and present led her to activism. Concerned about the inevitable loss of cultural knowledge, she sought to preserve as much of her culture as possible by adding more Native voices to the genre of fiction. Mourning Dove actively promoted awareness and understanding, instead of perpetuating negative stereotypes. By reconciling her two worlds, Mourning Dove opened a new world of possibility for Native American women activists, past and present.

NOTES

1. Russell Hellstern. "Mourning Dove (1885 (?)-1936: Colville Salishan Writer and Activist." Sharon Malinowski, ed., *Notable Native Americans* (Detroit: Gale Research Inc., 1995): 280.

2. Hellstern. "Mourning Dove (1885 (?)-1936: Colville Salishan Writer and Activist." Sharon Malinowski, ed., *Notable Native Americans* (Detroit: Gale Research Inc., 1995): 280

3. Mourning Dove, "Learning the Love Medicine," Clifford E. Trafer and Richard D. Scheuerman, eds., *Fiction International* 20 (1991): 142–156.

4. Dexter Fisher Cirillo, "Mourning Dove," Gretchen M. Bataille, ed., *Native American Women: A Biographical Dictionary*, 178; Hellstern. "Mourning Dove (1885 (?)–1936: Colville Salishan Writer and Activist." Sharon Malinowski, ed., *Notable Native Americans* (Detroit: Gale Research Inc., 1995): 280.

5. Cirillo, "Mourning Dove," Gretchen M. Bataille, ed., *Native American Women: A Biographical Dictionary*, 178-79; Hellstern. "Mourning Dove (1885 (?)–1936: Colville Salishan Writer and Activist." Sharon Malinowski, ed., *Notable Native Americans* (Detroit: Gale Research Inc., 1995): 280–281.

6. L.V. McWhorter Collection, Letters Sent and Letters Received, Manuscripts, Archives and Special Collections, Terrell Library, Washington State University, Pullman, Washington.

7. Hellstern. "Mourning Dove (1885 (?)–1936: Colville Salishan Writer and Activist." Sharon Malinowski, ed., *Notable Native Americans* (Detroit: Gale Research Inc., 1995): 281.

8. Cirillo, "Mourning Dove," Gretchen M. Bataille, ed., *Native American Women: A Biographical Dictionary*, 179.

BIBLIOGRAPHY

Champagne, Duane, ed. *The Native North American Almanac*. Detroit: Gale Research 1994.

Cirillo, Dexter Fisher. "Mourning Dove." Gretchen M. Bataille, ed. *Native American Women: A Biographical Dictionary*. New York: Garland Publishing, 1993.

Dove, Mourning. *Cogewea, the Half-Blood: A Depiction of the Great Montana Cattle Range*. London: University of Nebraska Press, 1990.

Dove, Mourning. *Coyote Stories*. Lincoln: Bison Books, 1990.

Dove, Mourning. *Mourning Dove: A Salishan Autobiography*, edited by Jay Miller. Lincoln: University of Nebraska Press, 1994.

Hellstern, Russell. "Mourning Dove (1885 (?)-1936: Colville Salishan Writer and Activist." Sharon Malinowski, ed. *Notable Native Americans*. Detroit: Gale Research Inc., 1995.

L.V. McWhorter Collection, Manuscripts, Archives and Special Collections, Terrell Library, Washington State University, Pullman, Washington.

Trafzer, Clifford E. and Richard Scheuerman, editors. *Mourning Dove's Stories*. San Diego: San Diego State University Press, 1991.

FURTHER READING

Champagne, Duane, ed. *The Native North American Almanac*. Detroit: Gale Research 1994.

Cirillo, Dexter Fisher. "Mourning Dove." Gretchen M. Bataille, ed. *Native American Women: A Biographical Dictionary*. New York: Garland Publishing, 1993.

Dove, Mourning. *Cogewea, the Half-Blood: A Depiction of the Great Montana Cattle Range*. Lincoln and London: University of Nebraska Press, 1991.

Dove, Mourning. *Coyote Stories*. Lincoln: Bison Books, 1990.

Dove, Mourning. "Learning the Love Medicine," Clifford E. Trafzer and Richard D. Scheuerman, eds., *Fiction International* 20 (1991).

Dove, Mourning. *Mourning Dove: A Salishan Autobiography*, edited by Jay Miller. Lincoln and London: University of Nebraska Press, 1990.

Hellstern, Russell. "Mourning Dove (1885 (?)–1936: Colville Salishan Writer and Activist."

Malinowski, Sharon ed. *Notable Native Americans*. Detroit: Gale Research Inc., 1995.

Trafzer, Clifford E. and Richard D. Scheuerman, editors. *Mourning Dove's Stories*. San Diego: San Diego State University Press, 1991.

Chapter Three

Premier Basket Artist

Elsie Comanche Allen (b. 1899–d. 1990)

Meranda Roberts

Pomo basket weaver Elsie Comanche Allen was born on September 22, 1899, to George and Annie Comanche (Burke) near Santa Rosa, California. As a child, Elsie lived with her maternal grandmother, Mary Arnold, in Cloverdale, California. From Mary Arnold, Elsie learned her people's ancestral stories as well as the importance of elderberry bushes and willows in the creation of Pomo objects. She learned how Pomo women used these plants to make baskets and homes. However, Elsie had to leave her grandmother's care after her father passed away and her mother's new husband moved the family to Hopland, California, to work as ranchers. While in the fields, Elsie began to learn how to speak Central Pomo, in addition to her native Southern Pomo.[1] She learned the Central Pomo dialect from tribal elders working in agriculture and ranching.[2] They also taught Elsie how to hunt, fish, and prepare wild plant foods. Unfortunately, these lessons came to a temporary halt, when at the age of eleven, a government agent convinced Annie Burke to enroll Elsie at the Indian boarding school on the Round Valley Reservation near Covelo, California.

Elsie's experience at the boarding school proved detrimental to her health. She suffered physical and mental abuse at the hands of her instructors, who wanted to transform Native children into assimilated Americans. They denigrated her Pomo culture and language to the extent that Elsie vowed to never teach her children Pomo languages, traditions, or values. Despite leaving this school after one year and returning home to her family, Elsie refrained from publicly acknowledging her Native heritage in American society until the 1960s.

When she turned thirteen, Elsie attended the Hopland Indian School, conveniently located near the ranch where her family worked. As a result of living in a Native community, she continued to learn from her elders about the old ways and important Pomo practices. As a young person, Elsie began to learn to weave baskets from her mother and Mary Arnold, who had learned to weave from Elsie's great-grandmother, *Gunsissie*. With their guidance, Elsie began to learn how to coil and twine burden, mortar, and canoe baskets. More importantly her mother and grandmother taught her to collect, store, and manage the natural materials used to create her baskets.[3] These lessons helped Elsie understand her place in the world and the prayers that she needed to use to thank the Creator for supplying bountiful amounts of plant materials for her baskets. Frustrated by only working as a ranch hand or farm worker most of her life, Elsie left Hopland at eighteen for a nursing position at the St. Joseph's Hospital in San Francisco, California.[4]

After nine months of work at St. Joseph's Hospital, Elsie contracted influenza and had to return to Hopland to recover. Elsie became one of the millions of people that caught the Spanish influenza of 1918–1919 during the global pandemic that killed millions of people around the world. Fortunately, Elsie survived after a lengthy and difficult convalescence. The prayers of her people, especially her family, helped heal the budding weaver. After making a full recovery in 1919, Elsie married Arthur Allen in a Catholic ceremony and then in an Indigenous ceremony.[5] Elsie and Arthur moved to a ranch north of Ukiah, California, where they began their family, eventually having four children.[6] The responsibility of raising her young family and providing for the family left little time for Elsie to collect basket materials or the time needed to assemble a fully formed basket.

In 1924, before passing away, Annie Burke asked Elsie to not burn her baskets upon her burial; an ancient Pomo tradition.[7] Annie recognized the cultural value of her baskets and wanted to leave them for others to study to continue the tradition of strong Pomo basket makers. Annie also wanted future basketry students to know the techniques she had used and how she had incorporated certain designs into baskets. She was particularly concerned that her daughter, Elsie, would have the baskets from which she could draw ideas and inspirations. Annie's forethought and actions helped insure the future generations of basket weavers among the Pomo and other nearly tribes. Annie asked Elsie to display the family's baskets in the local white community, so that non-Indians might learn to appreciate basketry as part of Pomo culture and civilization. Pomo basketry was high art, not a "primitive" art created by backward "savages." [8]

Throughout her life, Elsie carried the scars of discrimination against the Indigenous people of California. She remembered being punished for speaking her language at the Round Valley boarding school. She also worried about her own people criticizing her for publicly exhibiting her mother's baskets and those she had made herself. Displaying their baskets had never been their custom, but Elsie insisted on the change so that Native Americans and non-Natives might learn from her basket collection. In her autobiography, *Pomo Basketmaking: A Supreme Art for the Weaver,* Elsie revealed that she let go of these fears after taking her daughter, Genevieve, to a Chinese restaurant for dinner.[9] Elsie had expected that only Chinese people would be eating there but was shocked to see all the different ethnic groups represented in the café. She was more impressed with how much the Chinese openly embraced their cultural heritage and language, despite discrimination against them in Ukiah. From that moment forward, Elsie committed herself to ensuring that the art of Pomo basket weaving would never be lost and that she would do all that she could to teach others.

These affirmations helped Elsie honor her mother's wish to preserve her baskets. In 1962, her mother, Annie Burke, died. As Elsie made funeral arrangements, she openly and publicly refused to bury Annie's baskets and materials with her. Elsie wrote that at that time, "some of my Pomo people were not pleased with me. They felt these old ways should die and we should forget the past heritage."[10] Despite this backlash, Elsie used her mother's basket pieces to teach Pomo basket weaving at the California Mendocino Art Center. However, she had a hard time convincing young Native American girls to learn from her. These children did not want to dig in the mud for needed materials and did not want to dedicate any of their time to the practice of basket weaving. She eventually began to attract some of the local youth by announcing that, "Basket weaving needs dedication and interest and increasing skill and knowledge. It needs feeling and love and honor for the great weavers of the past who showed us the way. If you can rouse in yourself this interest feeling and dedication, you can create matchless beauty and help renew something that should never be lost."[11]

Susan Billy, Elsie's grandniece, became one of Elsie's greatest students. Susan studied with Elsie for five years and quickly realized that she could not separate basket weaving from Pomo history, traditions, customs, or religion. As Susan worked with Elsie Allen, she came to realize that all aspects of Pomo culture were connected to baskets, including gathering of materials, preparing the plant material, interacting with the basketry materials, and carefully weaving designs into the baskets. Elsie gave Susan some of the tools Annie had used to create her pieces during her lifetime. As a result of the Elsie's teachings and the use of tools once used by Annie, Susan felt that her grandmother's wisdom was being passed down to her and as a result she connected to weaving in a spiritual way, which she never anticipated.

Over the years, Elsie taught both Native and non-Natives how to weave Pomo baskets. She also showed her family's baskets in exhibitions around the United States. On some of her travels, Elsie was able to help properly identify and label baskets held in museum collections, which allowed these institutions to give accurate credit to a tribal community's history. In addition to her teaching, Elsie became the primary consultant for Sonoma State University's Warm Springs Cultural Resources Study, designed to document the history and culture of the Dry Creek and Cloverdale Pomo. One of the study's main goals was to prevent the United States Army Corp of Engineers from building a dam at Warm Springs that would have flooded the surrounding area and destroy Indigenous plants that Native peoples used for basket weaving, medicine, ceremony, or economic pursuits. As a member of the tribal council consulting with scholars, Elsie provided extensive knowledge about the endangered plants in the area and how the flooding of the proposed area would significantly alter the lives and traditions of Pomo people. In a bittersweet compromise, in 1985, Elsie was able to transplant some of the threatened plant species to an alternate location before the Corps of Engineers flooded the area.

In time, Elsie received an honorary Doctorate of Divinity as the "Pomo Sage." Though she passed away on December 31, 1990, at the age of 91, Elsie is still credited with keeping Pomo basket weaving from fading into obscurity and for being an inspiration for many of today's weavers, including many members of her family, who continue to fight to have their work acknowledged as more than a commercial art. According to Susan Billy, Elsie helped to give many of her students a purpose in life and for paving a path of understanding that Pomo basketry is a key element of Pomo culture and identity. Furthermore, Elsie's ability to save Indigenous foliage has influenced members of her community and other Indigenous people of California to teach farmers about the harm that pesticides and herbicides have on the vegetation that Pomo use for creating basketry. These same community members are committed to teaching museum curators about how the basket pieces in their collections are living beings with a story that must be told and respected. Without Elsie's fearlessness and determination, such strides in cultural preservation and understanding would not have been possible. Elsie Allen was a cultural activist, not just for the Pomo people, but for all traditional Indigenous artists living a life committed to preserving cultural traditions that are key elements to their spiritual and cultural arts and identities.

NOTES

1. Suzanne Abel-Vidor, Dot Brovarney, and Susan Billy. *Remember Your Relations: The Elsie Allen Baskets, Family & Friends* (Berkeley: Heyday Books, 1996), 23.

2. Elsie Comanche Allen and Vinson Brown, *Pomo Basketmaking: A Supreme Art for the Weaver* (Happy Camp, CA: Naturegraph, 1972), 9.

3. Suzanne Abel-Vidor, *Remember Your Relations: The Elsie Allen Baskets, Family & Friends*, 24.

4. Elsie Allen, *Pomo Basket Making: A Supreme Art for the Weaver,* 12.

5. Elsie Allen, *Pomo BasketMaking: A Supreme Art for the Weaver,* 12.

6. Elsie Allen, *Pomo Basket Making: A Supreme Art for the Weaver,* 13.

7. Elsie Allen, *Pomo Basket Making: A Supreme Art for the Weaver,* 12.

8. Elsie Allen, *Pomo Basket Making: A Supreme Art for the Weaver,* 13.

9. Elsie Allen, *Pomo Basket Making: A Supreme Art for the Weaver,* 14.

10. Elsie Allen, *Pomo Basket Making: A Supreme Art for the Weaver,* 14.

11. Elsie Allen, *Pomo Basket Making: A Supreme Art for the Weaver,* 15.

BIBLIOGRAPHY

Abel-Vidor, Suzanne and Susan Billy. *Remember Your Relations: The Elsie Allen Baskets, Family and Friends.* Berkeley: Heyday, 1996.

Allen, Elsie. *Pomo Basketmaking: A Supreme Art for the Weaver.* Happy Camp, CA: Naturegraph Publishers, 1972.

FURTHER READING

Abel-Vidor, Suzanne and Susan Billy. *Remember Your Relations: The Elsie Allen Baskets, Family and Friends.* Berkeley: Heyday, 1996.

Allen, Elsie. *Pomo Basketmaking: A Supreme Art for the Weaver.* Happy Camp, CA: Naturegraph Publishers, 1972.

Giese, Paula. "Elsie Allen (1899–1990) and Pomo Basket Family." Last modified July 7, 2011. http://www.kstrom.net/isk/art/basket/elsieall.html.

McAuliffe, Claudeen E., "Elsie Allen, 1899–1990." Malinowski, Sharon. *Notable Native Americans.* Detroit: Gale Research, 1995.

Sonoma State University Library. "Elsie Allen, 1899–1990." http://library.sonoma.edu/research/guides/regional/notablepeople/allen.

Chapter Four

Dancing Activist

Maria Tallchief (b. 1925–d. 2013)

Michelle Lorimer

As the best ballerinas emerged from Europe, particularly Russia, Maria Tallchief, an American Indian woman, became the first prima ballerina in the United States. Tallchief's graceful motions, designed under renowned choreographer George Balanchine, graced stages around the world. As one of the most distinguished ballerinas in American history, Tallchief received many honors including the Capezio Award in 1965 and Theodore Thomas History Maker Award for Distinction in the Performing Arts in 1999. Her collaboration with Balanchine precipitated the emergence of ballet as an institution in American art culture. The art of dance has reached an apex today as a direct result of Maria Tallchief. She credited her Native American heritage for her discipline and innate dancing abilities. She worked to preserve her Native culture while establishing herself as a professional ballerina of American Indian pedigree, never letting her background dictate the way people perceived her in the public sphere.

Maria Tallchief was born Elizabeth Marie Tall Chief on January 24, 1925. Maria's father was a wealthy Osage Indian named Alexander Joseph Tall Chief. Her mother was Ruth Porter Tall Chief, a Scots-Irish woman from Kansas. Maria's mother encouraged her and her sister to dance but she also emphasized the importance of their Osage heritage. Maria grew up in her hometown of Fairfax, Oklahoma. Although Maria and her family benefited from the wealth generated from oil found on Osage land, greed associated with large amounts of money spread among their people, resulting in less beneficial, even deadly outcomes. White American neighbors living outside the Osage community committed insurance fraud scams, intermarried with the Osage people, hired money-hungry lawyers to cash in on the oil boom, and threatened the persistence of Native society. Outsiders also murdered a number of Osage to get to their headrights. This invasion led to the death of over a quarter of Osage people during the early 1920s, a period now gruesomely known as the "Osage Reign of Terror." The Osages faced other destructive influences as a result of the leisure-filled lifestyle that money bought. For instance, Maria's mother expressed concern over the alcoholism and aimlessness that took hold of people in their community. Maria's parents kept the children close and directed them into the arts.[1]

In order to combat these social problems, Ruth enrolled Maria and Marjorie, Maria's younger sister, in ballet and piano lessons at an early age. Through a regimented daily routine Ruth instilled in the girls a strict sense of discipline and determination. This came naturally for the girls who enjoyed an innate sense of drive and determination due to their Osage heritage. Eventually, Ruth grew tired of Fairfax, her small hometown on the Osage Indian Reservation, which she did not envision as the best location for her children's artistic development. At age four, Maria began taking ballet lessons from a traveling instructor, who put her on point prematurely, a potentially dangerous action that a later instructor would try to mend. In 1933, the Tallchief family relocated to a suburb of Los Angeles, California, where Maria and Marjorie had more opportunities to enhance and develop their artistic abilities.[2]

In southern California, Ruth enrolled the girls in a local ballet school under Ernest Belcher, who took Maria off point and taught the girls the basics of ballet. After spending five years under Belcher's guidance, Ruth transferred the young dancers to a school operated by renowned choreographer and dancer Bronislava Nijinska near Beverly Hills, California. At Nijinska's school, twelve-year-old Maria expanded her passion for ballet. Maria refocused her earlier goal of becoming a concert pianist, to aspiring to become a professional ballerina. She thrived under Nijinska's disciplined and nonverbal instruction, a style that appealed to her sense of aesthetics. Maria again credited her Native American roots for her ability to thrive under Nijinska's demanding tutelage.

As proof of Maria's success under Madame Nijinska, the young ballerina danced the lead role in *Chopin Concerto*, which premiered at the famous Hollywood Bowl. After completing high school and five years learning under Madame Nijinska, Tallchief traveled to New York City with fellow dancer, Tatiana Riabouchinska, in hope of gaining an audition for Ballet Russe de Monte Carlo and Serge Denham. Initially rejected because Ballet Russe did not need dancers, a few days later Tallchief received a call informing her of an opening. She would need to leave immediately for a Canadian tour.

Maria danced in the Canadian dance tour, and she returned to New York where she received a permanent position with Ballet Russe. The company offered the position to Tallchief, who eagerly accepted. Her first break into the spotlight occurred early on when Ballet Russe added two of Madame Nijinska's ballets, *The Snow Maiden* and *Chopin Concerto,* the former of which Tallchief knew well. Madame Nijinska requested that Tallchief understudy the lead role in *Chopin Concerto* to the dismay of many Russian dancers in the company who thought themselves superior to the American dancer. For many months Tallchief danced in the ensembles for a variety of ballets. She constantly labored to improve her form and demonstrate her tireless work ethic. Finally, after the lead ballerina and Ballet Russe management suffered a falling out, Ballet Russe forced Tallchief to step into the position. She danced in this position while Ballet Russe toured and when it returned to New York. Tallchief earned positive reviews for this role, one of which came from John Martin, the preeminent dance critic in America who wrote for the *New York Times*.[3]

During her second year with Ballet Russe, Tallchief began to take on new roles, including lead positions. Also in 1942, Ballet Russe hired George Balanchine as a new choreographer, who later produced many ballets for the troupe. This visionary Russian choreographer, who opened the School of American Ballet and organized the American Ballet Company in New York City, looked to establish a ballet company in the United States to rival European ballets. Balanchine's ability to approach the ballet from the standpoint of a musician especially appealed to Tallchief, who had trained as a musician herself. Tallchief's relationship with Balanchine blossomed quickly through his constant guidance and her admiration and commitment to improve her dancing in order to please the choreographer. Balanchine rewarded Tallchief's hard work by giving her lead roles that challenged her still more.

As Tallchief and Balanchine's professional relationship evolved, so too did their personal relationship but on a subtler level. One night Balanchine, twenty years Tallchief's senior, expressed his feelings for Tallchief much more explicitly when he asked the twenty-year-old woman to be his wife. Tallchief, caught off guard by this proposal, was unaware of Balanchine's personal feelings toward her. Tallchief took some time to contemplate the proposal and asked for her mother's opinion. Tallchief's mother did not like the prospect of the young dancer marrying an older, divorced, man. Her father was also not interested in Tallchief marrying Balanchine, as he thought it best for Tallchief to focus on her dancing career, not marriage. The response Tallchief received from her parents discouraged the young woman, who returned to Balanchine's side. Nonetheless, on August 16, 1946, Tallchief and Balanchine married at the Manhattan County Courthouse, a ceremony her parents did not attend. Tallchief understood that the pair's personal and professional lives were intertwined, and that she was Balanchine's ballerina and muse just as much, if not more, than she was his wife.[4]

After completing the remainder of her contractual obligation to Ballet Russe in March 1947, Tallchief planned to join Balanchine's new company, Ballet Society—an exclusive group that performed for select audiences a few times each year. However, Tallchief's debut with Ballet Society was placed on hold because, soon after their marriage, Balanchine took a position with the Paris Opera Ballet, where Tallchief joined him. In Paris, Tallchief worked hard to improve her dancing, while she also took time to enjoy married life with her new husband. Life in France challenged the couple, as Tallchief had a difficult time adapting to the cultural differences, and Balanchine faced much criticism for his mix of classical and avant garde ballets. Despite these hardships, Tallchief also succeeded in France as the lead in *Apollo* on the Opera Ballet's opening night. Tallchief received attention and many positive reviews for this role, both as a stunning dancer and as a Native American woman. Tallchief's debut also commemorated the first time an American had danced at the Paris Opera in over a century.[5]

Living in Paris marked a turning point in Tallchief's ballet career. She noticed a substantial difference in her dancing skills, which she credited to Balanchine's instruction. After a season in Paris, the couple returned to New York to rejoin Ballet Society. Balanchine created many roles for Tallchief in his ballets, meant to challenge the twenty-two-year-old dancer. After three seasons, Tallchief took the role of lead ballerina of the Ballet Society following Mary Ellen Moylan's departure from the position for Ballet Russe.

After success with the exclusive ballet performances, Ballet Society decided to open their shows to the public with *Symphony in C*. Ballet Society experienced more success in *Orpheus*, a ballet derived from the Greek legend of a man who travels to the underworld to bring his wife back to life. Tallchief played the part of Eurydice, Orpheus's wife. *Orpheus*, a ballet produced through the collaboration of Balanchine and composer Igor Stravinski, has been credited as the piece that sparked the transformation of American ballet, with Tallchief standing at the forefront. Due to the success of *Orpheus*, Morton Baum, chairman of the Executive Committee of the City Center of Music and Drama Inc., asked Ballet Society to become the City Center's exclusive troupe, changing the name of the company to New York City Ballet.

New York City Ballet premiered on October 11, 1948, a night in which Tallchief danced for both *Orpheus* and *Symphony in C*. However, as time went on, Tallchief's limited dance schedule worried Balanchine, who helped her secure a concurrent position on tour with Ballet Theatre where she performed in *Swan Lake*, among others. After this tour, Tallchief studied further at Daphne Vane's studio in California for a summer. During their cross-country road trip back to New York, Tallchief and Balanchine visited Tallchief's hometown of Fairfax, Oklahoma to spend time with Tallchief's grandmother.

During this trip Tallchief shared aspects of her Native American heritage with her husband, who showed great interest in this important aspect of Tallchief's life. Tallchief never forgot her roots and continued to bring important people in her life back to visit her hometown to share her culture.

With the maturation of New York City Ballet, Balanchine allowed Tallchief to dance in the well-known ballet *Firebird*. Tallchief's role in *Firebird*, an iconic ballet that critics credit for solidifying New York City's role as a major ballet center, boosted Tallchief's career exponentially. Tallchief received rave reviews for her lead role as the firebird from such prominent periodicals as *Time, Newsweek*, and the *New York Times*. The public also lauded Tallchief's abilities. Her performance as the firebird inspired many people, as critics and writers for decades after noted the influential way in which Tallchief danced in this ballet. The increased publicity the New York City Ballet received as a result of *Firebird* created more opportunities for added performances and led to an invitation for the company to tour in England for a season. While the New York City Ballet did not receive as much praise from the international critics in London, their sheer presence on an international stage improved the company's reputation.[6]

At Tallchief's public notoriety grew, her personal relationship with Balanchine waned. Tallchief, in her mid-twenties, felt as though she needed more in her life than ballet. She expressed a desire for children—a notion Balanchine did not second as he thought his wife should not compromise her professional dancing career. The couple continued to drift until Tallchief and Balanchine publicly announced their separation after the New York City Ballet returned to the United States from their tour in Europe.

Despite their separation, Tallchief and Balanchine continued to build their successful professional relationship. Once they returned to New York, the company performed a series of successful ballets. Many of these ballets, such as Balanchine's *Swan Lake*, received rave reviews and again launched Tallchief's career to still higher levels. Balanchine persistently choreographed ballets that highlighted Tallchief's dancing abilities, as she became a fan favorite and ballet sensation. New York City Ballet returned to tour in Europe for a second time in 1952. The company performed in France, Italy, England, Germany, Netherlands, and Spain. They danced such favorites as *Firebird, Serenade, Lilac Garden, Swan Lake, La Valse*, and the controversial ballet *The Cage*. Furthermore, as technology advanced into the 1950s, Tallchief began to perform some of her most acclaimed roles for television shows and films.[7]

Tallchief garnered accolades when she danced for President Dwight D. Eisenhower at his inauguration on January 20, 1953. Later that same year, the Washington Press Club awarded Tallchief a Woman of the Year plaque, with the designation of Woman of Achievement. She further received a home-coming ceremony from Oklahoma and the Osage tribe, which declared June 29 Maria Tallchief day. The Osage inducted the dancer into the tribe with a new title, Princess Wa-Xthe-Thonba, chosen by Tallchief's grandmother. The new title, which translated to Princess Two Standards, represented Maria's double roles as a successful prima ballerina and an Osage woman. Tallchief took pride in her Osage heritage but tried to move professional focus away from this aspect of her life, as she did not want her culture to define her as a dancer.[8]

After a third European tour with New York Ballet in the summer of 1953, Tallchief and Balanchine began work on the legendary ballet, *The Nut-cracker*, with Tallchief as the Sugar Plum Fairy. Tallchief's success up to this point in her career set the stage for an extraordinary offer from Ballet Russe in 1954. Previously active for many seasons, the company wanted to reorganize for a tour in the United States. Its managers looked to Tallchief as a key player in realizing this goal. In return for her services, Ballet Russe, in conjunction with Columbia Artists, paid Tallchief the highest known salary in ballet's history. Tallchief received voluminous publicity from this deal, including a feature on the cover of *Newsweek*.

While Tallchief succeeded in her professional career, she continued to face hardships in her personal life. Following the legal termination of Tallchief's marriage to Balanchine in 1952, Tallchief quickly married for a second time to aviator Elmourza Natirboff, whom she had met before her separation to Balanchine. This marriage also fizzled rapidly, ending in 1954. Tallchief continued dating until she married for the final time at age thirty-one, to Henry "Buzz" Paschen. A season after their marriage in the summer of 1956, Tallchief returned for another tour of Europe with New York City Ballet, ac-companied by her husband. After only a short time on tour, Tallchief received word from her doctor that she was pregnant. Placed on bedrest, she could not continue with the company.[9]

The remainder of 1956 challenged New York City Ballet. Tallchief miscar-ried and polio paralyzed Balanchine's new ballerina wife. After recovering from these tragedies, Tallchief returned to New York City Ballet, embark-ing on a six-month tour of Asia and Australia. Tallchief agreed to tour only through Japan in order to maintain a closer relationship with her Chicago-based husband. In the summer of 1958, doctors informed Tallchief and Paschen that she had again become pregnant. This time Tallchief took numer-ous precautions to protect her baby while maintaining her ballet basics. After giving birth to her daughter, Elise Maria Paschen, Tallchief began training for her return to the ballet. Only seven months after Elise's birth, Tallchief began performing with New York City Ballet once more. However, along with the healthy birth of Tallchief's daughter came a pair of unfortunate events. Both Tallchief's and Paschen's fathers became very ill and passed away before Elise's first birthday.[10]

Despite these personal tragedies, Tallchief continued to perform, accepting a position on tour in Europe with Ballet Theatre. While it pained the dancer to be away from her daughter for six months, Tallchief knew it was important for an American ballet troupe to perform strongly and successfully on its diplomatic trip to the Soviet Union. The troupe received warm welcomes and positive reviews in the communist country, with many notable individuals joining the audiences, including Premier Nikita Khrushchev. After the troupe returned to the United States, Tallchief visited her husband and daughter in Chicago for a short time, only to leave time and time again for a series of performances in Europe and the United States with Ballet Theatre.[11]

Tallchief felt an emotional distance grow between herself and her husband after spending so much time away from him. Tallchief separated from Paschen, taking Elise and a nanny to Europe with her to study ballet. Tallchief accepted a position dancing at the Royal Danish Theater with her long-time partner Erik Bruch. Tallchief became the first American to dance at this theater. Eventually, she returned to America, settled in New York City, and reunited with New York City Ballet in order to establish a more sedentary life for her school-age daughter. Tallchief's position at the company shifted over the years. Into the mid-1960s she danced primarily in early bird matinees and focused more on teaching ballet. However, she maintained a high number of admirers and received a number of prominent invitations and awards. For instance, President Lyndon Johnson invited her to dance at the White House. Jacqueline Kennedy requested that Tallchief teach a ballet class for her daughter, Caroline. Along with teaching, Tallchief also began to lecture in conjunction with the New York City Ballet Education Department.[12]

After several more tours through Europe, both as a teacher and dancer, Tallchief contemplated retirement to preserve her family. Following a reconciliation with Paschen, Tallchief accepted only a handful of touring requests before she decided to retire to Chicago to become a more present mother and wife. Tallchief kept ballet alive in her daily routine, through personal practice at her home and as a teacher to young dance students. From this experience as an instructor, Tallchief became involved in the Chicago Lyric Opera Ballet and later developed it into the Chicago City Ballet. Tallchief worked diligently to teach in the same style as Balanchine, especially after his death in 1983. She also made efforts to keep his female focus of "ballet is woman" alive, in an age when men dominated ballet choreography and administration. In 1999, Tallchief received the National Medal of Arts.[13]

Maria Tallchief lived a long and active life as a dancer and instructor. She passed in 2013 at the age of 88. She was considered a national treasure and admired worldwide. Throughout her career, Maria Tallchief promoted preservation of Indian culture and tradition. She accepted a position on the board of Americans for Indian Opportunity, and worked with the television program, *One World* to bridge ballet culture and Native Americans. Although a boycott against Western art's infiltration into Native American cultures hampered this television program, Tallchief continued to develop her roots within the Native American community and became the first Osage to receive an Indian Achievement Award. Tallchief also kept her Native American roots alive within her own family. Many critics noted the interesting coincidence that America's first prima ballerina was, fittingly, a Native American woman. While Tallchief did not want this fact to define her career as a ballerina, she nonetheless continues respected her heritage and worked for the preservation of Native American art, culture, and history.

NOTES

1. Maria Tallchief and Larry Kaplan, *Maria Tallchief: America's Prima Ballerina* (New York: Henry Holt and Company, 1997), 8–12.

2. Maria Tallchief and Larry Kaplan, *Maria Tallchief: America's Prima Ballerina* (New York: Henry Holt and Company, 1997), 14–15.

3. Maria Tallchief and Larry Kaplan, *Maria Tallchief: America's Prima Ballerina* (New York: Henry Holt and Company, 1997), 23–27.

4. Maria Tallchief and Larry Kaplan, *Maria Tallchief: America's Prima Ballerina* (New York: Henry Holt and Company, 1997), 38–58.

5. Maria Tallchief and Larry Kaplan, *Maria Tallchief: America's Prima Ballerina* (New York: Henry Holt and Company, 1997), 73.

6. Joan Kufrin, *Uncommon Women* (Piscataway, New Jersey: New Century Publishers, 1981), 3–16.

7. Maria Tallchief and Larry Kaplan, *Maria Tallchief: America's Prima Ballerina* (New York: Henry Holt and Company, 1997), 134–149.

8. Maria Tallchief and Larry Kaplan, *Maria Tallchief: America's Prima Ballerina* (New York: Henry Holt and Company, 1997), 168–183.

9. Maria Tallchief and Larry Kaplan, *Maria Tallchief: America's Prima Ballerina* (New York: Henry Holt and Company, 1997), 193–229.

10. Maria Tallchief and Larry Kaplan, *Maria Tallchief: America's Prima Ballerina* (New York: Henry Holt and Company, 1997), 225–248.

11. Maria Tallchief and Larry Kaplan, *Maria Tallchief: America's Prima Ballerina* (New York: Henry Holt and Company, 1997), 250–272.

12. Maria Tallchief and Larry Kaplan, *Maria Tallchief: America's Prima Ballerina* (New York: Henry Holt and Company, 1997), 272–298.

13. Timothy Gilfoyle, "Creating a Dance: Interviews with Bruce Graham and Maria Tallchief," *Chicago History* 28 (2000), 54–65.

BIBLIOGRAPHY

Gilfoyle, Timothy. "Creating a Dance: Interviews with Bruce Graham and Maria Tallchief." *Chicago History* 28, no. 3 (2000): 54–65.

Kufrin, Joan. *Uncommon Women*. Piscataway, NJ: New Century Publishers, Inc., 1981.

Maria Tallchief. Produced by Sandra Osawa. DVD. Seattle, WA: Upstream Productions, 2007.

Tallchief, Maria, and Larry Kaplan. *Maria Tallchief: America's Prima Ballerina*. New York: Henry Holt and Company, 1997.

Tallchief Paschen, Maria. "Becoming Maria Tallchief." Carolyn Taylor, Emily Dial-Driver, Carole Burrage, and Sally Emmons-Featherston, editors. *Voices from the Heartland*. Norman: University of Oklahoma Press, 2007.

FURTHER READING

Tallchief, Maria, and Larry Kaplan. *Maria Tallchief: America's Prima Ballerina*. New York: Henry Holt and Company, 1997.

Tallchief Paschen, Maria. "Becoming Maria Tallchief." Carolyn Taylor, Emily Dial-Driver, Carole Burrage, and Sally Emmons-Featherston, editors. *Voices from the Heartland*. Norman: University of Oklahoma Press, 2007.

Chapter Five

Native Woman, Native Voices

Paula Gunn Allen (b. 1939–d. 2008)

Hal Hoffman and Clifford E. Trafzer

Paula Gunn Allen (born Paula Marie Francis) was a prominent Native American scholar, professor, poet, activist, novelist, and literary critic. She collected and interpreted Native American oral narratives and accounts. Allen advocated on behalf of American feminist and LGBT people, writers, and topics. During her life, she stood with antiwar and antinuclear organizations. Her list of publications is long and diverse and includes poetry, essays on feminist theory, and American history written from an American Indian perspective and understanding of culture, language, and oral traditions.

Born in Grants, New Mexico, on October 24, 1939, Allen grew up in Cubero, New Mexico, near her father's trading post.[1] Paula Francis spent her childhood in a small town near Laguna Pueblo located on an old Spanish land grant about fifty miles west of Albuquerque, New Mexico.[2] She often referred to herself as a multicultural event and wrote that the culture of the American Southwest and the ethnic and religious diversity of her family combined to shape many of her key ideas and dominant themes that appeared in her writings. Allen's great-grandfather, the Scottish-born, Kenneth Gunn, immigrated to New Mexico in the nineteenth century and married her great-grandmother, Meta Atseye of Laguna Pueblo.[3]

Her Presbyterian grandmother, who was half Laguna and half Scottish American, first married a Sioux and then remarried a German Jewish immigrant, Sidney Solomon Gottlieb. Her mother grew up speaking and writing both English and Spanish. Allen grew up in the shadow of Mount Taylor, a sacred mountain to her people and many Native Americans of the American Southwest. She was raised in New Mexico surrounded by people from multiple cultures and spoke Laguna, Spanish, Arabic, German, and Navajo. She was the middle of five children, with two older sisters and two younger brothers. Her father, Elias Lee Francis, owned the Cubero Trading Company and served as the lieutenant governor of New Mexico from 1967–1970.[4]

Elias Lee Francis was Lebanese American who spoke only Arabic and Spanish until he was ten years old. Allen's mother, Ethel Haines Gottlieb, was of Laguna Pueblo, Sioux, and Scots heritage, and converted to Catholicism from Presbyterianism to marry Francis. Her family members included people who were Roman Catholics, Jews, Protestants, and atheists. Others believed in the old faith of Laguna Pueblo and supported the ceremonial calendar of Laguna people. These influences, and many others, shaped her ideas, inspired her activism, and empowered her to make rich contributions to Native American literature.[5]

Allen's early childhood education provided her with a variety of experiences and influences. She attended St. Vincent's Academy in Albuquerque and mission schools in Cubero and San Fidel. However, she completed most of her schooling at a Sisters of Charity boarding school in Albuquerque where she graduated from high school in 1957. She became interested in writing in high school when she discovered and tried to imitate the works of Gertrude Stein, Percy Bysshe Shelley, and John Keats. Conflicts between her Catholic background and other religious influences in her life, such as Native American, Protestant, Jewish, and Maronite faiths, profoundly influenced her early writing and thinking.

After attending mission schools in rural Cubero, San Fidel, and Albuquerque, and taking classes at Colorado Women's College, Allen enrolled in the University of Oregon where she received her Bachelor of Arts in English in 1966. Two years later, she earned a master's in fine arts in creative writing from the University of Oregon. After college, she married, had two children (a son and a daughter), and subsequently divorced. A second marriage produced twin sons, one of whom died in infancy. This marriage also ended in divorce. While in Eugene, feeling isolated and suicidal, Allen read N. Scott Momaday's Pulitzer Prize winning *House Made of Dawn*, a story she claimed saved her life and gave her voice as a Native American writer. Momaday's novel helped her understand that she was sane and not crazy, and if she was crazy, then thousands of people around the world were just as nutty as Paula. Momaday's novel centered in the American Southwest helped Paula return to the land of her youth, the hills, mountains, rivers, and people of the American Southwest where she had grown up. Momaday's novel helped Allen refocus her life and consider again the many cultures of the Southwest. Momaday's landmark book forced Paula to embrace her own heritage and the land of her Laguna ancestors. She no longer wanted to write in the Eurocentric manner of other writers. She could form her own literary style, content, and way of presentation based on her own cultural background as a mixed blood Laguna person.[6]

Allen returned to Albuquerque to continue her education and she became more serious about her writing. She enrolled in the doctoral program at the University of New Mexico and was teaching there in 1974 when she published *The Blind Lion*, her first book of poetry. She came to a turning point in her educational career when she read Robert Creeley's *For Love* and discovered that he was teaching at the University of New Mexico. By the late 1960s, Creeley had become interested in mentoring promising young poets, and Allen studied under him for two years. At the time, she considered herself a prose writer, but Creeley help Paula unleash the poet inside of this Laguna woman. Creeley was part of the Black Mountain poets, and he introduced Allen to the writings of several influential American modernist authors such as Denise Levertov and Charles Olson and Beat writers such as Allen Ginsberg. In the 1960s, the Vietnam War inspired Denise Levertov to write remarkable works of rage and sadness. Charles Olson's compelling writings on many topics, including gender and sexuality and the importance of community activism, established him as one of the central figures of mid-twentieth-century American poetry. These activist, avant-garde writers and poets became Allen's early literary models. Recent influences upon her work and thought have been Adrienne Rich, Patricia Clark Smith, and E. A. Mares.[7]

In 1975, Allen graduated with a PhD in American Studies with an emphasis in Native American Studies from the University of New Mexico. Her degree was in American Studies because the English Department had no field in Native American literature. During the 1960s, university programs found no legitimacy in Native American history, culture, literature, music, art, or any other discipline. Promising students like Paula Gunn Allen had to create their own paths to earn a PhD in Native American Studies.

Allen had a remarkable teaching career and a long and significant life as a writer, poet, and activist. While completing her doctorate, she taught at the University of New Mexico and spent her postdoctoral years at the University of California, Los Angeles (UCLA), and in 1984 at the University of California at Berkeley, where she received grants from the Ford Foundation and National Research Council. She taught at San Francisco State University where she was the Director of the Native American Studies Program and was an Associate Fellow at the Stanford University Humanities Institute. Other teaching positions included Fort Lewis College, the College of San Mateo, De Anza Community College, and San Diego State University.[8]

For over thirty years, Allen was an academic activist who promoted Native American literature. She wrote poetry, literary criticism, essays, short stories, a novel, and various scholarly works. Her concern for the plight of Native American culture and literature began during her early college years. In the late 1960s and early 1970s, a new spirit of political militancy arose among the First Americans. They were the nation's poorest minority group with the highest suicide rates. They held lands coveted by corporations. Paula Gunn Allen understood the connection between the socioeconomic troubles of American Indians and lower levels of education. Colleges and universities provided little opportunities for Native American students, and academics had little respect for the study of Native Americans.

During the 1960s, most colleges and universities denied the existence of Native American literature, culture, and history, so Allen directed her energies toward changing the literary world. Through her books and articles as well as her activism, Allen offered a lifelong commitment to promoting the work of Native American writers while advocating for the inclusion of Indian voices in the mainstream of American literature. Allen's thirty years of writing and activism produced significant changes for many minority authors. She was one of the people primarily responsible for altering the required reading lists of literature classes on American college campuses. She helped change the canon. Allen wanted the world to understand that Native American cultures were alive and well throughout the Western Hemisphere.

The list of Allen's publications reflects the wide range of intellectual and spiritual inquiry. She often promoted feminist ideas and consistently attacked stereotyping of Native American women. She never hesitated to challenge the status quo. Many of her early writings explored the conflicts she had with her own multiculturalism. In *Shadow Country* (1982), Allen used a collection of poems and the theme of shadows to explain her experiences as a woman with a multicultural heritage.[9]

In 1983, Allen published *Studies in American Indian Literature: Critical Essays and Course Designs*, a book with an extensive bibliography and detailed information on teaching Native American literature courses. This seminal work laid the foundation for the field of Native American Studies in higher education. Three years later, Allen again broke new ground with a controversial book that became a cornerstone in the study of American Indian culture and gender, *The Sacred Hoop: Recovering the Feminine in American Indian Traditions* (1986). In this work, she highlighted many of the differences between Euro-American and Native American literature, and she attacked the stereotypical portrayals of American Indian women with provocative essays examining female deities, the honored place of lesbians, and the importance of mothers and grandmothers to Indian identity.[10]

Allen made a bold statement about the position of women in American Indian cultures, arguing that phallogocentric European explorers and colonizers subverted traditional American Indian lifestyles and beliefs, and that Indian societies are more often gynocratic (governed by women) than not, and they are never patriarchal. These ideas sparked a spirited debate, but there was no denying that women played key roles in all Native American tribes and communities, a role heretofore ignored by non-Indians.[11]

In 2003, Allen wrote a historical biography of the women she called, the Mother of our Nation. In *Pocahontas: Medicine Woman, Spy, Entrepreneur, Diplomat*, she told the story of early seventeenth century America and the Algonquin woman who formed groundbreaking relations among American Indians and English colonists. Allen's innovative approach to biography writing earned her a Pulitzer Prize nomination for this book. In an effort to "nativize" the story, Allen drew from American Indian oral traditions to go beyond the facts to study Pocahontas within her own spirit-centered world. In the introduction, Allen wrote that any biography of Pocahontas had to explain her life history through a supernatural lens of spirits, myths, and ghosts, all of which informed people of her life and character. Allen's activism was a common element in all of her writings, and with *Pocahontas*, she continued her fight to teach readers about the key roles of women in Indian societies.[12]

During her lifetime, Allen earned many awards. In 1990, she received the American Book Award from the Before Columbus Foundation for *Spider Woman's Granddaughters: Traditional Tales and Contemporary Writing*. She won the Hubbell Prize for Lifetime Achievement in American Literary Studies from the Modern Language Association and the Susan Koppelman Award from the Popular Culture Association. In 2001, she won the Native Writer's Circle Lifetime Achievement Award. She received fellowships from the National Endowment for the Arts, Ford Foundation, Lannan Foundation, and National Research Council. The University of Oregon named Allen CAS Alumni Fellow. Allen won other awards and honors.[13]

Several important people and events have influenced Allen's writings and activism throughout the course of her life. Early in her career, the writings of her mother's uncle, John Gunn, an anthropologist provided a major source of information for her work. Her sister, poet Carol Lee Sanchez, and her cousin, writer Leslie Marmon Silko, share Allen's Laguna Pueblo cultural heritage and both authors influenced her ideas.

In addition, her brother, Lee Francis, created the Wordcraft Circle of Native American Writers and Storytellers and was a notable author. Allen often marveled at her good fortune because the wind, sky, rocks, canyons, stars, and trees influenced her ability to speak, write, and teach. When her poetry teaches about the spiritual relationships between Indian people and their country, the land itself is always central to her storytelling. She explained that much of her mind and work centered on the lands of the American Southwest. She felt that people were the backdrop of the land. The single greatest influence upon Allen's thought and writing has been her multicultural heritage, which she often wrote about. Her novel, *The Woman Who Owned the Shadows* (1983), drew from her experience of growing up in a Catholic home with Protestant, Jewish, and Maronite family members. Throughout her career she embraced her multiculturalism, but she also struggled against it.

In some of her writings, she explored the concept of mixed blood within her personal and educational backgrounds. She defined breeds as people alien to both traditional Native Americans and whites, and she identified with other mixed bloods of different racial and ethnic backgrounds. While she was of mixed blood, she considered herself an outsider, separated from Native America by white blood. Her outsider status provided her a unique perspective from which to view the world. She was at once, Native American and white American. She related to both cultures and understood both to some degree, which served her well.[14]

Allen helped shatter long-held stereotypes of Native Americans as savage warriors or demure squaws. She pioneered the fields of Native American Studies and literature, drawing on her strong spiritual beliefs. She demonstrated that the literature of Native authors was unique, diverse, and vibrant. Allen's contributions as the foremost Native American lesbian-feminist theorist have been significant and controversial. Her ideas challenged many dearly held beliefs about Native Americans. Her assertions about Native American women were not without opposition, especially by Lakota people.[15] Allen observed that the Western patriarchal culture had successfully eroded respect for gays and lesbians in Native American culture as well as the acknowledgment of women's central position in many societies. Allen successfully connected the political goals of American feminists to the ongoing political struggles of Native Americans.[16]

During her last years, Allen shared drinks and conversations in a bar in New Mexico, saying that she hoped her work had made an impact on her people and the academy. As she chain-smoked cigarette after cigarette, Paula pondered her role as a writer and activist. In her later years, she battled cancer, bronchitis, and chronic fatigue syndrome. As much as she wanted to continue writing and speaking out, she had to slow down. Her long career of teaching, writing, and activism ended with her death. Paula Gunn Allen died at her home in Fort Bragg, California, on May 29, 2008, remembering her childhood, running and playing in the hills and arroyos under the towering heights of Mount Taylor.

NOTES

1. According to some accounts, Paula was born in Albuquerque, but in conversation with Clifford Trafzer, her brother, Lee Francis, explained that his sister was

born in Grants, New Mexico, in the shadow of her beloved Mount Taylor along old Highway 66.

2. Annette Van Dyke, "Paula Gunn Allen," in Sharon Malinowski, ed., *Notable Native Americans* (Detroit: Gale Researchers, Inc., 1995), 6–7.

3. Jocelyn Y. Stewart, "Champion of Native American Literature," *Los Angeles Times*, June 7, 2008.

4. Van Dyke, "Paula Gunn Allen," 6–7.

5. Stewart, "Champion of Native American Literature."

6. Jackson R. Bryer, "Report of the Hubbell Committee," Hubbel Medal Award Ceremony for Paula Gunn Allen.

7. Van Dyke, "Paula Gunn Allen," 8.

8. A. LaVonne Ruoff, *American Indian Literatures* (New York: Modern Language Association, 1990), 92–94.

9. Paula Gunn Allen, *Shadow Country* (Los Angeles: American Indian Studies Center, 1982), 1–23. Elaine Jahner, Review of *Shadow Country*, *American Indian Quarterly* 7, No. 1 (1983), 84–86.

10. Paula Gunn Allen, *The Sacred Hoop: Recovering the Feminine in American Indian Traditions*. Boston: Beacon Press, 1986), 1–66.

11. Clifford E. Trafzer, *As Long as the Grass Shall Grow and Rivers Flow* (Fort Worth: Harcourt, 2000), 475, 481, 483.

12. Paula Gunn Allen, *Pocahontas: Medicine Woman, Spy, Entrepreneur, Diplomat* (New York: HarperCollins Press, 2003), 1–12; Review of *Pocahontas: Medicine Woman, Spy, Entrepreneur, Diplomat*, *Publishers Weekly*, September 1, 2003; Review of *Pocahontas: Medicine Woman, Spy, Entrepreneur, Diplomat*, *Los Angeles Times*, July 16, 2004.

13. Bryer, "Report of the Hubbell Committee," Hubbel Medal Award Ceremony for Paula Gunn Allen; Brian Swann and Arnold Krupat, eds. *I Tell You Now: Autobiographical Essays by Native American Writers* (Lincoln: University of Nebraska Press, 1987), 92–94.

14. Laura Coltelli, "Paula Gunn Allen," in Gretchen Bataille, ed., *Native Amerian Women: A Biographical Dictionary* (New York: Garland Publishers, 1993), 6–8.

15. Swann and Krupat, eds. *I Tell You Now*, 92-94; "Paula Gunn Allen," in C. F. Crawford, John F. William Balassi, and Annie O. Ersturox, eds., *This Is About Vision: Interviews of Southwestern Writers* (Albuquerque: University of New Mexico Press, 1990), 95–107.

16. "Paula Gunn Allen," in Crawford, Balassi, and Ersturox, eds., *This Is About Vision*, 95–107.

BIBLIOGRAPHY

Allen, Paula Gunn. *The Woman Who Owned the Shadows*. San Francisco: Spinsters/ Aunt Lute Books, 1983.

Allen, Paula Gunn. *Studies in American Indian Literature: Critical Essays and Course Designs*. New York: Modern Language Association, 1983.

Allen, Paula Gunn. *The Sacred Hoop: Recovering the Feminine in American Indian Traditions*. Boston: Beacon Press, 1986.

Allen, Paula Gunn. *Spider Woman's Granddaughters: Traditional Tales and Contemporary Writing by Native American Women*. New York: Fawcett Press, 1990.

Allen, Paula Gunn. *Pocahontas: Medicine Woman, Spy, Entrepreneur, Diplomat*. New York: HarperCollins Press, 2003.

Bryer, Jackson R. "Report of the Hubbell Committee." Hubbel Medal Award Ceremony for Paula Gunn Allen. December 9, 2015.

Coltelli, Laura. "Paula Gunn Allen." In Gretchen Bataille, ed. *Native American Women: A Biographical Dictionary*. New York: Garland Publishers, 1993, 6–8.

Crawford, C. F., John F. William Balassi, and Annie O. Ersturox, eds. *This Is About Vision: Interviews of Southwestern Writers*. Albuquerque: University of New Mexico Press, 1990.

Jahner, Elaine. Review of *Shadow Country*. *American Indian Quarterly* 7, No. 1, 1983, 84–86.

Ruoff, A. LaVonne. *American Indian Literatures*. New York: Modern Language Association, 1990, 92–94.

Stewart, Jocelyn Y. "Champion of Native American Literature." *Los Angeles Times*, June 7, 2008.

Swann, Brian and Arnold Krupat, eds. *I Tell You Now: Autobiographical Essays by Native American Writers*. Lincoln: University of Nebraska Press, 1987.

Trafzer, Clifford E. *As Long as the Grass Shall Grow and Rivers Flow*. Fort Worth: Harcourt, 2000.

Van Dyke, Annette. "Paula Gunn Allen," in Sharon Malinowski, ed. *Notable Native Americans*. Detroit: Gale Researchers, Inc., 1995, 6–7.

FURTHER READING

Allen, Paula Gunn. *The Woman Who Owned the Shadows*. San Francisco: Spinsters/ Aunt Lute Books, 1983.

Allen, Paula Gunn. *Studies in American Indian Literature: Critical Essays and Course Designs*. New York: Modern Language Association, 1983.

Allen, Paula Gunn. *The Sacred Hoop: Recovering the Feminine in American Indian Traditions*. Boston: Beacon Press, 1986.

Allen, Paula Gunn. *Spider Woman's Granddaughters: Traditional Tales and Contemporary Writing by Native American Women*. New York: Fawcett Press, 1990.

Allen, Paula Gunn. *Pocahontas: Medicine Woman, Spy, Entrepreneur, Diplomat*. New York: HarperCollins Press, 2003.

Swann, Brian and Arnold Krupat, eds. *I Tell You Now: Autobiographical Essays by Native American Writers*. Lincoln: University of Nebraska Press, 1987.

Trafzer, Clifford E. *As Long as the Grass Shall Grow and Rivers Flow* (Fort Worth: Thompson, 2000).

Van Dyke, Annette. "Paula Gunn Allen," in Sharon Malinowski, ed. *Notable Native Americans*. Detroit: Gale Researchers, Inc., 1995, 6–7.

Chapter Six

Poet Warrior

Joy Harjo (b. 1951–)

Christie Time Firtha

Joy Harjo is truly a force. Referring to poetry as "soul talk," she is the first Native American person to serve as Poet Laureate of the United States, a position she has held for three terms so far. Born on May 9, 1951, in Tulsa, Oklahoma, to Wynema Baker and Allen W. Foster, Joy Harjo is an enrolled member of the Muscogee Creek Nation and is also of Cherokee, French, and Scots-Irish heritage. She is the oldest of four children and descends from a long line of tribal leaders on her father's side, most notably Monahwee, who was a leader of the Red Stick War and fought against Andrew Jackson. At the age of 19 and with her parents' blessing, Joy adopted the last name of her maternal grandmother, Naomi Harjo, visibly linking herself to her great aunt Lois Harjo, whom Joy credits as the source of her teachings about her identity as a Muscogee/Creek woman. Through her own work as a teacher, poet, and musician, Harjo upholds her family's tradition as a courageous and powerful spokesperson for America's Indigenous peoples, offering her stories, poems and songs "as gifts for challenge, for inspiration, for sustenance."[1] Her activism is her art, as artistic works feed the hope and validate the fears and experiences, the very the human tribulations, of Indigenous peoples. Her goal through her art is to help people become the best human beings possible.

Harjo's project as poet lareueate is a testment to her dedication in this area. "Living Nations, Living Words" is an online literary map hosted by the Library of Congress. It charts the Unites States according to Indigenous poets and their homelands. Harjo's stated goal is to "counter damaging false assumptions—that indigenous peoples of our country are often invisible or are not seen as human."[2] Harjo is concerned by the lack of Native American voices in what she calls "the American Book of Poetry," and writes that "Native Nations poets use the tools of knowledge and creativity to ride the waves of language, even as we also tend to our indigenous cultural systems and communities."[3] The resulting map features 47 Native Nations poets, with short biographies and links to their respective poems and commentaries, all housed for posterity within the Library of Congress.

Harjo, herself, is a well-rounded artist. In March 2021, in the midst of a global pandemic, she released the beautifully performed *I Pray for My Enemies,* which features an elegant combination of music, singing, and the spoken word. Harjo describes that the album was conceived from "an urgent need to deal with discord, opposition."[4] In a similar vane, her recent project *We Were There When Jazz Was Invented* reminds us that musical forms originating in the United States, specifically Jazz and Blues, were in part shaped by Southeastern Indigenous people. She has also recently published a number of books, including *An American Sunrise* (2019), *Conflict Resolution for Holy Beings* (2015), and *Crazy Brave* (2012), which won the 2013 PEN Center USA literary prize for creative nonfiction.

By the time she was four, Harjo had developed a love of music and poetry, and she soon after began to develop her own talents in these arenas to later become an award-winning poet and writer, who was named one of the Outstanding Young Women of America in both 1978 and 1984. In 2005, she was named the Wordcraft Circle of Native Writers and Storytellers' Film Scripts Writer of the Year for her script, *A Thousand Roads*, an honor which she also held the previous year for her CD, *Native Joy for Real*. Her other recent awards include the 2003 Arrell Gibson Lifetime Achievement Award and the 2003–2004 Writer of the Year in Poetry for *How We Became Human: New and Selected Poems 1975–2001*. Harjo also co-edited *Reinventing the Enemy's Language: Native Women's Writing of North America*, an anthology of contemporary Native women's writing, which was pronounced one of the London *Observer*'s Best Books of 1997. She has also received the "William Carlos Williams Award" from the Poetry Society of America for the best book of poetry in 1991; the "Oakland PEN, Josephine Miles Poetry Award" in 1991; "Bravo Award" from the Albuquerque Arts Alliance in 1996; the "Oklahoma Book Award" in 1995 for *The Woman Who Fell from the Sky*; the Witter Bynner Poetry Fellowship in 1994; the Woodrow Wilson Fellowship at Green Mountain College in Poultney, Vermont in 1993; and an honorary doctorate from Benedictine College in 1992. Her work has been included in the Pushcart Prize Poetry Anthologies XV and XIII. She also wrote an award-winning children's book, *The Good Luck Cat*.

Harjo has also successfully delved into the arts of painting and documentary filmmaking. Taking after her great-aunt and grandmother, both of whom were reputable artists, Harjo originally intended to become a painter, and she has received the 1st and 2nd Place Awards in Drawing at the University of New Mexico Kiva Club Nizhoni Days Art Show in 1976. She is now a member of the Hui Nalu Canoe Club and is training to become competitive at open-sea outrigger-canoeing.

Harjo's early love of music and poetry initially manifested in her desire to become a missionary. After her parents' divorce when she was eight, Harjo began to devote increasing amounts of energy to the church. She read the Bible three times, organized biblical performances, and gave sermons in her community. Her interest in missionary work dissipated, however, when she witnessed a minister insult two Mexican girls for being noisy and told them to leave. Harjo, herself, left the church shortly after this incident. Not too long afterwards, Harjo left Oklahoma to attend boarding school at the Institute of American Indian Arts in Santa Fe, where she found people who would support her artistic ambitions and help develop them. "I arrived there barely alive," she says. "I was suicidal. At IAIA I was given permission to be an Indian artist. I was given permission to be human. That was no small thing."[5]

While Harjo was in high school, she became pregnant with her son, Phil, and she moved back to Oklahoma. A few years later in 1973, she had another child, this time a daughter, whom she named Rainy Dawn. This was a tough time for Harjo. She was raising two small children, dealing with their alcoholic and abusive father, and all the while, trying to complete college and scrape a living together through various jobs as a waitress, service-station attendant, janitor at a hospital, nurse's assistant, and dance teacher. Harjo remarks about this time in her life that it was "difficult even to swallow, and each step had to be calculated."[6] Harjo calculated well, and in 1976, she graduated from the University of New Mexico with a BA in English. In 1978, she graduated from the University of Iowa with a MFA in Poetry.

Harjo currently lives in Tulsa, Oklahoma, and has held the prestigious Joseph Russo endowed professorship at the University of New Mexico. She has also held teaching positions at the Institute of American Indian Arts, the University of Colorado, the University of Arizona, the University of Hawaii, and the University of California, Los Angeles. Despite the impressive positions she has held, Harjo expresses a sense of ambivalence at working in the university environment. She states "I feel conflicted when I step into a University. I never even had plans to attend college, but here I am in the classroom. So I approach it like an artist who is helping other young artists become the best human beings possible."[7]

Afraid that she was going to "lose her Poetry" to the demands and atmosphere of a university position, Harjo began playing the saxophone to maintain balance.[8] She also began "writing poetry and songs that were influenced by Southwestern Indian music, Nat King Cole, Charlie Parker, native philosophies and the American Indian rights movement."[9] She has since formed two bands, Poetic Justice and the Joy Harjo Band, with whom she tours regularly.

In 2002, she co-produced the "Eagle Song" music video, which was nominated for best music video at the American Indian Film Festival. The American Indian Film Festival awarded her the Eagle Spirit Achievement Award that year, and a song from her CD, *Winding Through the Milky Way*, released in September of 2008, won the New Mexico Music Award.

Renowned for its musical and eclectic qualities—its combination of jazz and blues, as well as African, Native American, and European poetic traditions—Joy Harjo's writing, like her music, often incorporates themes of survivance and resistance to violence. Born in Oklahoma, the land formerly stolen and set aside as "Indian Territory," Harjo is keenly aware of the scars marring the face of this continent. In one of her many performances, this one at UCLA, she states, "violence seems to be a prevalent theme in the history of this land. . . . This country as we know it is built on violence."[10] On this same idea, she writes in *Ploughshares*, "for many of us in these lands now called America, imagining this place has been a tricky feat, because there is no place that hasn't or won't get stolen, polluted, or destroyed, and for all of us now, planted here, the foundation is shaky, because though it is strong with vision, this country was founded on violent theft."[11]

While her music and metaphors speak of the Native Nations' experiences of past, present, and future violence and destruction, her work also expands to address healing and the enduring presence of justice, even in spaces where hopelessness abides. In her video diary called "Joy Harjo's 'Reality Show,'" Harjo articulates "songs, poetry and art of renewal will carry us forward despite the rough path."[12] Harjo believes that the act of writing is an act of creation. It is through this act of creation that Harjo deals with violence and brutality of being Native American, a woman of color, and a citizen of an exploitive "over-culture" that speaks to many people globally. "'My audience,' Harjo says, 'starts with my tribal nation, spreads out to include those who are also trying to find a way through this particularly rough layer of the world.'"[13]

In her poem, "I Give You Back" from *She Had Some Horses,* Harjo writes of a pain and fear that are representative of American Indian experiences of loss and violence, and she writes of her release from the fear that haunts her as a witness and as the descendant of witnesses of imperialistic scenes of violence. She captures and personalizes in writing the "white soldiers/ who burned down my home, beheaded my children,/ raped and sodomized my brothers and sisters . . . who stole the/ food from our plates when we were starving."[14] The white soldiers have no face, but are present in her history and memories, just like they are for so many others—for Native Americans forcedly dispossessed of their lands during the many Indian wars of the nineteenth century, for African Americans stolen from their homes and families, for others around the world suffering the burden of living under imperial eyes. As an Indigenous woman, Harjo was tormented by her family's and friends' stories of white soldiers. Even in school, she would have opened her history books to see the pictures of American "triumph" over Native Americans, which to her would resonate as images of conquer, like the photos of the dead and frozen Lakota women, children and enfeebled who were left half buried in the snow at the Battle of Wounded Knee. Like others who had family members suffer in such ways, she saw these images. As happened to others, these images made her afraid.

But despite the oppressive images of violence and fear that "hold these scenes in front of [her],"[15] "I Give You Back" is a poem about healing and justice through the release of fear. Harjo writes, "I release you, my beautiful and terrible/ fear. I release you. You were my beloved/ and hated twin, but now, I don't know you/ as myself."[16] This release, though, is not a denial of events passed, nor is it forgiveness. Rather, it is a refusal to be bound and burdened by the inhumane actions others have inflicted upon her and other oppressed peoples. In this poem, she releases "fear, so [it] can no longer keep [her] naked and frozen in the winter" like the frozen mother and child and Wounded Knee and she develops a new mantra to replace her former fear, "I am not afraid to be angry/ I am not afraid to rejoice/ I am not afraid. . . ."[17] This disowning of fear is a claiming of rights and power. It is a rejection of the idea that people need permission to be angry about the depredations committed against them and their families; it is a validation of that anger. It is also a validation of re-creation, of moving beyond assaults and death to being fully alive. This rejection of fear and validation of emotions allows her to take back one of the important things that is too often stolen during conquests or lost in their legacy: security in one's sense of self. She writes, "I take myself back, fear."[18] She takes back her rights to herself, her rights to live, her rights to the human experience.

The poem ends on a note of retribution, a karmic sort of justice, for a world that is notably lacking in legal justice. Having released her fear and reclaimed herself from it, Harjo metaphorically faces fear, saying "come here, fear/ I am alive and you are so afraid/ of dying."[19] This challenge to her fears illustrates that not only has she overcome the fears that oppress her, the fears she had been shown, but also that these fears can no longer be used against her. Those that used fear to control and oppress her no longer have the power to do so. Instead, the things that have made her afraid, the images used to keep oppressed peoples subordinate, are dying. This recognition of the systemic way in which fear is used to enforce people's suppression contains a larger threat—when the fear used to control people and keep them oppressed is recognized and no longer operable, revolution is at hand. For Harjo, this is not a threat of violence, but of move towards compassionately re-constructing the world. In an interview with Bill Nevins of *Albuquerque Arts Magazine*, Harjo states "those who write are assisting in constructing the next world, the next consciousness."[20] For Harjo, this new world would be a just one.

These themes of justice and reconstruction are echoed in several of Harjo's other poems, notably "Transformations." In "Transformations," Harjo writes, "what I mean is that hatred can be turned into something else."[21] Like fear, hatred haunts people. It keeps them blind, encourages violence, and does no good. As Harjo says almost proverbially, "Bone splintered in the eye of the one you chose to name your enemy won't make it better for you to see"[22]— basically, harming those whom you have decided for whatever reason are you enemy won't make your life better; hatred only creates wounds. But however damaging, Harjo realizes that hatred can be transformed by words and meanings. She writes, "I know you can turn a poem into something/ else. This poem could be a bear treading the far northern tundra."[23] Just as Harjo has taken control of the words and meaning of a poem to make it not metaphorically trace the experiences of a bear, people can take control of their hatred for the people they identify as their enemies and turn that hatred into compassion for others, whom they've ceased to regard as "enemy."

The vividness and clarity of the images in these poems are characteristic of Harjo's poetic style. Her conscious effort and, as she terms it, "responsibility" as a poet is "to be clear and alive in my work, to not add to the confusion."[24] In the words of William Pitt Root, Harjo "has steadily intensified her efforts to contain language in ever more musical forms, to make it go, like music alone, straight to the heart with as little mediation as possible."[25] Perhaps this desire to reach easily and directly to the hearts of people stems from her abiding interest in music. Indeed, Harjo states, "it was in song that [she] first found poetry, or it found [her], alone at the breaking of dawn under the huge elm sheltering my childhood house, within range of the radio, of [her] mother's voice."[26]

Music and song have most definitely influenced Harjos's career as a teacher and poet, and music provides another venue for Harjo to speak out about violence, justice, and healing, as evinced in the name of her band, Poetic Justice. According to Sheila Nopper, Poetic Justice is "a name [Harjo] defines in the liner notes [to one of her albums] as 'a term of grace, expressing how justice can appear in the world despite forces of confusion and destruction.'"[27] One reason for the strong link in the themes of Harjo's work in poetry and music is that Harjo has turned many of her poems into songs. In an interview with terrain.org, she states:

> I happened on the direct relationship between poetry and music when I realized
> that most of the poetry in my tribe, and with most peoples of the world isn't

found in books, it's oral. Then I began to consider how to make that bridge—I didn't do so with a direct plan—it was a natural outgrowth of being a contemporary Mvskoke poet who had picked up a saxophone.[28]

Among the poems she has set to music are "I Give You Back," on *She Had Some Horses*, her first album named after the book in which the poem originally appeared, and her elating, award-winning "Eagle's Song."

To Joy Harjo, poetry and music are both "song art." She realizes that "with whatever you say or do, you are making a stand, one way or the other."[29] In taking a stand against violence and for healing with her carefully chosen words, Joy Harjo is following in the footsteps of her warrior ancestors. She states, "I believe those so-called "womanly" traits are traits of the warrior. . . . The word, warrior, it applies to women just as well. I don't see it as exclusive to a male society . . . . They've stood up in the face of danger, in the face of hopelessness. They've been brave-not in the national headlines, but they've been true to themselves."[30] In her unique and eclectic combination of poetry, music and visual art, Joy Harjo has been nothing if not true to herself. Harjo is indeed a "poet warrior," a woman who fights violence and oppression with her words, like Audre Lorde and Richard Hugo, the poets she so admires.

NOTES

1. Joy Harjo, "Introduction," *Ploughshares* (Boston: Emerson College Press, 2004), 8.

2. Harjo, Joy. "Story Map Cascade." *Living Nations, Living Worlds*, Library of Congress, 2020, www.loc.gov/ghe/cascade/index.html?appid=be31c5cfc7614d6680e 6fa4 7be888dc3&bookmark=Introduction.

3. Harjo, Joy. "Story Map Cascade." *Living Nations, Living Worlds*, Library of Congress, 2020, www.loc.gov/ghe/cascade/index.html?appid=be31c5cfc7614d6680e 6fa4 7be888dc3&bookmark=Introduction.

4. Harjo, Joy. "I Pray for My Enemies." *Joy Harjo*, JoyHarjo.com, 2021, www. joyharjo.com /music/i-pray-for-my-enemies.

5. Joy Harjo in William Pitt Root, "About Joy Harjo," *Ploughshares* Boston: Emerson College Press, 2004), 183.

6. Joy Harjo in William Pitt Root, "About Joy Harjo," *Ploughshares* Boston: Emerson College Press, 2004), 182.

7. Joy Harjo, "Joy Harjo's 'Reality Show': A Video Diary," *Joy Harjo Channel Youtube* (November 05, 2007).

8. Leslie Ullman, Interview, *Kenyan Review*, 1993.

9. "Joy Harjo and the Arrow Dynamics Band," *Santafe.com*.

10. Joy Harjo, "Nearly Unbearable Grace: The Poetry of Joy Harjo," *Uctelevision* (January 31, 2008).

11. Joy Harjo in William Pitt Root, "About Joy Harjo," *Ploughshares* Boston: Emerson College Press, 2004), 8.

12. Harjo, "Joy Harjo's Reality Show."

13. Joy Harjo in William Pitt Root, "About Joy Harjo," *Ploughshares* Boston: Emerson College Press, 2004), 181.

14. Joy Harjo, "I Give You Back," *She Had Some Horses* (Middleton, Conn.: Wesleyan University Press, 1990), 469.

15. Harjo, "I Give You Back," *She Had Some Horses* (Middleton, Conn.: Wesleyan University Press, 1990), 69.

16. Harjo, "I Give You Back," *She Had Some Horses* (Middleton, Conn.: Wesleyan University Press, 1990), 69.

17. Harjo, "I Give You Back," *She Had Some Horses* (Middleton, Conn.: Wesleyan University Press, 1990), 70.

18. Harjo, "I Give You Back," *She Had Some Horses* (Middleton, Conn.: Wesleyan University Press, 1990), 77–8.

19. Harjo, "I Give You Back," *She Had Some Horses* (Middleton, Conn.: Wesleyan University Press, 1990), 78.

20. Bill Nevins, *"'Milky Way,' Joy Harjo's Multi-talented World"* Albuquerque Arts 12:7 (August 2008), 13. For music created by Joy Harjo, see *I Pray for My Enemies.* Sunyata Records/Sony Orchard Distribution, 202; *Red Dreams, Trail Beyond Tears.* Mekko Productions Inc., 2010; *Winding through the Milky Way. Fast Horse;* Recordings 2008, Mekko Productions Inc., 2009; *She had some Horses.* Mekko Productions, Inc., 2006; Native Joy for Real. Mekko Productions, Inc., 2004; Letter from the End of the Twentieth Century. Mekko Productions, Inc., 1997; Native American Currents. *Silver Wave, 1997; Heartbeat 2.* Smithsonian Folkways, 1998; Weaving the Strands. *Red Feather, 1998.*

21. Joy Harjo, "Transformations," *In Mad Love and War* (Middletown, Conn.: Wesleyan University Press, 1990), 59.

22. Harjo, "Transformations," *In Mad Love and War* (Middletown, Conn.: Wesleyan University Press, 1990), 59.

23. Harjo, "Transformations," *In Mad Love and War* (Middletown, Conn.: Wesleyan University Press, 1990), 59.

24. Joy Harjo, "The Woman Hanging from the Thirteenth Floor Window," *Wicazo Sa Review* 1, no. 1 (Spring, 1985), 39.

25. Joy Harjo in William Pitt Root, "About Joy Harjo," *Ploughshares* Boston: Emerson College Press, 2004), 183, 184.

26. Harjo, "Introduction," 7.

27. Sheila Nopper, "Joy Harjo and the Poetic Justice," *Herizons* 11, no. 3 (Summer 1997), 42.

28. Joy Harjo, "Joy Harjo: Muscogee Poet and Musician," *Terrain.org.*

29. Harjo in Nevins, "Milky Way," 13.

30. Joy Harjo in Helen Jaskowski, "A MELUS Interview: Joy Harjo," *MELUS* 16 (1989–90), 11.

BIBILIOGRAPHY

Eyre, Chris. *A Thousand Roads*. Written by Joy Harjo. Product Details, 2005.

Harjo, Joy. *A Map to the Next World: Poems and Tales*. New York: W. W. Norton & Company, 2001.

Harjo, Joy. *An American Sunrise: Poems*. New York: W. W. Norton & Company, 2020.

Harjo, Joy. *Conflict Resolution for Holy Beings: Poems*. New York: W. W. Norton & Company, 2020.

Harjo, Joy. *Crazy Brave: A Memoir*. New York: W. W. Norton & Company, 2012.

Harjo, Joy. *"Eagle Song."* http://www.youtube.com/user/joyharjo. November 05, 2007. July 20, 2008. http://www.youtube.com/watch?v=y8mEdBmC9Jo.

Harjo, Joy. *"Eagle Song."* http://www.youtube.com/user/joyharjo. November 05, 2007. July 20, 2008.

Harjo, Joy. *For a Girl Becoming*. Tucson : University of Arizona Press, 2009.

Harjo, Joy. *How We Became Human: New and Selected Poems: 1975-2001:* New York: W. W. Norton & Company, 2002.

Harjo, Joy. *In Mad Love and War*. Middleton, Conn.: Wesleyan University Press, 1990.

Harjo, Joy, *Secrets from the Center of the World*. Tucson: University of Arizona Press, 1989.

Harjo, Joy. *She Had Some Horses,* Middleton, Conn.: Wesleyan University Press, 1990.

Harjo, Joy. *The Good Luck Cat*. Florida: Harcourt Children's Books, 2000.

Harjo, Joy. *The Last Song*. Puerto Del Sol, 1975.

Harjo, Joy. *The Woman Who Fell from the Sky:* New York: W. W. Norton & Company, 1996.

Harjo, Joy. *What Moon Drove Me to This?* New York: Reed, Cannon & Johnson Publishers, 1979.

Harjo, Joy and Gloria Bird. *Reinventing the Enemy's Language: Contemporary Native American Women's Writings of North America*. New York: W. W. Norton & Company, 1998.

Harjo, Joy and Laura Coltelli. *The Spiral of Memory: Interviews*. Ann Arbor: University of Michigan Press, 1996.

FURTHER READING

Bernardin, Susan. *"Soul Talk, Song Language: Conversations with* Joy Harjo.*"* *World Literature Today* 86, no. 3 (June 2012): 77–78.

Bruchac, Joseph. "Interview with Joy Harjo." *North Dakota Quarterly* 53 (1985): 220–234.

Harjo, Joy. "Introduction." *Ploughshares*. Boston: Emerson College Press, 2004. 7–8.

Harjo, Joy. "The Woman Hanging from the Thirteenth Floor Window." *Wicazo Sa Review* 1, no. 1 (Spring, 1985): 38–40.

Harjo, Joy and Tanaya Winder. *Soul Talk, Song Language: Conversations with Joy Harjo.* Middletown, Conn.: Wesleyan University Press, 2011.

Jackowski, Helen. "A MELUS Interview: Joy Harjo." *MELUS* 16, no. 1 (Spring 1989–1990): 5–13.

Kallet, Marilyn. "In Love and War and Music." *Kenyon Review* 15. (1993): 57–66.

Lang, Nancy. "'Twin Gods Bending Over': Joy Harjo and Poetic Memory." *MELUS* 18, no. 3 (Autumn, 1993): 41–49.

Pettit, Rhonda. *Joy Harjo.* Idaho: Boise State University Press, 1998.

Root, William Pitt. "About Joy Harjo." *Ploughshares* (Boston: Emerson College Press, 2004): 180–185.

Waxman, Olivia B. "Joy Harjo The first Native American U.S. poet laureate on her new book, An American Sunrise, and the state of poetry." *TIME* 194, no. 8–9 (September 2019): 115–116.

Chapter Seven

Civil Justice

Louise Erdrich (b. 1954–)

Christie Time Firtha

Old Tallow, a central character in Louise Erdrich's children's novel *Birchbark House,* speaks of the importance of community and good actions coming full circle. Eleven years in the past, this remarkable, tough Ojibwe woman saved an infant Omakayas from an island whose other inhabitants has been killed by smallpox, placing the small girl in a family. Then when the pox descends on her foster family, Omakayas is immune and able to seek Old Tallow's help to save them. It is at this point that Old Tallow reflects on the reciprocity of good works. This human kindness of taking in an orphaned child ends up saving the family and speaks to the way in which one might effect concrete changes in the lives of individuals through one's actions. Pulitzer Prize winning writer/storyteller Louise Erdrich lives this lesson; she effects concrete changes in individuals' lives on a community and grassroots basis. Through her writing and through her community-based book store Birchbark Books in Minneapolis, Minnesota, her ancestral territory, Erdrich promotes what has been described as civil justice. She supports the work of Native American artists, providing them with space and encouragement to develop their voices and destabilize the stereotypes that mainstream audiences have of indigenous peoples.

Karen Louise Erdrich was born June 7, 1954, to Ralph and Rita Erdrich in Little Falls, Minnesota. She is an enrolled member of the Turtle Mountain Band of the Anishinaabe Nation and the eldest of seven children. Although Erdrich never lived on the reservation as a child, she lived nearby and spent a good amount of time with her large extended family, whose constant storytelling affected her writing life from an early age. Her father, Ralph, who according to family lore was born in a tornado, was German-American. Her mother, Rita, was French and Anishinaabe. Erdrich's grandfather, Patrick Gourneau, from whom she began learning *Ojibwemowin* (the language of the

Anishinaabe) as he used it in his prayers, served as a tribal chairman for the Turtle Mountain Band of Chippewa Indians.

Erdrich describes her childhood as "very sweet." "'I lived a very sheltered childhood . . .' she says. 'We used to go for walks outdoors. I spent a lot of time around animals. I grew up without television.'"[1] Both of Erdrich's parents were educators, moving to Wahpeton, North Dakota, to teach at a Bureau of Indian Affairs school. They both encouraged her to write and supported her aspirations, as Erdrich herself would later do for others. As a teacher himself, Erdrich's father introduced her at young age to William Shakespeare's plays "and encouraged [her] and her sisters to write their own stories."[2] He also "encouraged his children to memorise the poems of Frost, Tennyson, Robert Service and Longfellow, paying them a nickel for every poem they could recite. Not surprisingly, two other Erdrichs are writers—Lise, a children's author, and Heid, the author of three poetry collections."[3] Erdrich's mother encouraged her writing also by weaving "strips of construction paper together and stapl[ing] them into book covers. So at an early age [Erdrich] felt [her] self to be a published author earning substantial royalties."[4]

In 1972, Erdrich began attending Dartmouth College. She was one of the first women admitted to the Ivy League school that began as a boarding school for Native Americans, a distressing topic, the significance of which Erdrich would later address in her writings. There she earned a BA in 1976 and met the man who was to be her future husband, the Modoc anthropologist and writer Michael Dorris. After completing her undergraduate degree, Erdrich taught poetry and writing to young people through a position at the State Arts Council of North Dakota. She worked a variety of jobs, some of which appear as the occupations of characters in her writing, including waitressing, life guarding, teaching poetry in prisons, weighing trucks on the interstate, and serving as editor for *The Circle* (a newspaper produced by and for the urban Native population in Boston), before she graduated with her MA degree in Creative Writing from Johns Hopkins University in 1979.

It was around this time that Erdrich found herself reacquainted with Michael Dorris, when she was invited to Dartmouth to give a reading. They exchanged addresses, wrote to each other, exchanged manuscripts, and then reunited the following year. In October 1981, they married. Dorris returned to Dartmouth, and Erdrich became a writer-in-residence there. The couple had six children. Dorris had adopted Reynold Abel, Jeffrey Sava, and Madeline Hannah before he met Erdrich. After their marriage, Erdrich adopted the children also, and the couple had three more daughters together, Persia Andromeda, Pallas Antigone, and Aza Marion.

In 1991, the couple's son Reynold Abel, the subject of Dorris' book *The Broken Cord*, was hit by a car and killed at the age of 23. Shortly after this,

Dorris and Erdrich unsuccessfully pursued an extortion case against their other son, Jeffrey, who had accused them both of child abuse. In 1995, soon after the failed court case, the couple filed for divorce. On April 11, 1997, Michael Dorris committed suicide in a motor lodge in Concord, New Hampshire. Erdrich had been aware of Dorris' ongoing battle with depression since the second year of their marriage.

In 1984, when she was thirty years old, Louise Erdrich published her first two books—*Jacklight*, a volume of poetry, and *Love Medicine*, a novel—with the help of her husband, who wrote to recommend her books on "Michael Dorris Agency" letterhead. Despite her enduring love of poetry, Erdrich considers herself to be a storyteller. She states, "I began as a poet, writing poetry, I began to tell stories in the poems and then realized that there was not enough room in a poem unless you are a John Milton and write enormous volumes of poetry."[5] Since 1984, Erdrich has gone on to write seventeen more novels and two more volumes of poetry.

In 2020, Erdrich won the Pulitzer Prize for her novel *The Night Watchman,* a story inspired by the life of her maternal grandfather. But her literary acheivements date back to 1982, when Erdrich won her first major award—the Nelson Algren Fiction Competition for her story "The World's Greatest Fisherman," which later became the first chapter of *Love Medicine. Love Medicine* is considered the first novel in a tetralogy, followed by the *The Beet Queen, Tracks*, and finally, *Bingo Palace. Love Medicine* won the National Book Critics Circle Award. *The Birchbark House*, a story that is continued in a subsequent children's novel, was a National Book Award finalist. Erdrich did eventually win the National Book Award in 2012 for her novel *The Roundhouse. The Game of Silence* was the winner of the Scott O'Dell Award for Historical Fiction. Erdrich also co-wrote a novel with Michael Dorris entitled *The Crown of Columbus*. Erdrich holds an additional honor not common among those in her profession; she was once named one of *People Magazine's* most beautiful people.

Though Erdrich's stories highlight the survivance[6] of American Indians, her stories focus more on the American experience in all of its diversity. Often incorporating themes of everyday revenge, everyday language, and everyday memory, Erdrich's books are almost Joycian in their exploration of select daily minutiae. As Erdrich continues to learn her mother's tongue *Ojibwemowin*, this aspect of her writing deepens. For instance, in an article for the *New York Times* entitled "Two Languages in Mind, but Just One in the Heart," Erdrich writes,

> The [*Ojibwemowin*] word for stone, *asin*, is animate . . . . Once I began to think of stones as animate, I started to wonder whether I was picking up a stone or it was putting itself into my hand. Stones are not the same as they were to me

in English. I can't write about a stone without considering it in Ojibwa and acknowledging that the Anishinaabe universe began with a conversation between
stones.[7]

It is this attention to the meanings embedded in the mundane and everyday
that is, perhaps, Louise Erdrich's greatest contribution to the field of Native
American literature, for in focusing on the plain, daily lives of her characters,
she writes against the stereotypes that are still commonplace in American
life, if not the old-fashioned image of the Indian chief in war bonnet, then
the casino-rich Indian. As Erdrich states, "There seems to be very little mainstream awareness of Native Americans as contemporary people. Most people
still think in stereotypes."[8]

Indeed, critic E. Shelley Reid acknowledges the challenges Erdrich must
continually overcome as a Native American woman writer. She states, "Erdrich faces a textual and cultural challenge: to reclaim a Native American
identity from the Coopers and Disneys of Euro-American culture, and then
to find a way to share it with an audience that suspects that she and her
culture are on the brink of extinction."[9] Through her storytelling, Erdrich
moves beyond stereotypes and the myth of extinction by showing the usual-
ness of everyday life for Native peoples and how Native peoples are in fact
incorporated into the work-a-day world. At the same time, she balances this
demythification with respect for individual Native cultures by exploring how
specific modes of thought create various worldviews that do not necessarily
accord with those of the dominant culture, but are disjointedly and imper-
fectly incorporated into that culture nevertheless.

The characters and events presented in Erdrich's first book *Love Medicine*
go a long way toward diffusing stereotypes of the Native Americans living
just outside the fictive, Great Plains town of Argus, North Dakota, even while
the tribe in question is represented in their uniqueness. The characters in *Love
Medicine* want to become nuns, torment themselves in love triangles, suffer
from alcoholism, deal with difficult mother-in-laws, accidentally burn each
other's houses down, retreat to the wilderness, and seek solace and healing
from doctors—both medical doctors in the Western tradition and traditional
Chippewa healers. This is where the Erdrich's deft balancing of the everyday
aspects of life in rural North Dakota and attention to Native people's beliefs
becomes apparent. She represents a group of impoverished people dealing
with the messes that commonly muddle peoples' lives, while also attending
to her characters as a group of tribal people, bound together by common
beliefs and the long, interconnected histories of their Chippewa families. In
the words of Erdrich's belated ex-husband, "*Love Medicine* is a story about a
contemporary group of people that are in some ways indistinguishable from

other rural North Dakota people who are not rich, but in other ways they are very much unique."[10]

Love Medicine centers around the stories of three families, the Kashpaws, Morrisseys, and Lamartines, as these families struggle with each other and struggle to survive in an American world which, by fiat, devalues their very existence. Sadly, the chapter is also about June Morrissey's death and how her family deals with it. In effect, Erdrich reveals much about the way that this group of Chippewa people live in then contemporary 1980s U.S. Albertine Johnson, June's niece who is away at an unnamed university studying medicine, hears of June's death and funeral after they happen because, as Albertine's mother says "we knew you probably couldn't get away from your studies for the funeral."[11] Albertine is far off the reservation studying to become a doctor. This lack of communication is a passive-aggressive slight again Albertine for her decision to leave the reservation and go to a university, a slight which reflects a common occurrence in Native American history—often, those who moved off the reservation to get an education did not return. Ever since Indian boarding schools were established, this has been a social pattern, only becoming less so recently. Children would go away to school, learn a trade, learn to speak and read English, and then return to the reservation to find that they no longer fit in. While many returnees did eventually readjust, there were many who did not and found employment off the reservation. This tendency of educated Indians to leave the reservation and the reception they receive as a result of this tendency echoes in the first chapter of *Love Medicine.* The government sponsored Indian boarding schools are an often ignored part of American history. With the culturally genocidal official policy of "kill the Indian . . . save the man," the purpose of the boarding schools was to expunge Native American cultures from the country, a very traumatic and oppressive experience for Indigenous peoples. By exploring the impacts of this experience through her characters, Erdrich opens a forum in which past traumas can be addrsessed, as is the purpose of many activits, so that Native and non-Native communities can work toward redress.

Where many critics talk of the incorporation of magic into the book as magical realism, Erdrich does not see it as such. For her and other Ojibwa, it is part of the everyday. She states,

> My work has never really seemed fantastical to me . . . although it was interesting to me that the more unusual occurrences . . . were based on bits of historical research. I found mention of an early priest whose organ playing really did attract snakes. It was considered a great wonder. And every Ojibwa knows someone who's hitched a canoe ride on the rack of a swimming moose.[12]

By introducing Grandma Kashpaw as someone who "is constantly being told things . . . . One time she told Gordie never to ride with a crazy Lamartine boy. She had seen something in the polished- tin of her bread toaster . . . . Thanks to Grandma's toaster, Gordie was probably spared,"[13] Erdrich is introducing readers to a part of everyday contemporary Chippewa life that they likely would not have conceived of before reading the book. In refusing to classify her work as part of the genre of magical realism, Erdrich is validating that experiences of Native peoples are parts of daily life rather than as famtasical events. Though to mainstream audiences, "being told things,"[14] bespeaks a connection to the supernatural that exist beyond the realm of the norm, to indigenous audiences, the beliefs are a way of life, a way of being in the world, a realtionship to the world. The idea of magical realism is that it qualifies experiences as something beyond real. Erdrich's refusal to speak of her work as magical realism effectively refuses the idea that indigenous belif systems are anything other than normal, valid, everyday experiences that have continued to exist despite centuries of attempts at extermination.

Erdrich takes her depiction of this sort of cultural integration a step further in *Tracks*, showing that Native beliefs have not in fact lost power even though that power might exist in a somewhat different context. That after all is the way of culture and belief; they are living and ever-changing. In *Tracks,* Erdrich depicts a woman with powers named Fleur, who uses her powers to call the wind. After she is raped in revenge for winning a poker game, she uses her magics to punish those who assaulted her. She calls a hot August wind and a storm to descend upon Argus. The storm leaves the town unblemished, but the men who raped her, fearing the storm, lock themselves into a freezer for shelter and there they end up freezing to death. In this instance, Fleur appears to transcend understanding and the integration of practices of the dominant culture into her own life. Like many native peoples, she has learned to use the beliefs and practices of the dominant culture for her own gain and in such a way as to garner the upperhand in the conflict. The men simply don't understand the storm. They lock themselves away as they had been taught to do rather than being able to recognize the storm for what it is. This is why they get locked into the freezer and this is why they die. Fleur has used their beliefs against them.[15]

Erdrich does not merely address her concerns to adults. She writes children's novels as well, thus, extending awareness of the lives of Indigenous peoples to the youths of the world. A large and significant part of activism, after all, is education. In her children's novel *The Birchbark House*, Erdrich depicts the daily life of Omakayas, an adolescent girl living at the end of the nineteenth century. Omakayas is a member of the Turtle Band of the Anishinaabe, who live on an island in Lake Superior called the Golden-Breasted woodpecker. Her story represents the changing ways of life during this time period, as the *chimookoman*, white people, increase in number on Lake Superior, bringing disease with them and forcing her people to adapt or starve. Erdrich tells of Fishtail, who is going to the mission school to learn English so that he will know what the treaties say; Deydey, Omakayas' father, who is half white and loathes and ridicules even while he trades with them for his living; and Old Tallow, a powerful woman who rescues Omakayas from the island where all of her relatives died, presumably from smallpox.[16]

Despite the disease and changes in lifeways that are being wrought within her community, Omakayas feels herself somewhat removed from the influence of the *chimookoman*. As a survivor of smallpox and a savior of her adopted family during a harsh winter, Omakayas finds a joy and place within that are untouchable by outside influences. Like the characters in *Love Medicine*, Omakayas and her very extended family are survivors. As Lawrence Gross argues in "The Trickster and World Maintenance: An Anishinaabe Reading of Louise Erdrich's *Tracks*," "if there is one overriding characteristic of the characters in the corpus of Erdrich's works, it is that they are survivors."[17] They are characters that are very much like the real people who "adhere to traditional culture while adjusting themselves to broader society."[18] While *The Birchbark House* is a story of survival, it is also a story of remembrance. "In the beginning, the whites had all the power," Erdrich says, "but as one reviewer put it: The Indians have the history."[19] It is the history that is shown in *Birchbark House*. And it is through old, family stories like those Erdrich listened to while growing up and through new stories about old traditions, like Omakayas' story, that people are taught to remember. Her work speaks to the survivance of the people despite years of oppression. In speaking to the youth, she is developing understandings of America's Indigenous peoples in the minds of the next generation of leaders, both Native and non-Native.

It is evident in her books that Erdrich's life is dedicated to the sharing of stories and to educating people about the everyday lives of Native peoples. She has helped this objective to materialize beyond the world of her own writing by helping Native peoples share their stories with the public at her bookstore Birchbark Books in Minneapolis, Minnesota. This independent bookstore is a joint venture with Native Arts, and together they promote local book lovers, writers, Native American artists, neighborhood artisans, carpenters, and painters. They are also a teaching bookstore, willing to answer questions about books and displays. The bookstores' mission, thus, reflects a theme common in Erdrich's works, that of responsible pedagogy. According to Margaret Toth, Erdrich's "responsible pedagogy is not simply one that does 'justice' to the text but one that works toward civic justice. That is, such pedagogy produces not only careful and informed readers but also active allies."[20]

As a teacher, poet, writer, mother, and conscientious community member, Erdrich has accomplished something profound on behalf of Native peoples— she has humanized her subjects and opened a window for mainstream America to view Native peoples as something other than stereotypes. Even in their most magical moments, Erdrich's characters are represented as ordinary, fallible people, not war-bonnet-wearing heros, not shaman stereotypes, just everyday people, who like the rest of us, are just trying to make it through life.

NOTES

1. "Louise Erdrich, Secrets in the Indian File," *The Independent,* (June 20, 2008).

2. James R. and Wanda Giles, (ed), *The Dictionary of Literary Biography* (Detroit: Gale Research, Incorporated, 1995), 44.

3. "Louise Erdrich: Secrets in the Indian File."

4. Brigham Narins, "Louise Erdrich," *Contemporary Authors New Revision Series* 62 (Detroit: Gale Research, 1998).

5. Louise Erdrich in Laura Coltelli, "Louise Erdrich and Michael Dorris," *Winged Word: American Indian Writers Speak* (Lincoln: University of Nebraska Press, 1990), 45.

6. In *Manifest Manners,* Geraldo Vizenor uses the term "survivance" to refer to the active, continual process of survival that Native American people go through to maintain their daily lives, traditions, and cultures in the face of "dominant" American culture, which would just as soon write Native peoples out of existence. Gerald Vizenor, *Manifest Manners: Narratives on Postindian Survivance* (Nebraska: University of Nebraska Press, 1999).

7. Lousie Erdrich, "Two Languages in Mind, but Just One in the Heart," *Writers on Writing: New York Times on the Web* (May 22, 2000).

8. Katie Bacon, "An Emissary of the Between-World: A Conversation with Louise Erdrich, whose Stories Occur in the 'margin where cultures mix and collide,'" *The Altantic* (January 17, 2001).

9. E. Shelley Reid, "The Stories We Tell: Louise Erdrich's Identity Narratives," *MELUS,* 25, no. 3/4 Revising Traditions Double Issue (Autumn–Winter, 2000), 65–86.

10. Dorris as found in Louise Erdrich in Laura Coltelli, "Louise Erdrich and Michael Dorris," *Winged Word: American Indian Writers Speak* (Lincoln: University of Nebraska Press, 1990), 45.

11. Louise Erdrich, *Love Medicine* (New York: Harper Perennial, 2001), 7.

12. Bacon, "An Emissary of the Between-World: A Conversation with Louise Erdrich, whose Stories Occur in the 'margin where cultures mix and collide,'" *The Altantic* (January 17, 2001).

13. Erdrich, *Love Medicine,* 240.

14. Erdrich, *Love Medicine,* 240.

15. Louise Erdrich, *Tracks (*New York: Harper Perennial, 1989).

16. Louise Erdrich, *The Birchbark House* (New York: Hyperion, 1999).

17. Lawrence Gross, "The Trickster and World Maintenance: An Anishinaabe Reading of Louise Erdrich's Tracks," *Sail* 17, no. 3 (Fall 2005), 48.

18. Lawrence Gross, "The Trickster and World Maintenance: An Anishinaabe Reading of Louise Erdrich's Tracks," *Sail* 17, no. 3 (Fall 2005), 48.

19. Erdrich, quoted in *The Independent* referencing *The Birchbark House* (1999).

20. Margaret Toth, "Decolonizing Pedagogy: Teaching Louise Erdrich's The Bingo Palace," *Sail* 19, no. 1 (Spring 2007), 106.

BIBLIOGRAPHY

Bacon, Katie. "An Emissary of the Between-World: A Conversation with Louise Erdrich, whose Stories Occur in the 'margin where cultures mix and collide,'" *The Altantic* (January 17, 2001).

Coltelli, Laura. "Louise Erdrich and Michael Dorris," *Winged Word: American Indian Writers Speak*. Lincoln: University of Nebraska Press, 1990.

Erdrich, Louise. *Love Medicine.* New York: Harper Perennial, 2001.

Erdrich, Louise. *The Birchbark House.* New York: Hyperion, 1999.

Erdrich, Louise. *Tracks.* New York: Harper Perennial, 1989.

Erdrich, Louise. "Two Languages in Mind, but Just One in the Heart," *Writers on Writing: New York Times on the Web* (May 22, 2000).

Giles, James R. and Wanda Giles, (eds.), *The Dictionary of Literary Biography*. Detroit: Gale Research, Incorporated, 1995.

Gross, Lawrence. "The Trickster and World Maintenance: An Anishinaabe Reading of Louise Erdrich's Tracks," *Sail* 17, no. 3 (Fall 2005), 48.

"Louise Erdrich, Secrets in the Indian File," *The Independent* (June 20, 2008).

Narins, Brigham. "Louise Erdrich," *Contemporary Authors New Revision Series* 62. Detroit: Gale Research, 1998.

Reid, E. Shelley. "The Stories We Tell: Louise Erdrich's Identity Narratives," *MELUS*, 25, no. 3/4 Revising Traditions Double Issue (Autumn–Winter, 2000).

Toth, Margaret, "Decolonizing Pedagogy: Teaching Louise Erdrich's The Bingo Palace," *Sail* 19, no. 1 (Spring 2007), 106.

Vizenor, Gerald. *Manifest Manners: Narratives on Postindian Survivance.* Nebraska: University of Nebraska Press, 1999.

FURTHER READING

Erdrich, Louise and Michael Dorris. *Crown of Columbus.* New York: Harper Perrenial, 1991.

Erdrich, Louise and Michael Dorris. *Route Two.* Northridge, Ca: Lord John Press, 1991.

Erdrich, Louise. *Baptism of Desire.* New York: Harper Perennial, 1990.

Erdrich, Louise. *Books and Islands in Ojibwe Country.* New York: Harper Perennial, 2003.

Erdrich, Louise. *Chickadee.* New York: HarperCollins, 2012.

Erdrich, Louise. *Four Souls.* New York: Harper Perennial, 2005.

Erdrich, Louise. *Future Home of the Living God.* New York: Harper Collins, 2017.

Erdrich, Louise. *Grandmother's Pigeon.* New York: Hyperion, 1999.

Erdrich, Louise. *Jacklight.* New York: Flamingo, 1996.

Erdrich, Louise. *LaRose.* New York: HarperCollins, 2016.

Erdrich, Louise. *Love Medicine.* New York: Perennial, 2001.

Erdrich, Louise. *Makoons.* New York: HarperCollins, 2016.

Erdrich, Louise. *Original Fire: Selected and New Poems.* New York: HarperCollins, 2003, reprint 2018.

Erdrich, Louise. *Painted Drum.* New York: Harper Perennial, 2006.

Erdrich, Louise. *Tales of Burning Love.* New York: Harper Perennial, 1997.

Erdrich, Louise. *The Antelope Wife.* New York: Harper Perennial, 1999.

Erdrich, Louise. *The Beet Queen.* New York: Perennial, 1998.

Erdrich, Louise. *The Bingo Palace.* New York: Perennial, 2006.

Erdrich, Louise. *The Birchbark House.* New York: Hyperion, 1999.

Erdrich, Louise. *The Blue Jay's Dance: A Birthyear.* Harper Perennial, 1995.

Erdrich, Louise. *The Last Report on the Miracles at Little No Horse.* New York: Harper Perennial, 2002.

Erdrich, Louise. *The Master Butchers Singing Club.* New York: Harper Perennial, 2005.

Erdrich, Louise. *The Night Watchman.* New York: HarperCollins, 2021.

Erdrich, Louise. *The Plague of Doves.* New York: Harper, 2008.

Erdrich, Louise. *The Porcupine Year.* New York: HarperCollins, 2008.

Erdrich, Louise. *The Range Eternal.* New York: Hyperion, 2002.

Erdrich, Louise. *The Round House.* New York: HarperCollins, 2012.

Erdrich, Louise. *Tracks.* New York: Harper Perennial, 1989.

Erdrich, Louise. "Two Languages in Mind, but Just One in the Heart." *Writers on Writing: The New York Times*, *The New York Times*, May 22, 2000. archive.nytimes.com/www.nytimes.com/library/books/052200erdrich-writing.html.

Chapter Eight

The Voice of a Generation

Indigenous Singer-Songwriter, Actor, Activist and Icon, Buffy Sainte-Marie (b. 1941–)

Kimberly Norris Guerrero

Growing up in rural Oklahoma, I remember there being a "voice" present that helped me understand my place in the world as a little girl. As a little *Indian* girl. It didn't belong to my mother, grandmother or a teacher, the particular voice I'm referring to belonged to someone I watched religiously on television and latched on to like a long-lost relative. The voice belonged to Buffy Sainte-Marie—an activist, musician, actor, artist, educator, and one of *the* seminal voices representing Native American and First Nations people during the mid-to-late twentieth century.

Buffy Sainte-Marie's origin story is as mythic as her hauntingly inimitable singing voice. Born in the early 1940s on the Piapot Reserve in Canada, she was orphaned as an infant and— like thousands of other aboriginal children born during that period—was adopted out. She was sent 3,500 miles away to Wakefield, Massachusetts, with no accompanying birth certificate or any kind of official paperwork. Alfred and Winifred Sainte-Marie became her adoptive parents and named her Beverly; but the world would come to know her by her nickname—Buffy.

The cheerful name belied the reality of her difficult upbringing. At a very young age, Buffy was made aware of her adoption and her Indigenous heritage. Though Winifred herself was part Mi'kmaq, she would skirt Buffy's questions about her cultural roots and tell her to find out for herself when she was older. Closed off to any meaningful connection with her tribal heritage, Sainte-Marie was left on her own to face the daily challenges of growing up brown in a predominantly white town. She would face racists taunts in the streets and ignorance in the classroom as teachers spoke of Natives as if they were extinct relics of the past, and then there was her town's red-faced, big-nosed, high school mascot—the Wakefield Warrior.

Sadly, the challenges facing Buffy didn't just lie outside her home. Sainte-Marie shared that there were not only predators stalking her disadvantaged neighborhood, but they were also in her own family, in her own house. In Joan Prowse's documentary on Sainte-Marie's life, Buffy confesses that, "In many ways I was not treated well in that town, or in my family . . . so I grew up kind of as a child on my own."[1] Fortunately, in the midst of all that darkness and isolation, Buffy found a "playmate."

At three years old, the perennially inquisitive, astoundingly bright Buffy taught herself to play the piano. At four, she set one of her poems to music. With no formal boundaries, Buffy began an experimental exploration of sound that would become a fundamental aspect of her music. In an interview with *Vogue* magazine, Sainte-Marie recalled, "I could play fake Beethoven, and do other things with strange chords that other people didn't use, but that I liked. I banged on pots and pans, I'd play with rubber bands, I'd blow on grass, I played the mouth bow."[2] When she turned sixteen Buffy began playing the guitar, creating thirty-two original ways to tune it which only compounded her already unique sound. With a guitar in her hands and deep longings, observations, questions and pain welling up in her spirit, Buffy began to pour everything out into song—and then the real magic began to happen.

Having emerged from the crucible of growing up in Wakefield, Sainte-Marie flourished as an undergraduate at the University of Massachusetts, Amherst. Buffy would play and sing her songs for the girls in her dorm. They, along with their housemother, Theresa de Kerpely, would sit and listen, transfixed. De Kerpely, who was European, introduced Buffy to the music of iconic French singer, Edith Piaf, and the powerful Flamenco singer/dancer, Carmen Amaya. Inspired by the power and fierce femininity of these women, Buffy began to see herself in context of the wider world, realizing that like Piaf and Amaya, she too had a unique voice to share with the world. As a young indigenous woman, Sainte-Marie sensed she could help provide a voice to an entire people group who had been silenced by the ravages of colonialism. By the time she began playing the local coffeehouses, Buffy Sainte-Marie was a force to be reckoned with.

As she was developing as an artist, Buffy was also prospering academically and graduated with honors with a degree in Eastern Philosophy. Though her plan was to travel to India and continue with her Peace Studies, friends pleaded with her to stay and sing; they believed that her voice and the messages in her songs needed to be heard. It was, after all, 1962 and the counterculture movement was ready to explode—and no one was more counterculture than Buffy Sainte-Marie. Within months, Buffy would move to the very epicenter of conscious music and thought, New York City.

During this pivotal period, Buffy was invited to visit her reserve in Canada. Emile Piapot, youngest son of the revered Southern Cree Chief Piapot, worked with Buffy trying to locate her family. Unfortunately, her birth re-cords had all been destroyed, but many in the Piapot family believed Buffy was indeed, their relative. Buffy was certainly exemplifying the traits of the infamous Chief Piapot, who had himself had been raised away from his tribe and family. Years after being kidnapped and raised by another tribe, Piapot returned to his people and become a courageous and outspoken political and spiritual leader, utterly unafraid to challenge the status quo. Emile and his wife, Clara, would go on to adopt Buffy according to Cree tradition—they gave her the name Medicine Bird Singing.[3]

Full of purpose and resolve, Buffy returned to the United States and im-mersed herself in the coffeehouse scene in New York City. One day, folk wunderkind Bob Dylan walked in, heard Buffy sing, and then insisted she go straight to the famed Greenwich Village hangout, the Gaslight, and ask to play. As luck would have it, the *New York Times* critic, Robert Shelton, was in the audience the very first time Buffy took the stage at the Gaslight. In his next article, he would herald Buffy Sainte-Marie as "one of the most promising new talents on the folk scene."[4] She was immediately signed to Vanguard Records and released her first album, appropriately titled, *It's My Way!* in 1964.

In the painfully raw, achingly beautiful songs on her debut album, Buffy tackled issues from cultural genocide ("Now That the Buffalo's Gone"), to incest ("The Incest Song"), to addiction ("Cod'ine"). The debut album also included "The Universal Soldier," a song that would become an anthem of the anti-war movement after being recorded by Donovan. *It's My Way!* received critical acclaim and *Billboard* magazine put Buffy on their cover, hailing her as the "Best New Artist" of 1964—the same year four lads from Liverpool arrived on America's shores.

In 1965, Buffy recorded her sophomore album, *Many a Mile,* which fea-tured a love song that would catapult her into previously unimagined finan-cial success. "Until It's Time for You to Go" would be re-recorded by some of the music industry's greatest voices including Neil Diamond, Barbra Strei-sand, Johnny Mathis, and "the King" himself, Elvis Presley, who considered Buffy's tune his and his wife Priscilla's personal love song.

With "plenty of money to eat two meals a day"[5] for the rest of her life, Buffy started a non-profit organization called the Nihewan Foundation for American Indian Education. The foundation would provide practical support and financial scholarships to help Indian students make the leap from high school to college. But Buffy's generous spirit was not just shared amongst her own people, she also supported fellow artists. There was one particular songwriter Buffy truly believed in, so she took the singer's tape around New York City, playing it for all the heavy hitters on the folk music scene. But no one was interested. Finally, just as Buffy was about to run out of options, a manager in her own office heard the tape, caught the vision, and at long last thanks to Buffy's help, Joni Mitchell was "discovered."

During the latter half of the 60s, Buffy's music evolved from acoustic folk to country to rock. In fact, by the end of the decade Buffy found herself tapping into the experimental creative instinct she'd developed as a child. In 1969, Buffy recorded *Illuminations*, the first quadrophonic electronic album ever recorded. For some reason, even though her skills as a singer, songwriter and performer were growing stronger, her music was no longer garnering radio play. It would be years before Sainte-Marie would find out she'd been placed on a blacklist by the Johnson and Nixon administrations, her music pulled from the airwaves because it was deemed dangerous, and Buffy herself, "a loose cannon."[6] And to some degree, she was: loose, armed . . . and focused.

Buffy threw herself into supporting Indigenous causes using her voice draw attention to a wide array of Indigenous and environmental issues. From protesting the Kinzua Dam President Kennedy had sanctioned, which threatened to displace one third of the Seneca reservation, to demanding that if director Leo Penn (Sean's father) wanted to cast her for a television episode of *The Virginian,* he would have to hire Native actors for the Native roles, to performing concerts to raise financial support for the American Indian Movement's occupation of Alcatraz, Buffy moved out of the 1960s and into the 1970s in the spirit of Chief Piapot—unafraid of challenging the status quo.

Throughout the 70s, Buffy Sainte-Marie continued making albums, scoring films and adding to what would become a 33-page long file the FBI kept on the singer/activist. Buffy continued her staunch, vocal protest of the aberrant treatment of Native peoples by the United States government, through her support of the Trail of Broken Treaties (1972), the Occupation of Wounded Knee (1973) and the Longest Walk (1978). During this tumultuous decade, one of the most effective decisions Sainte-Marie made was to appear as herself in an episode of the popular children's television show, *Sesame Street.* Buffy saw the opportunity as the perfect venue to teach the children who were watching—both in America and the 73 countries that aired the show—that Indians were real, live human beings. Though she was only hired to appear in one show, it became immediately apparent to producers that Buffy Sainte-Marie belonged on *Sesame Street.*

From 1976 to 1981, Buffy, her husband Sheldon Wolfchild and their son Cody, appeared regularly on the show. Perhaps the most groundbreaking aspect of their presence was that they weren't Native American characters, per se. They were simply people, a normal family, who just happened to be Native American. Speaking from experience as an Indigenous actor, there is a subtle but powerful difference. Buffy and her family were allowed to simply *be.* And in that freedom to be, Buffy broke other barriers as well, such as being the first woman to breast-feed her child on television. Thanks to Buffy's years spent on *Sesame Street*, a generation of children grew up knowing that Native Americans didn't just live in history books, they were alive and well and best friends with Big Bird!

In 1981, during her last year on *Sesame Street*, Buffy began using an Apple computer to record her music. That same year, she was also asked to co-write a theme song for a film starring up-and-coming actor, Richard Gere. Joining forces with Will Jennings and Jack Nitzsche, Buffy wrote the title track to *An Officer and A Gentleman*, which was recorded by Joe Cocker and Jennifer Warren. "Up Where We Belong" went on to win the Academy Award for Best Song in a Motion Picture, rendering Buffy Sainte-Marie the very first Native American to win an Oscar.

Three years later, Buffy began to use her computer not only for creating music, but for expanding her practice of making visual art. Having begun painting around the same time she learned to play guitar as a teenager, Buffy began experimenting with graphic design programs like MacPaint. While following her simple instinct to play and create, Sainte-Marie became a pioneer in digital art. Her work has been shown in galleries across North America and her images are immortalized in the permanent collections of the American Indian Arts Museum, First Nations University, and the Tucson Art Museum. Buffy encouraged other artists not to be afraid of the computer, but to use it like any other medium or tool. It was as if she presaged the great leveling of the creative playing field about to occur, as what had previously been extraordinary technology was finding its way into the hands of ordinary people.

With that ever-evolving technology at her fingertips, Buffy began working on her first album in sixteen years, *Coincidence (and Likely Stories)* (1992). She recorded it on her computer at her home studio in Hawaii and sent the tracks to her producer in London. This ground-breaking file sharing was reportedly the first album ever to utilize the world wide web in its production. At the same time, Sainte-Marie began thinking it would be interesting to connect classrooms near her home in Hawaii, with First Nations students back on the reserves in Canada.

The educational exchange proved so successful that in 1997, Buffy expanded her Nihewan Foundation to include digital resources for educators who wanted to improve the way Native American history and culture was taught to both Native and non-Native youth—and the Cradleboard Teaching Project was born. Utilizing digital connectivity that Buffy christened, the Electronic Powwow, the Cradleboard Teaching Project partnered Indian and non-Indian teachers and students across the continent. Because of its success at promoting intercultural understanding, the project garnered national acclaim by President Clinton's One America Initiative on Race. The honor buoyed Sainte-Marie's foundation which continues to support education in Indian Country. In fact, when asked about the various awards she'd received over the years—from her Oscar to several honorary doctorates—Buffy commented, "My biggest honor was to find out that two of my early scholarship recipients had gone on to found tribal colleges. Can you imagine that kind of thrill?"[7]

In the last four decades of the twentieth century, Buffy Sainte Marie used her voice to bring creative expression and activism into perfect harmony. There was no album on which Buffy didn't address issues burdening her Native people or celebrate their vibrant culture. There was no television, radio or magazine interview over those many years in which she would do anything less than speak the truth—and sometimes sing it—in order to dispel ignorance and breed understanding and peace. If the powers that be told her she was only to sing one of her love songs and refrain from mentioning any political or social issues, she would politely but firmly say no. She championed the cause of changing the antiquated colonial history being taught to children and was a pioneer of utilizing digital connectivity to enhance education.

Buffy's voice changed the way the world viewed Indigenous people of North America. Buffy's voice resounds with the undying courage and ingenuity of her ancestors. Buffy's voice was, is, and will continue to be, a powerful vibration capable of tearing down walls of ignorance while it builds up the human spirit. That very same voice was present the day I was "born" into the professional world of acting.

In 1991, I was cast in my first television production—a big-budget miniseries called, *Son of the Morning Star*. I played a young Cheyenne woman, Kate Bighead, who was an eyewitness to the Battle of the Little Bighorn. On screen the audience would see me, but off screen they would hear the voice of an older Kate as she recounted her memories. The night the show aired, I discovered with delighted shock that the voice telling Kate's side of the story would be none other than Buffy Sainte-Marie. In retrospect the "voice" that had been there for me in my formative years *had* been something a mother, grandmother, and teacher—and not just to me, but countless others around the world who have been forever touched by the music, activism, acting, art, and philanthropy of Buffy Sainte-Marie—*Medicine Bird Singing*.

NOTES

1. *Buffy Sainte-Marie, A Multimedia Life*. Joan Prowse. Performers Buffy Sainte-Marie, Joni Mitchell, Robbie Robertson. True North Productions, 2014.

2. Alex Frank, "Buffy Sainte-Marie on Her New Album and Legacy as a Native American Activist," *Vogue* (May 27, 2015), https://www.vogue.com/article/buffy-sainte-marie-power-in-the-blood.

3. Andrea Warner, "Buffy Sainte-Marie at 80," *Chatelaine* (March 22, 2021), https://www.chatelaine.com/living/buffy-sainte-marie-at-80/.

4. Brian Wright-McLeod, *Encyclopedia of Native Music* (Tucson: University of Arizona Press, 2005), 170.

5. Alex Frank. "Buffy Sainte-Marie on Her New Album and Legacy as a Native American Activist," *Vogue* (May 27, 2015), https://www.vogue.com/article/buffy-sainte-marie-power-in-the-blood.

6. Alex Heigel, "Activist and Musician Buffy Sainte-Marie on Her New Album and Reading Her FBI File," *People* (May 6, 2015), https://people.com/celebrity/buffy-sainte-marie-power-in-the-blood-out-may-12/.

7. Alex Frank, "Buffy Sainte-Marie on Her New Album and Legacy as a Native American Activist," *Vogue* (May 27, 2015), https://www.vogue.com/article/buffy-sainte-marie-power-in-the-blood.

BIBLIOGRAPHY

Buffy Sainte-Marie, A Multimedia Life. Joan Prowse. Performers Buffy Sainte-Marie, Joni Mitchell, Robbie Robertson. True North Productions, 2014.

Frank, Alex. "Buffy Sainte-Marie on Her New Album and Legacy as a Native American Activist." *Vogue*. May 27, 2015. https://www.vogue.com/article/buffy-sainte-marie-power-in-the-blood.

Heigel, Alex. "Activist and Musician Buffy Sainte-Marie on Her New Album and Reading Her FBI File." *People*. May 6, 2015. https://people.com/celebrity/buffy-sainte-marie-power-in-the-blood-out-may-12/.

Stonechild, Blair. *Buffy Sainte-Marie: It's My Way*. Markham: Fifth House, 2012.

Warner, Andrea. "Buffy Sainte-Marie at 80." *Chatelaine*. March 22, 2021. https://www.chatelaine.com/living/buffy-sainte-marie-at-80/.

FURTHER READING

Heigel, Alex. "Activist and Musician Buffy Sainte-Marie on Her New Album and Reading Her FBI File." *People*. May 6, 2015. https://people.com/celebrity/buffy-sainte-marie-power-in-the-blood-out-may-12/.

Warner, Andrea and Joni Mitchell. *Buffy Sainte-Marie: The Authorized Biography*. Vancouver: Greystone, 2021.

Chapter Nine

A Woman of Vision

Vivienne Jake (b. 1939–d. 2016)

Daisy Ocampo

To the Southern Paiute, Earth as we know it today, originated from the body of *Hutsipamamau'u* (Ocean Woman) at the beginning of time when she descended from the sky in the form of a worm. Taking skin and dirt from her own body, Ocean Woman made a ball of mud, skin, and oil to create this land.[1] While still in the form of a worm, she began stretching and molding her body in various directions to make the Americas and constructed the beautiful plateaus where the *Nuwuvi* (Southern Paiute) call home. With the help of *Shinav* (Coyote), Ocean Woman perfected these lands, which are currently Arizona, Utah, California, and Nevada. Later, in a journey through the Pacific Ocean, from an island off the coast, a female elder instructed *Shinav* to transport a basket to his brother, *Tivatsi* (Wolf).

Despite being warned not to open this basket, *Shinav's* impulsiveness led him to untie the basket. Immediately, several people ran out from inside the basket. *Shinav* was unable to keep control and retie the basket, and the "womb of Mankind" gave birth to the first people.[2] Each person made their way home across the Americas. *Shinav* was curious to know if the basket was empty. *Shinav* then peaked at the bottom of the basket. There he saw people crushed and quickly retied the basket. Upon receiving the basket, *Tivatsi* scolded *Shinav. Tivatsi* took the crushed people from the basket and held them close and blew his powerful breath medicine on them. This medicine made these people strong, pragmatic, and adaptive, essential qualities to live in the Mojave Desert. These were the first *Nuwuvi* people.[3]

Much like the elders before her, the history of this land and its people have been inseparable for Vivienne Caron Jake. Her *Nuwuvi* people of the Kaibab Plateau are part of the origin story, and Vivienne continued the process of creation and preservation. Vivienne Jake's life trajectory included serving her community and protecting Kaibab Paiute ancestral territory. She, like many others of her tribe, are entrusted with the responsibility of the Salt Songs, which are sacred. The Salt Songs are a spatially complex that anchors *Nuwuvi* people to their ancestral homelands. She was an example of Native American women in leadership positions, which allows for women to occupy political, cultural, and environmental spaces that advance Indigenous sovereignty and strengthens the overall well-being of Native communities.

Vivienne Jake was born on February 23, 1939, in Kanab, Utah, just miles from the Kaibab Reservation. As a child she attended the Kaibab Day School and went on to school in White Rocks, Uinta, before transferring to the Phoenix Indian School in Encanto Village in Phoenix, Arizona.[4] After graduating high school at the Phoenix Indian School, she continued her education at Arizona State University and later graduated from the University of Indiana. She became one of the first Native women in higher education, inspiring a new generation of Native woman scholars. Her daughter, Brittanni Wero, remembers her mother as a smart, insightful, and resourceful woman. Vivienne saw higher education as a reciprocal space where students brought Native knowledge in the classroom, and in return, universities would invest academic resources back into Native communities. While working as a social worker on the Hopi Reservation, Vivienne knew that for life to be meaningful, she must always be of service to others, especially her community.

Later, in service to her family, community, and land, she served in the United States Marine Corps during the Vietnam War from 1968 to 1971. She, like other Native veterans, have historically fought to protect their lands and communities. Her decision to serve began when Vivienne's family received a letter from Vietnam where her brother was stationed. In this letter, he narrated the perilous experience as a frontline soldier. The family knew he may not make it back home. Vivienne immediately began writing letters to legislative officials, urging them to bring him home. In these letters, Vivienne pleaded for his return and expressed her concern that her elderly parents would not survive the heartbreak of losing a son. Vivienne promised to serve in the military if her brother was allowed to return home. Although not a decision based on her letter, her brother eventually returned home. When he did, Vivienne fulfilled her promise, packed her bags, and enlisted into the Marines.

Vivienne's brother urged her to not enlist in the military, and she responded that it was too late.[5] For Vivienne, serving in the military was more of a promise than a family tradition. It was something she knew had to do, primarily, because she had given her word. Veterans like Vivienne are distinguished members in their communities and are often honored in events, such as Powwows, for their service. Friend and colleague Cliff Trafzer remembers learning of her military service from accounts given by Native American staff at the University of Arizona, and later at the Chunkchansi Gold Resort and

Casino in Yokuk County for a Tribal Environmental Protection Agency (EPA) meeting. Trafzer learned that Vivienne was truly a visionary for her work in environmental protection and partnerships with scholars such as Professor Richard Stoffel (foundational ethnographer for Southern Paiute landscapes).[6] Her vision and persistence made Vivienne a woman of note and leadership among *Nuwuvi* people.

In providing professional social services, Vivienne sought to incorporate cultural practices and connections to the land in her community-based work to promote well-being. Given the impacts of colonization on tribal lands and communities, she fought for Native rights on many fronts. In addition to her professional work, she served for over forty years Vivienne served the Kaibab Paiute people in numerous political capacities for forty years. She served terms as Tribal Chairwoman (1975–1977), Director of Social Services (1980–1988), Director of Native American Graves Protection and Repatriation Act (NAGPRA, 1990–1997), Environmental Director (1998–2003), and as a tribal Council Member (2009–2011). In all her roles, she advocated for the preservation and protection of the land. As tribal chairwoman, she secured recognition of *Avi Nava/ Ting-ai-ay* (House Rock) as traditional Kaibab territory—a sacred place where the journey of the Salt Songs begins.[7]

Later in 1989, Vivienne formed a Kaibab-Paiute environmental organization named the Paiute Earthkeepers as a way to advocate for Kaibab ancestral lands and successfully overturned Waste-Tech Services' (a major waste disposal company) proposal for an incinerator plant.[8] The waste disposal industry is notorious for targeting tribal reservations to build incinerator plants that skirt state and local safety regulations. This incinerator would have impacted the local springs, air quality, and ultimately undermined tribal sovereignty, traditions, and culture. Vivienne and the Paiute Earthkeepers worked tirelessly until the tribal council officially rejected the hazardous waste incinerator proposal in 1991.

As a tribal historian, Vivienne also sought to address historical inaccuracies of events such as the Mountain Meadows and Circleville Massacres. In the case of the Mountain Meadows Massacre, at the height of westward expansion in the 1850s, Paiute people became scapegoats for an attack that began between Mormon settlers and Methodist emigrants.[9] The Mormons blamed Paiute people for the massacre of federal troops—a lie that the Mormon Church protected for more than one hundred years.[10] Western narratives of the "savage" Indian often became blanket cover ups for violent outbreaks where Native people were wrongfully blamed. People who passed as White were given the benefit of the doubt, while Native people were typecast as inferior, savage, and uncivilized—natural perpetrators of violence. These strong negative stereotypes and historical inaccuracies continue to impact Indigenous

people today. Utilizing archaeological and historical records, Vivienne overturned outdated historical narratives that presumed White innocence and assumed Native criminality during both these massacres. Vivienne's re-writing
of history brought dignity, historical accuracy, and healing to the Kaibab
community.[11] Vivienne's leadership demonstrates the importance of centering
Native voices. Indeed, Native women have been at the forefront of revitalization and reclamation efforts. This was certainly true of her participation in
preserving the sacred Salt Songs.

Preserving the Salt Songs was one of the concerns and ancestral responsibilities Vivienne confronted. The Salt Songs are an ancient cultural tradition shared by the thirteen bands of Southern Paiute people. The Salt Songs
include an old complex of approximately one hundred and forty songs. The
Salt Songs express themselves in two different ways: as specific physical
trails and as spiritual trails traveled by the spirit of the *Nuwuvi* person at the
time of death.[12] These songs are sacred because they are sung at the time of
someone's passing, and functional in their denotation of a knowledge system
of plants and animals of the Southwest desert landscape. Professor Trafzer
explains the spiritual sense of the Songs, reporting that during special *Yagapi*
ceremonies, singers unite their songs with those from other *Nuwuvi* territo-
ries.[13] These songs intersect to build strength and the momentum needed for
a person's last journey through Southern Paiute homelands to the person's
final resting place, the Milky Way. Geographically, the Salt Songs begin their
journey at *Avi Nava* or *Ting-ai-ay* (Rock House), a sacred cave at the conflu-
ence of the Bill Williams and Colorado Rivers. The songs travel through the
Kaibab and Colorado Plateau for one thousand miles. They continue west to
the great mountain of *Nuva Kiav* near Mt. Charleston in the Spring Mountains of southern Nevada. The origin place of *Nuwuvi* people also serves as
the launching area for souls into the Milky Way.[14] The Salt Songs then travel
further south and west before turning east through mountains like the Old
Woman Mountains in the Mojave Desert, and finally back to their place of
origin, *Ting-ai-ay*.

Vivienne's daughter remembers her mother as a woman who lived a life
dedicated to the protections of the land and sacred sites.[15] Reminiscing on
a Salt Song Gathering with numerous singers, Trafzer shares, "Whenever
I heard her [Vivienne] speak, she would calmly state that she was sharing
what she had learned and that we as humans had an obligation to take care
of, including the lands, plants, animals, and spaces in between sacred places,
like the space between Mt. Charleston and the Old Woman Mountains. That
space was part of the sacred web or network of power that came from Ocean
Woman; the power concentrated in places and spaces."[16] This network of
sacred places, which spans the states of California, Arizona, Nevada, and

Utah, together invoke the power of the spirits that live there. This power is known as *puha* and is concentrated in certain locations. *Puha* is described like a spider web, because the power spirals into a cone-like shape with a broad opening at top and narrowing to the bottom.[17] These invisible spider webs and spirals encircle the earth, but also concentrate power in certain places like Mt. Charleston, Old Woman Mountains, and Rock House.

The Salt Songs are a binding oral document that creates the cultural fabric of the Southern Paiute. These songs establish proprietary rights, outline in-tertribal relationships, and tie people with the land and water sources along the physical and spiritual trails across the desert. All Southern Paiute people mark their territory with songs. Southern Paiutes who inherited a song gained access to an ancestral oral document, a cultural survey of the land, as well as the family obligation to steward it. It is one of the ways that Nuwuvi people establish kinship ties.[18]

Each person is entrusted with the Salt Songs to their respective homelands by the Creator. Singing the Salt Songs is an important cultural marker that makes space for identity and place to merge and inform each other. These songs are spatial, anchoring of Creation Stories and in turn narrate revered places that express spiritual power, movement, relationships, memories, and ancestral histories. Vivienne shares that when the people sing the songs, the spirits that dwell in these certain locations know that they haven't been forgotten.[19] By singing the Salt Songs, the Spirits have been honored—and in that process the landscape becomes activated, bringing health and vitality back to the people. Vivienne viewed the Salt Songs as a way of putting the world back together after so many years of turmoil.

Vivienne Jake encouraged the youth to learn the Salt Songs, but also gently encouraged the singers to bring them back from their dormant state. Vivienne made a call to elders to take leadership over their revitalization. Kaibab elders wondered where the good times went when the Salt Songs were sung every-where. During a memorial service, Matthew Hanks Leivas (Chemehuevi), an old friend of Vivienne's, remembers when he met her, he was still learning the songs. Vivienne repeatedly told the elders that the songs needed to be taught in order for them to be learned by people like Matt Leivas. Yet the reality was that there were few singers left. Some had passed, while others were greatly impacted by boarding schools: where Native students subject to westerniza-tion and an assimilationist education, with the goal to "kill the Indian in him, and save the man." Vivienne had an opportunity to change this and took it.[20]

Vivienne's elder, Willis Mayo, also known as Uncle Willy to her family, asked to speak to her one day. Vivienne knew that Willis Mayo, lead Salt Song Singer, was in his eighties at the time and few singers were left. Willis Mayo learned the Salt Songs from Steward Snow and he had no one to teach the songs to. Willis allowed family members to informally record his songs, yet he feared that he would be an end point in the history of Salt Songs. During Vivienne's visit, Willis expressed concern and uncertainty about the survival of the Salt Songs. Willis approached certain individuals to take on this responsibility, a decision not to be taken lightly. Lead singers must travel to funerals, be of service to the multiple Southern Paiute nations, and teach the songs to the next generation. One individual he approached refused, opting instead to work, start a family, and live a mainstream life. One young man named showed great promise. Although he did not traditionally learn the songs from the caves or know the exact sequence, he sang well, and Vivienne was particularly proud of him. Unfortunately, he passed away in the middle of his learning process. There remained a need for a lead singer. Other potential students simply did not have the right make-up for this important position and responsibility. Afraid of losing the Salt Songs, Willis told Vivienne that it was now her responsibility to do something.[21] Vivienne took Willis' directive seriously. According to her daughter, Brittanni, her mother as a woman of her word when it came to spiritual matters. She approached decisions with strength, strict adherence to truth, and intelligence.[22]

Vivienne decided that the best means to preserve the songs was to record them and create a mechanism that would protect the Salt Songs for Southern Paiute People. There have been instances when some of these early recordings of Willis Mayo were for sale at powwows. This altered its purpose from its cultural context to a commercial one. Vivienne shared her preservation interests with her friends Matthew Leivas, Betty Cornelius, and Larry Eddy. Together they called an informal meeting with a few people in an 8 by 10 room in Flagstaff, Arizona, to discuss preservation efforts.[23] This small and humble gathering marked the birthplace of the Salt Song Project with Co-Directors Vivienne Jake and Matt Leivas. This group then partnered with Melissa Nelson and Philip Klasky from the Cultural Conservancy to conduct the official recordings.

The Salt Song Project produced numerous copies of the recordings for tribal members, retained copyrights to the recordings, and archived the recordings in a repository where Southern Paiute people could gain access to them. Many Southern Paiute nations did not agree with the recording of the Salt Songs. Traditionally, these songs were part of a vibrant cultural institution that required initiates to learn the songs in the oral tradition and engage with the land, especially caves, in order to gain the power to make the Salt Songs work. Colonization heavily disrupted this cultural practice. Although the Salt Songs were not extinct, the community knew they were at grave risk. Matt Leivas and Vivienne's goal with the recordings was to create a place holder until a new generation revitalized and fully maintained the songs.

When lead singers are unavailable for funerals, families play the CD record-ing. The recordings serve as a guide for recent revitalization efforts across Southern Paiute lands. Vivienne's vision of using the Salt Songs to bring healing continued as a central undertaking of the Salt Song Project.

Vivienne believed that the Salt Songs should visit places in need of heal-ing first. One of these places was Sherman Indian High School in Riverside, California, one of the many boarding schools established by the United States government. Vivienne stressed the importance of bringing the Salt Songs to boarding schools to assist the spirits of students that had died at the school and were never taken home for burial to find a pathway to the spirit world. Vivienne herself had attended boarding school at the age of eleven in north-ern Utah and at Phoenix Indian School. Vivienne recounted to her daughter the visceral memories of boarding school when administrators conducted roll-call outdoors in the snow. Vivienne remembers not having shoes, lined up barefoot in the snow, all while waiting for their names to be called and dismissed.[24] Despite these early traumatic experiences with education, sing-ing the Salt Songs would bring healing back to the community to address the intergenerational trauma of boarding schools.[25]

During the late nineteenth and early twentieth centuries, the United States government established several off-reservation boarding schools for Native children to replace their cultural identities with a Western agenda of civili-zation and assimilation, both forms of cultural genocide. This was done by instituting a curriculum that stressed economic progress and Western civility into the minds and spirits of young Native children. Schools such as Sherman Institute (today, Sherman Indian High School) first opened its doors in Perris, California, in 1892, and later moved to Riverside. Administrators forcibly removed children from their families, prohibited them from speaking their languages, and prohibited them from practicing traditions such as the Salt Songs. Students secretly continued singing the Salt Songs, not knowing they would become the generation to revitalize the songs back home.

At the boarding schools, administrators and teachers instituted trade edu-cations for Native children focused on trades such as baking, cleaning, and childcare. The school's goal was to bring Native students into the American workforce and make them "productive citizens."[26] During this time, students created new identities that tied them to sports, nursing, military, and various trades. Workplace negligence often surfaced at the boarding schools. Some administrators notoriously kept these cases from families and other cases of neglect involved infectious disease, particularly tuberculosis. Families received notice from Sherman's administrators that their child had broken a bone, or contracted smallpox, measles, or typhoid fever.[27] In some deeply heart-wrenching cases, administrators wrote letters to parents informing them of their child's death, followed by instructions for the recovery of their bodies or burial at the school cemetery. Due to the economic hardship on reservations, some parents had no means to recover their children's bodies. The number of dead children at Sherman Institute multiplied and administrators created a cemetery. These children did not have Indigenous funeral services. They left behind grieving loved ones. Family members never received the closure to confront the reality of such a violent loss.

Vivienne Jake and other Southern Paiute elders believed the spirits of these children did not depart this world. Instead, the spirits of these children wandered. Both Jake and Matt Leivas as well as other Nuwuvi people were former boarding school students. Salt Singers took on the responsibility to guide the spirits of former boarding school children to the Milky Way. Chemehuevi Salt Song Singer, Larry Eddy shared how the songs were received: "The Creator told us, I'm going to teach you these songs, but before I teach you these songs, I'm going to break your heart."[28] Vivienne Jake explained, "sometimes our hearts need to be broken, I suppose it would be one of the ways the Creator would tell us we are living beings. He gave us feelings. We just go through life without thinking, without observing, without feeling and those things need to be brought back to us."[29] Salt Songs offered souls a pathway to the spirit world as well as healing prayers. In 2002, Southern Paiute singers met at Sherman Indian High School Cemetery to sing for former students.

Vivienne Jake had a vision to preserve the Salt Songs by visiting and singing to sacred sites along the Salt Song Trail in present-day California, Arizona, Nevada, and Utah. She and a group of Salt Song singers, in conjunction with the Native American Land Conservancy and Cultural Conservancy, sang to the Old Woman Mountain, a sacred mountain range with a medicine cave, springs, and other cultural sites. Vivienne supported the Native American Land Conservancy (NALC), which stewards the Old Woman Mountain Preserve and creates Healing and Learning Landscape Programs for youth.[30] In 1998, thirteen Salt Song singers, led by Jake, Larry Eddy, and Matt Leivas, came together at the Old Woman Mountain to sing. The Cultural Conservancy created a visual and audio recording of the singers performing songs to support the teaching of various audiences, including young singers.[31] Due to Jake's efforts, several young people have joined the ranks of Salt Song singers to keep the songs alive.[32]

Vivienne Jake believed the Salt Songs would bring *Nuwuvi* people back together. The Native American Land Conservancy (NALC) supports education for Native youth, the revitalization of the Salt Songs, and preservation of the landscape. Like Vivienne, the NALC is motivated by an urgent call to protect Native American sacred sites from unprecedented levels of development that endangers landscapes due to the lack of protection under state and federal laws. Current laws and land use management policies fail to protect Native cultural resources. This puts Native peoples in constant environmental litigation, having to weigh the protection of their ancestral lands against resource extraction that creates various forms of environmental degradations. To alleviate this strain to Native people, NALC acquires at-risk sites, provides protective land management, and scientific studies.[33] NALC's mission of healing from intergenerational trauma understands the need to connect people back to the land. Sacred places found throughout the Salt Song Trail are landscapes of belonging. Jake understood that the Salt Songs remind people of their responsibility, purpose and identity. While working together with the NALC, Vivienne Jake affirmed her faith and vision in the power of the Salt Songs to bring the people back together:

> These songs are very powerful. They are the songs that are going to unite our people again. It's going to be a spiritual awakening of the Native American people, especially other Paiute people. It has to happen. It has been prophesied. How do you stop prophecy? You can't stop prophecy.[34]

Part of Vivienne's journey with the Salt Song Project included creating a Salt Song map. How do you create a map that properly conceptualizes Native cultural resources, sacred geographies and centers Southern Paiute? From a colonial and Western framework, maps became legal documents that would be used to claim property and outline settlements that would eventually become towns, cities and contemporary states. Spanish, Mexican, and Americans created colonial maps as a tool to claim land, yet they also inadvertently left proof of Native land dispossession. These maps altered the spatial history of sacred Indigenous places with new ideas of legal property and territory, which claim the seemingly, westernized perspective of barren landscapes. Maps can be seen as expressions of power. Vivienne believed that power came out of revitalization. A team from the Cultural Conservancy and Salt Song singers created a multi-dimensional map that reflects the movement of the Salt Songs throughout today's states of California, Arizona, Utah, and Nevada.[35] This Salt Song map indicates the various cultural resources and sacred sites along the physical trail. This map establishes the *Nuwuvi's* historical presence and invites an imaginative engagement with the land that includes people and traditions. The Salt Song map has been reproduced as a poster and proudly displayed in community centers, living rooms, schools, universities, senior centers, health clinics and tribal headquarters.

Vivienne Jake's scholarly and community work enhanced the lives of Southern Paiute people and friends of *Nuwuvi* people. Native people have been relegated as "exotic Indians" and part of a vanishing and backward culture. This is due to the colonial perceptions of the racial inferiority of

Native people and deep-seated stereotypes and beliefs. Jake challenged negative beliefs and actions threatening Native Americans, and she worked diligently to bring knowledge and understanding to Southern Paiute people. She was a community agent for positive and constructive change through her preservation efforts. After living with dialysis for years, Vivienne surrendered to her fate. While riding in a car with her daughter, Brittanni Wero, through Cedar Ridge Hill along the Grand Canyon, Vivienne sang songs as they made their way to the reservation, including her beloved Salt Songs. Not long afterwards, Vivienne Caron Jake passed away on February 23, 2016, in her home in Eagle Mountain Village, Arizona. Singers gathered to honor her passing with Salt Songs, sending her soul to *Nuva Kiav* in the Spring Mountains of Nevada. Before making her journey, Vivienne shared these last words.

> Come and touch me, said Mother Earth
> So I removed my shoes and walked.
> Come and sing a song with me, said the Bird
> And I did so.
> Sit and rest awhile beside me," said the Brook
> And I sat and meditated beside it.
> Tell me, how is your day going?" asked the Tree.
> I leaned up against it and whispered how wonderfully good it was.
> The Sun called out, "Did you miss me?"
> My reply was quick and firm,
> It has been a long winter and I have waited for your shining warmth.[36]

NOTES

1. Clifford E. Trafzer, *A Chemehuevi Song: The Resilience of a Southern Paiute Tribe* (Seattle: University of Washington Press, 2015), 21–23.
2. Carobeth Laird, *Mirror and Pattern: George Laird's World of Chemehuevi Mythology* (Banning: Malki Museum Press, 1984), 43.
3. Clifford Trafzer, *Chemehuevi Indians: Historic Properties of Traditional Lands on the Yuma Proving Grounds* (Riverside: California Center for Native Nations, 2013), 37.
4. *Southern Utah News*, Obituaries, February 25, 2016.
5. Ocampo Field Notes, telephone interview with Brittanni Wero, January 3, 2021, Author's Collection.
6. Email Communication between Clifford E. Trafzer and Daisy Ocampo, December 19, 2020, Author's Collection.
7. *Southern Utah News*, Obituaries, February 25, 2016.
8. Kathleen L. McCoy, *Cultures at a Crossroads: An Administrative History of Pipe Spring National* (Denver: National Parks Services, 2000), 617–618.

9. Sarah B. Gordon and Jan Shipps, "Fatal Convergence in the Kingdom of God: The Mountain Meadows Massacre in American History," *Journal of the Early Republic* 37, no. 2 (2017): 307–47.

10. https://www.pbs.org/wgbh/americanexperience/features/mormons-massacre/.

11. Linda T. Smith, *Decolonizing Methodologies: Research and Indigenous Peoples* (London: Zed Books, 2012), 29–39.

12. Daisy Ocampo, "Spiritual Geographies of Indigenous Sovereignty: Connections of Caxcan with Tlachialoyantepec and Chemehuevi with Mamapukaib," (PhD Diss., University of California, Riverside, 2019), 30–31.

13. Trafzer, *Chemehuevi Indians*, 93.

14. Ocampo, "Spiritual Geographies of Indigenous Sovereignty," 32.

15. Ocampo Field Notes. Telephone interview with Brittanni Wero, January 3, 2021, Author's Collection.

16. Trafzer Interview, December 19, 2020, Author's Collection.

17. Clifford E. Trafzer and Matthew Leivas, *Where Puha Sits: Salt Songs, Power, and the Oasis of Mara* (Riverside: Rupert Costo Endowment, 2018), 4–5.

18. Ocampo, "Spiritual Geographies of Indigenous Sovereignty," 14–67.

19. Cultural Conservancy, 2005.

20. Clifford E. Trafzer, Jeffrey Smith, and Lorene Sisquoc, *Shadows of Sherman Institute* (Pechanga Reservation, California: Great Oak Press, 2017), 4–6. .

21. Ocampo Field Notes. Telephone interview with Brittanni Wero, January 3, 2021, Author's Collection.

22. Ocampo Field Notes. Telephone interview with Brittanni Wero, January 4, 2021, Author's Collection.

23. Personal Communication of Matthew Leivas with Daisy Ocampo circa 2016.

24. Ocampo Field Notes. Telephone interview with Brittanni Wero, January 3, 2021, Author's Collection.

25. Melissa K. Nelson, "Oral Tradition, Identity, and Intergenerational Healing through the Southern Paiute Salt Songs" in *Cultural Representation in Native America* ed. Andrew Jolivette (Lanham: AltaMira Press, 2006), 104.

26. Kevin Whalen, *Native Students at Work: American Indian Labor and Sherman Institute's Outing Program, 1900–1945* (Seattle: University of Washington Press, 2016), 3–28.

27. Jean A. Keller, *Empty Beds: Indian Student Health at Sherman Institute, 1902–1922* (East Lansing: Michigan State University Press, 2002), 121–150.

28. *The Salt Song Trail: Bringing Creation Back Together*. Cultural Conservancy Documentary Film, 2005.

29. *The Salt Song Trail: Bringing Creation Back Together*. Cultural Conservancy Documentary Film, 2005.

30. Clifford E. Trafzer, ed., *Painted Rock and the Old Woman Mountain: A Learning Landscape* (Riverside: California Center for Native Nations, 2008).

31. Salt Song Trail Map, Author's Collection.

32. *The Salt Song Trail: Bringing Creation Back Together*. Cultural Conservancy Documentary Film, 2005; Personal Communication of Matthew Leivas with Daisy Ocampo circa 2016.

33. Kurt William Russo, *In the Land of Three Peaks: The Old Woman Mountain Preserve* (California: Native American Land Conservancy, 2005).

34. Nelson, "Oral Tradition, Identity, and Intergenerational Healing through the Southern Paiute Salt Songs," 105.

35. Salt Song Tail Map. Author's Collection.

36. William Logan Hebner, *Southern Paiute*: *A Portrait* (Logan: Utah State University Press, 2010), 185.

BIBLIOGRAPHY

Gordon, Sarah B. and Jan Shipps, "Fatal Convergence in the Kingdom of God: The Mountain Meadows Massacre in American History," *Journal of the Early Republic* 37, no. 2 (2017).

Hebner, William Logan. *Southern Paiute, A Portrait*. Logan: Utah State University Press, 2010.

Keller, Jean A. *Empty Beds: Indian Student Health at Sherman Institute, 1902–1922*. East Lansing: Michigan State University Press, 2002.

Laird, Carobeth. *Mirror and Pattern: George Laird's World of Chemehuevi Mythology,* Banning: Malki Museum Press, 1984.

McCoy, Kathleen L. *Cultures at a Crossroads: An Administrative History of Pipe Spring National*. Denver: National Parks Services, 2000.

Melissa K. Nelson, "Oral Tradition, Identity, and Intergenerational Healing through the Southern Paiute Salt Songs" in *Cultural Representation in Native America* ed. Andrew Jolivette. Lanham: AltaMira Press, 2006.

Ocampo, Daisy. "Spiritual Geographies of Indigenous Sovereignty: Connections of Caxcan with Tlachialoyantepec and Chemehuevi with Mamapukaib." PhD Dissertation University of California, Riverside, 2019.

Ocampo Field Notes, telephone interview with Brittanni Wero, January 3–4, 2021, Author's Collection.

Personal Communication of Matthew Leivas with Daisy Ocampo circa 2016.

Russo, Kurt. *In the Land of Three Peaks: The Old Woman Mountain Preserve*. California: Native American Land Conservancy, 2005.

Salt Song Trail Map, Author's Collection.

Smith, Linda T. *Decolonizing Methodologies: Research and Indigenous Peoples*, (London: Zed Books, 2012.

Southern Utah News, Obituaries, February 25, 2016.

The Salt Song Trail: Bringing Creation Back Together. Cultural Conservancy Documentary Film, 2005.

Trafzer, Clifford E., Jeffrey Smith, and Lorene Sisquoc, eds. *Shadows of Sherman Institute.* Pechanga Reservation, California: Great Oak Press, 2017.

Trafzer, Clifford E. and Matthew Leivas, *Where Puha Sits: Salt Songs, Power, and the Oasis of Mara.* Riverside: Rupert Costo Endowment, 2018.

Trafzer, Clifford E. *A Chemehuevi Song: The Resilience of a Southern Paiute Tribe*. Seattle: University of Washington Press, 2015.

Trafzer, Clifford E. *Chemehuevi Indians: Historic Properties of Traditional Lands on the Yuma Proving Grounds.* Riverside: California Center for Native Nations, 2013.

Trafzer, Clifford E. ed., *Painted Rock and the Old Woman Mountain: A Learning Landscape* (Riverside: California Center for Native Nations, 2008.

Trafzer Interview, December 19, 2020, Author's Collection.

Whalen, *Native Students at Work: American Indian Labor and Sherman Institute's Outing Program, 1900–1945.* Seattle: University of Washington Press, 2016.

FURTHER READING

Hebner, William Logan. *Southern Paiute, A Portrait.* Logan: Utah State University Press, 2010.

Russo, Kurt. *In the Land of Three Peaks: The Old Woman Mountain Preserve.* California: Native American Land Conservancy, 2005.

Trafzer, Clifford E. *A Chemehuevi Song: The Resilience of a Southern Paiute Tribe.* Seattle: University of Washington Press, 2015.

Trafzer, Clifford E. and Matthew Leivas, *Where Puha Sits: Salt Songs, Power, and the Oasis of Mara.* Riverside: Rupert Costo Endowment, 2018.

Trafzer, Clifford E, Jeffrey Smith, and Lorene Sisquoc, eds. *Shadows of Sherman Institute.* Pechanga Reservation, California: Great Oak Press, 2017

Chapter Ten

Preserving the Memory of Snake River Country

Mary Jim Chapman (Xínstanik)
(c. 1910–2000)

Benjamin T. Jenkins

In the landscape of Snake River country, memory, death, and survivance flow together to shape Native lives, past and present. Historically, the Snake River-Palouse people lived along the lower Snake River between the Clearwater and Columbia Rivers. Although white intervention drastically reconstituted this landscape through damming and flooding, culturally enlightened conservators preserved Native views of the region. Among the most vocal of these advocates during the twentieth century was Mary Jim, a Snake River-Palouse woman who fought to educate society about her people's history and to protect her ancestors and their home from interlopers. To Mary, the landscape, memory, and caring for the dead intermingled. One could not understand Palouse history without knowing the geography of Snake River. Furthermore, Mary viewed it as her sacred duty to care for the dead and went to great lengths to protect remains and the spirits of deceased Palouse buried near the river. Because these aspects of existence had become so closely intertwined, Mary spent her life educating the world about the Snake River-Palouse people as products of nature and history, which she shared with Native peoples and so that they might better understand this region and its peoples.[1]

Mary Jim, or Xínstanik, was born around 1910 to Thomas Jim (Alíwiya, a Nez Perce name) and Annie Jim (Liplíptkwin) at *Samayúya,* a Palouse village on the lower Snake River. From her earliest years, Snake River became a defining feature of Mary's life. "I love my Snake River," she once commented. "That is where I should be, at Snake River. My river sings to me. That song is my Snake River."[2] As they did to other Native peoples of the Columbia Plateau, Americans stole the Palouse landscape along Snake River, making claims on their lands without consultation or permission. Mary Jim's family, like other Native families along the river systems, refused to remove to reservations until the twentieth century. Nevertheless, as Mary proved through her storytelling and cultural activism, the Palouse and other groups from the Pacific Northwest refused to abandon the landscape of their ancestors, which they still claim as their homelands. The land had meaning and memory to Mary Jim and members of her family.

Throughout her life, Mary maintained strong connections to Snake River and to previous generations of Palouse. She was the granddaughter of *Cawa-w'tiak*, or Fishhook Jim, a historically significant Palouse man from Snake River. "He was a kind man," Mary later recounted. "He was always taking care of his life, serving the Creator all the time."[3] When he passed in 1922, Fishhook Jim was buried in a canoe on an island in the Snake River not far from Mary's village and home on the banks of Snake River. This waterway was also a source of life. Mary spent most of her life living off the environment just as her ancestors before her. She fished Snake River for salmon and eels; she traveled each spring to root grounds where she gathered nutritious varieties of roots; in the fall she supported men on hunting expeditions and traveled with women to the mountains slopes where they gathered berries and other plant foods. For many years, Mary lived at Leavy along the river. Three islands emerged from its waters near Leavy, including Big Island, "where Fishhook Jim caught salmon and where [a] graveyard was."[4] He took care of the dead at Fishhook Bend, approximately five miles up the Snake River from Fishhook Island. Even in death, the Palouse remained linked to their river, a fact that had great meaning to Mary and her kin.[5]

Neighboring Native groups shared the bounty that the water provided. "We were Snake River and Palouse Indians," Mary once explained, "and Naxíyampam and Palúspam, and Wanapams and Yakamas and Nez Perce. Yes, all mixed up!"[6] Mary's family and relatives were from multiple tribes and traditions of the Columbia Plateau. Mary lived among this mixed population of Native peoples for decades, until the 1960s when her world came crashing down and the government forced her to abandon her home and move to the Yakama Reservation. However, before her removal, Mary raised her family in a large tent on the southern banks of Snake River. Because of her immersion in this multiethnic environment Inland Pacific Northwest, she raised her children to appreciate Native values and cultures. In particular, her daughter, Carrie Jim, learned to speak Palouse, Nez Perce, and English. Mary's husband, Alex Chapman, had been a former student at Chemawa Indian School in Salem, Oregon, where he distinguished himself as a talented musician. Carrie would ultimately take her place as the matriarch of the family, bringing forward the cultural teachings of her mother.

Mary Jim and Alex started their family, living on Snake River in the old ways of seasonal rounds. Life became a challenge for Mary, separated from Alex at time, but Mary persevered and raised her family. Mary Jim had many children. Tragically, four of them died as infants. Pearl, Mary's oldest daughter, succumbed in 1927. Mary's daughter Anna and son Tyrone also passed away tragically. Her son, Tom Estimo, attended boarding school at Fort Simcoe on the Yakama Reservation. Later, he distinguished himself as a horse trainer in California. Unlike Carrie who grew up and lived with Mary throughout much of her life, Tom found his own way and made his mark in the outside world.

Throughout the early twentieth century, Mary Jim, her father, Thomas Jim, and their family lived peacefully along the banks of Snake River. During the 1950s, the government and private interests planned the building of dams on Snake River, thereby disturbing the salmon runs and flow of water into the Columbia River and Pacific Ocean. More disturbing, non-Native peoples in Washington state put into motion a series of acts leading to the building of Ice Harbor Dam on the lower Snake River, a dam that threatened Mary Jim's home and way of life. Before beginning construction, the Army Corps of Engineers hired archaeologists to recover cultural resources before the river flooded.

During the 1950s, archaeologists began digging human remains and artifacts, taking them to universities for analysis and storage. On one occasion, archeologists from a state university drove an amphibius vehicle onto Big Island and began digging the grave of Fishhook Jim. On shore, Mary Jim and her family called out to the ghouls to go away, and her relative Harry Jim took his canoe to the island to tell the archaeologists to leave. After physically pushing Harry Jim, the archaeologists forced Harry off the island and onto the mainland. They outnumbered Harry and claimed authority over the situation. The white ghouls exhumed the canoe burial and stole the remains of Fishhook Jim. As of 2022, the family has never found their relative to return his remains to the earth, although Washington State University has returned the remains of several Palouse for reburial along the banks of Snake River. In 1977–1978, Richard Scheuerman and Clifford Trafzer began their work on a history of the Palouse; they interviewed Mary Jim numerous times. During every consultation, Mary Jim would break down and cry, remembering the theft of his grandfather's canoe burial and the flooding of Big Island behind Ice Harbor Dam. Her mother and many relatives lie under the water of Lake Sacajawea on the Lower Snake River.[7]

Archaeologists from a university explained that the Corps of Engineers had hired them to conduct salvage archaeology and took the Ancestors from their graves before the Army Corps of Engineers built Ice Harbor Dam on Snake River. To compensate them for their losses, the government paid $130 for the 160 acres belonging to Mary's family. Neither Mary nor any member of the Jim family agreed to the sale of their homeland, but the government condemned their property and planned to remove Mary, Harry, Carrie, and the remainder of the Jim family from Snake River. As Mary explained, "Money is not worth land."[8] She refused the offer, never taking money for her land. She tried her best to remain at her home on the river, but eventually, "the law" forced her off her ancestral lands. While the number of fish in the river dwindled and Indian fishing rights came under assault, Mary Jim refused to abandon her home until the 1960s, when "the law," including state police and county sheriffs, forced Mary, Harry, Carrie, and the family out of their home and into cars. They were taken to the Yakama Reservation and left there. Fortunately, the family had close friends on the reservation who took them in and shared land with the Jim family. Mary made her home there, but her heart was always on Snake River. Once the dam was built and much of the land around Mary's home flooded, water destroyed Native home sites. Today, Mary's former home is under the waters of Snake River below a prominent bluff and farmland, no longer visible. But Mary never forgot this place on earth, her home and that of her ancestors. The Snake River that had defined so much of Mary Jim's early life now spread across the graves of her mother and many other friends and family members.

By the 1960s, after the theft of her grandfather and many other Palouse, Mary Jim faced the same struggle as Native peoples across the United States: a battle for the repatriation of stolen human remains. For decades prior to the removal of Fishhook Jim, white invaders had stolen tens of thousands of Natives from burial sites. This dated back to the nineteenth century, when the Smithsonian Institution started collecting Native skeletons. The trend intensi-fied in the 1940s, as the government of the United States began to improve its infrastructure and thus had to dig up Native sites to prepare new road-ways, waterways, communication towers, etc. By that time, as she became a Palouse elder, Mary Jim conceived of herself as a caretaker for the dead. Disturbing human remains, Mary Jim and other Palouse believed, upset the journey to the afterlife. "I respect the dead," Jim once opined in an interview, "because they came here first and lived here. God put them here to live and they had the land and everything . . . . Now they flood the area and I didn't know all the time they were stealing my land."[9]

Following the flooding of her land, the loss of her home, desecration of her forebears, and her family's forced removal from Snake River, Mary and her family moved to the Yakama Reservation. She reflected on the Walla Walla Council of 1855, when whites had first confined Native peoples of the Co-lumbia Plateau to reservations. The United States had used the treaties made at the Walla Walla Council to remove many non-reservation Indians. Mary saw this as an unfair act and believed that the Natives who had taken part in the Walla Walla Council had no right to speak on behalf of the Snake River-

Palouse. Nevertheless, such treaties had laid foundation for forced removal and reservations across the Pacific Northwest.

Although she had been forced to abandon her home, Mary was head of her clan. She took an active role in educating people about Palouse culture. Mary worked closely with Carrie Jim Schuster, her daughter, whom she groomed to inherit the mantle of Palouse leadership and protection of the dead. Together, from the 1950s to 1980s, Mary and Carrie petitioned the Army Corps of Engineers and Washington State University, which had become the repository of the Snake River-Palouse remains, for the repatriation of stolen human remains. Furthermore, Mary devoted much of her time to preserving Native identity among the living. Mary was a master artist, and she shared her knowledge and life experiences with Richard D. Scheuerman and Clifford E. Trafzer, which was published in 1986 as *Renegade Tribe: The Palouse Indians and the Invasion of the Inland Northwest,* a book that won the Governor's Book Award. In 2016, Washington State University Press reprinted and updated an enlarged version of the book as *The Snake River-Palouse and the Invasion of the Inland Northwest*. Although entering her eighth decade by the 1980s, Mary retained vivid memories of Native families from her childhood. People came to her to ask for family histories, and she shared information with them on Palouse burial sites. Mary also continued her traditional weaving, and recited prayers as a way of keeping her culture alive and instilling Native values to the next generation.

Perhaps most strikingly, even at an advanced age, Mary remained willing to fight to return her ancestors to Snake River, traveling across the country in the process. In 1988, the United States Senate began hearings on fishing rights for Native peoples in the Northwest. Although this had nothing to do with Mary and Carrie's quest, Carrie realized this opportunity could fix national attention on her mother's work. When she became aware of the hearings, Carrie booked tickets to the capital and brought Mary to Washington, D.C. Mary Jim took the floor of the Senate as leader of the Snake River-Palouse people and sang to members of Congress before sharing her story. Following her testimony, senators vowed to help her, sending an aide with Mary and Carrie to the National Museum of Natural History to secure the remains of Native peoples. Sadly, that component of the Smithsonian Institution maintained that it had no bones from Fishhook Island. Mary and Carrie returned to Washington State disappointed.

Thankfully, Mary's struggle did not end at the National Museum of Natural History. As the 1980s waned, the older anthropologists at Washington State University who had taken remains from Snake River began to retire. In their place came younger professors who expressed willingness to work with Native communities to return human remains stolen decades earlier. Critical in this endeavor was Roderick Sprague, an anthropologist who had taken part in the excavations in the Snake River during the 1950s before leaving to teach at the University of Idaho. Sprague approached Mary Jim about returning the remains of Snake River-Palouse taken from Fishhook Island. Although many remains were never accounted for, thanks to Jim's partnership with Sprague, others returned to their homeland. As late as 2006, 150 additional remains of Snake River-Palouse from Washington State University and Idaho were reburied outside Page, Washington. Mary and Carrie Jim were largely responsible for the return of ancestors to the earth near Snake River.

Mary Jim's passion for her people extended beyond her stewardship over the dead. Unlike many Indigenous peoples across the globe, who often fear sharing their stories and histories with outsiders, Mary Jim openly discussed her life, ancestors, and Palouse culture with scholars. She gave oral histories of her people to historians Richard D. Scheuerman and Clifford E. Trafzer. In the numerous interviews she granted these scholars in the 1970s and 1980s, Mary stressed power of landscape in the Palouse worldview. She explained that she was strongly connected to *Samúya* and *Tasawiks*, her villages, and her power mountain, *Yumushtah*, settlers called Steptoe Butte. Through her detailed testimony, Mary offered outsiders an unprecedentedly vivid glimpse into Snake River country.

Although Mary's Native activist spirit manifested most clearly in the struggle to reclaim lost Palouse remains, she championed other causes, as well. She particularly emphasized the restoration of Native economic resources, particularly fishing rights. Growing up along the Snake River, fishing had been a defining activity during Mary's childhood. Mary once equated the protection of fishing rights among Palouse and other Native groups with her quest to reinter the dead. "We didn't want to leave our buried people and where we grew up," Mary once commented. "We didn't want to leave our fishing rights because that was important to catch and dry the fish and put it away for winter." [10]

In 2000, approaching the age of 90, Mary Jim passed way in Toppenish, Washington. Thanks to the fact that she had shared Palouse stories and traditions with countless Palouse people and historians, her memory has contributed to scholars' understanding of the Palouse world. In 2015, Richard D. Scheuerman and Clifford E. Trafzer published *River Song*, a book containing the recollections of Palouse elders. In this volume, Scheuerman and Trafzer included Mary's recollections of her life, as well as Palouse stories she had shared with them. Even after her passing, then, Mary's passion for educating her people and the world continues to inspire Native and non-Native audiences. During an oral history interview with Trafzer and Scheuerman, Mary succinctly summarized her life's work and her mission. "I'm calling for our land and everything else to pray and ask Him," Mary stated. "I like to reach out for my children, and their children, because some children now have no homes."[11] To Mary, learning about Snake River and its people reverberated across generations, from the dead such as *Cawa-w'tiak* to her daughter Carrie and her family. All the Palouse wanted was "to have a piece of our background and have our homes again." Thanks to Mary's tireless spirit, many Palouse ancestors have returned to those homes, and the Palouse have proudly reclaimed the background she dedicated her life to preserving.

During Mary's life, she called her people together every spring to meet at Fishhook Jim Park on the south banks of Snake River to celebrate their survival as Palouse people and to remember. After Mary's death, Carrie brought the people together, and today, Mary's granddaughter Ione Irons brings the people together in an all-day ceremony. In May of each year, Washat drummers and singers join in the Palouse gathering and sing their sacred songs. The people lament the loss of their loved ones and their homeland. They pray for their Ancestors and for all Palouse people today. They cry and lament, remembering the past and their people. Then they give Indian names to newborns and to honored guests. At the most recent gathering, Ione remembered her childhood and being raised with her *Kuthla*, Mary Jim. As she spoke of her grandmother, tears came to many eyes, remembering Mary and her contribution to the preservation of the people of Snake River.[12]

NOTES

1. Clifford E. Trafzer and Richard D. Scheuerman, *The Snake River-Palouse and the Invasion of the Inland Northwest* (Pullman: Washington State University Press, 2016): 50–51, 169–173, 189. The author wishes to thank Dr. Richard D. Scheuerman for peer reviewing this essay and returning it to me with recommendations on August 31, 2021.

2. Richard D. Scheuerman and Clifford E. Trafzer, eds., *River Song: Naxiyamtáma (Snake River-Palouse) Oral Traditions from Mary Jim, Andrew George, Gordon Fisher, and Emily Peone* (Pullman: Washington State University Press, 2015), xvii.

3. Scheuerman and Trafzer, eds., *River Song*, 47.

4. Scheuerman and Trafzer, eds., *River Song*, 49.

5. Trafzer and Scheuerman, *The Snake River-Palouse*, 154, 161, 165, 169, 173.

6. Scheuerman and Trafzer, eds., *River Song*, 48.

7. Telephone Interview with Clifford E. Trafzer, August 28, 2021.

8. Scheuerman and Trafzer, eds., *River Song*, 15.

9. Scheuerman and Trafzer, eds., *River Song*, 55.

10. Scheuerman and Trafzer, eds., *River Song*, 53.

11. Scheuerman and Trafzer, eds., *River Song*, 55.

12. Trafzer Interview, August 28, 2021.

BIBLIOGRAPHY

Scheuerman, Richard D. and Clifford E. Trafzer, eds., *River Song: Naxiyamtáma (Snake River-Palouse) Oral Traditions from Mary Jim, Andrew George, Gordon Fisher, and Emily Peone*. Pullman: Washington State University Press, 2015.

Scheuerman, Richard E. and Michael Finely, *Finding Kamiakin: The Life and Legacy of a Northwest Patriot*. Pullman: Washington State University Press, 2008.

Trafzer, Clifford E. "The Legacy of the Walla Walla Council, 1855." *Oregon Historical Quarterly* 106, no. 3 (Fall 2005).

Trafzer, Clifford E. and Richard D. Scheuerman, *The Snake River-Palouse and the Invasion of the Inland Northwest*. Pullman: Washington State University Press, 2016.

FURTHER READING

Scheuerman, Richard D. and Clifford E. Trafzer, eds., *River Song: Naxiyamtáma (Snake River-Palouse) Oral Traditions from Mary Jim, Andrew George, Gordon Fisher, and Emily Peone*. Pullman: Washington State University Press, 2015.

Smith, Gary. "Keepers of the Past." *Audubon* 95, no. 3 (May–June 1993): 88–99.

Trafzer, Clifford E. "The Legacy of the Walla Walla Council, 1855." *Oregon Historical Quarterly* 106, no. 3 (Fall 2005): 398–411.

Trafzer, Clifford E., and Richard D. Scheuerman. *The Snake River-Palouse and the Invasion of the Inland Northwest*. Pullman: Washington State University Press, 2016.

Chapter Eleven

Cultural Historian, Linguist, and Ethnobotanist

Katherine Siva Saubel (b. 1920–d. 2011)

Lisa Riggin

Katherine Siva Saubel was a nationally and internationally respected Native American cultural leader of the Cahuilla tribe in Southern California who once commented that when people know their languages, they know who they are. As an author, activist, scholar, and educator, Saubel committed her life to preserving her tribal history, oral literature, language, and culture. In 1940, she was the first Native American female to graduate from Palm Springs High School. Years later, in 1993, she became the first Native American woman to be inducted into the National Women's Hall of Fame in Seneca Falls, New York. She was a published author and a teacher of Cahuilla history, literature, and culture at various universities, including the University of Cologne in Germany, one of the largest and oldest of its kind in Europe. She also helped establish the first nonprofit tribal museum on a California Indian reservation and received numerous prestigious awards.

Katherine Siva was born in the spring of 1920 at *Pa'chahualpa* on the 29,000-acre Los Coyotes Reservation in San Diego County. This decade brought great excitement for many Americans due to the ratification of the Nineteenth Amendment that allowed women to vote, the American Indian Citizenship Act, and a national recovery after the Great War. Yet life on California's Indian reservations remained much the same as it had been for generations. Residents enjoyed few roads, poor housing, lack of sanitation, ill health, contaminated drinking water, no electricity, and no plumbing. Katherine, one of eleven children, born to Melana Sawaxell and Juan C. Siva, grew up with these struggles of reservation life. Her family originated in Coyote Canyon between present-day Anza, California, and the Anza Borrego State Park in the Colorado Desert. When Katherine was four, the family moved to Palm Springs, California, where Juan found work, and they lived on the Agua Caliente Reservation. Her father mastered several languages, including

Cahuilla, Spanish, Latin, and English. Her mother Melana, who spoke only
Cahuilla, enrolled Katherine in Palm Springs elementary school. At the time,
Katherine also spoke only Cahuilla and struggled with the English language.
It took her a year before she could communicate in English, but she enjoyed
learning and was determined to go to high school. Even though her family
lacked the funds to provide her with school clothes and supplies, Saubel insisted she would make do, and attended school anyway. Proudly, in 1940, she
became the first Native American female to graduate from Palm Springs High
School. That same year, while attending a ceremony at the Agua Caliente's
tribal Big House, she met the man who would become her lifelong partner,
Mariano Saubel. They were married in a Catholic ceremony and moved to the
Morongo Reservation, where they raised their son, Allen and became active
voices in the community.[1]

The love of learning and the desire to educate stayed with Saubel as a
lifelong aspiration. As a high school student, Katherine began cataloging
Cahuilla names and applications of plants and herbs her mother used. She
documented location, preparation, and use of plants, which would become
the basis of her first book, *Temalpakh,* meaning of the Earth. Katherine recalled that she and her siblings never went to the doctor during their youths
because their mother, Melana Sawaxell, was a medicine woman with great
knowledge of medicinal plants. If something serious happened, the shamans
would take over.

As in ancient times, Cahuilla women gathered food, such as seeds, herbs,
and pods, while the men hunted. Together, they also farmed small gardens. As
a child, Katherine recalled being taught respect for the natural world, and the
Indigenous responsibility to care for and protect plants, trees, and rocks. During the Great Depression of the 1930s and into the Second World War, Saubel's
family depended on traditional foods such as the barrel cactus, yucca blossoms,
acorns, and mesquite. "We went back to our own food," she recalled, that way
"we didn't have to depend on buying at the store." Still, even as a young girl
she understood traditional ways and the language of the Cahuilla were disap-
pearing. The new generation of her people no longer lived by the traditions of
previous generations. "It is still important to us elders—to me," she declared,
"because I was raised traditionally, and I know what is being lost."[2]

> [We]used plants for food, for medicine, for housing, for clothing—for every-
> thing . . . the ones that come from the mountains are the best medicines that can
> be used. That is why I fight so much to preserve all this, so we can continue to
> use these things. . . . I would like to have it protected.[3]

Influenced by her mother, Katherine followed her passion and become an
ethno-botanist. In 1962, Lowell John Bean, an anthropologist from California

State University, Hayward, came to the reservation to document the abundant use of plants by the Cahuilla. Saubel's descriptive notebook of Cahuilla plants and herbs from her time in high school proved invaluable to Bean. Katherine supplied knowledge of Cahuilla culture, and Bean provided "all the Latin names." Their ten-year collaborated effort culminated in 1972 in the publication of *Temalpakh: Cahuilla Indian Knowledge and Usage of Plants*, a book that has remained in print today. This informative book, considered a classic, received positive reviews for its appeal to wide audiences, including professional anthropologists, the general public and, most importantly, as a historical document for the Cahuilla people.[4]

Saubel's fear of losing her tribal language was not unfounded. According to Douglas Whalen, Chairman of the Endangered Languages Fund at Yale University's Haskins Laboratory, "every American Indian language is endangered." In the second half of the nineteenth century, the federal government of the United States sent Native American children to Indian boarding schools such as Sherman Institute in Riverside, California, where white teachers forced them to speak English. The government wanted to use boarding schools to assimilate and acculturate Indian children into white society. Students were forbidden to speak their native language, practice their religion, or wear traditional clothing, and in most cases, they were not allowed to go home during the summer.[5]

Rising up in the late-nineteenth century, reformers from the middle class voiced displeasure with government Indian policies and demanded change. In 1899, renowned journalist and editor for the *Los Angeles Times,* Charles F. Lummis, began a long campaign against the Indian Schools with a series of articles entitled "My Brother's Keeper." Lummis, a determined advocate for Indian rights concluded that "the Bureau of Indian Affairs was administered by men who did not know their business and who were concerned with the Indians as statistics rather than as human beings." The practices did not abate until after 1928, when a report titled *The Problems of Indian Administration*, was produced. Also known as the Merriam Report, this document blasted governmental policies toward Indian education and boarding schools. At one time, California boasted the highest concentration of Indigenous languages in North America. By 2000, according to a *Los Angeles Times* report, of the 100 Native American languages once spoken in the state, only 50 remain, and of those 17 have no fluent speakers. In a 1999 article, Professor Leanne Hinton of the University of California, Berkeley, determined that no "language endemic to California is being learned at home by children; most are spoken by elders." Fortunately, this trend has changed after 2000 when some tribes made a major effort to teach their languages to children.[6]

As a native of the Golden State, Katherine Saubel became determined to save the Cahuilla language. In 1962, she began working with William Bright, professor emeritus of Linguistics and Anthropology at the University of California, Los Angeles, on his study of Native American languages, specifically the Cahuilla language. While at UCLA, Saubel assisted Professor Bright as well as Professor Pamela Munro in the classroom, and co-authored with Munro *Chem'I'vullu: Let's Speak Cahuilla*, published by the University of California in 1981. Saubel took the opportunity to audit classes at the university, including archaeology, geology, and anthropology. In 1962, Saubel received the J. F. Kennedy Scholarship for Native Americans and continued her education in anthropology. An honorary PhD from La Sierra University, Riverside, California, vindicated her efforts. She became the most significant advocate for the preservation of the Cahuilla language, which culminated in major publications.[7]

Beginning in 1964, Saubel's work brought her together with German linguist Hansjakop Seiler of the University of Cologne. This research took her to both the University of Cologne in Germany and Hachinohe University in Japan, and resulted in the publication of three volumes, including a Cahuilla grammar book and dictionary published by the University of Indiana Press in 1981. Together, Saubel and Seiler created an authentic translation of the Cahuilla language, which previously existed only in spoken form. Saubel went on to publish her own dictionary, *I'sniyatam: A Cahuilla Design Book* with Malki Museum Press in 1981. In 2004, Katherine worked with linguist Eric Elliot and published *Isill Heqwas Waxizh: A Dried Coyote's Tail*, a hefty two-volume bilingual text of thirteen hundred pages. As the last fluent speaker of Cahuilla since the death of her husband Mariano in 1985, Saubel remarked that "there is no one here to converse with." However, in addition to written texts, and to further ensure that the next generation will have access to the Cahuilla language, she recorded word pronunciation, songs, and stories as a resource of tribal memory. According to scholars, it has become increasingly important to preserve this sense of place, language, and history for Native American people. As historian Clifford Trafzer noted, Native Americans "understand clearly they are part of today's world, but that their tribal traditions, languages, ceremonies, and stories create a relationship to this land that" remains unequaled.[8]

The need for a local community center to house and promote tribal preservation became evident early in Katherine's career. In 1963, she worked with Jean Penn, Lowell Bean, Harry Lawton, and her husband Mariano to establish the Malki Museum at the Morongo Reservation to meet long-term goals of traditional and cultural preservation. Malki Museum started "on a shoestring" and with donated artifacts, but rapidly became a site for Cahuilla culture and learning. The museum, named Malki, the Cahuilla word for "dodging" the original name for the Morongo Reservation, is "not just for Indians," Katherine once remarked. It "really helps people understand who" historically occupied the area "and what they have done." Over 1,000 Indians and non-Indians attended the official opening and dedication in 1965. To date, the Malki Museum is the first all Native American Museum to be created and maintained by Native Americans on a reservation in California.[9]

Since the institution opened its doors, and until her death, Katherine Saubel served as president of the Malki Museum, overseeing continuous expansion. This included the construction of a permanent adobe brick building, the Temalpakh Ethnobotanical Garden (which houses the plants used by the Cahuilla for food, medicine, and housing), and educational projects and scholarships to Native American students. In addition, the museum proudly displays an impressive collection of basketry, pottery, photographs, and hunting artifacts. Formed in 1965 to promote Cahuilla culture and tradition, the institution formed the Malki Museum Press, publisher of the *Journal of California and Great Basin Anthropology*. In 2005, the museum acquired Ballena Press to continue the promotion of quality literary works of California Indian cultures.

Over the course of her life, Dr. Saubel has served on numerous boards, committees, and agencies. In 1982, Governor Jerry Brown appointed her to the California Native American Heritage Commission to preserve and protect sacred sites and Indian remains. Local awards include Riverside County Historian of the Year (1986); Elder of the Year (1987); Regents Scholar, UCR (1991–92); Women of Achievement Award, YMCA (2000); Desert Protective Council Award (2000); and Bridge to Peace: Latino and Native American Hall of Fame, Riverside, CA (2000). In 1994, she became the first recipient of the Smithsonian Institution, National Museum of the American Indian, Art and Culture Award. In 2002, the University of California, Riverside, honored Saubel with the Chancellor's Medal, the highest award given by the University. David Warren, the acting chancellor, stated this prestigious award was in recognition for her "extraordinary education and cultural contributions to the world."[10]

Almost until the end of her life, Katherine Saubel continued as president of the Malki Museum and remained an activist and scholar. As chairwoman of the Los Coyotes Band of Cahuilla and Cupeño Indians, she fought for a series of projects that would expand Indian gaming in the state and allow the Los Coyotes Band to build a $160 million casino complex in the town of Barstow. Saubel, sharply disappointed when the proposal failed after heavy lobbying by larger Indian bands, retorted, "we have always shared . . . but not anymore." Despite this misgiving, she continued to lobby the state on behalf of the Los Coyotes Band. The wealth generated by a casino, Saubel believed, would provide economic salvation for her tribe. Saubel continued her work documenting, recording, and preserving the Cahuilla language, overseeing the Malki Museum and planning cultural and traditional events. She passed away in 2011 and her relatives performed a traditional all-night wake attended by many admirers. Katherine's focus always returned to the land, and "Indian culture," she stated, "is the only way to live with the respect of everything around you . . . yourself and the people." For Katherine Siva Saubel the land was the "most important thing you can think of," and "without that, you are nothing."[11]

NOTES

1. Robert Lee Hotz, "The Struggle to Save Dying Languages; Global Pressure Threaten Them, But More Voices Are Being Raised to Keep Them Alive," *Los Angeles Times*, January 25, 2000; Leigh Podgorski, producer, writer, and editor "We are Still Here: Katherine Siva Saubel and the Cahuilla Indians of Southern California" (Malki Museum Press, 2007).

2. Deborah Dozier, *The Heart of Fire* (Berkeley, Ca: Heyday Books, 1998), 35, 41, 73, 77.

3. Dozier, *The Heart of Fire*, 69.

4. Michael Kearney, "Review of Temalpakh: Cahuilla Indian Knowledge and Usage of Plants by Lowell John Bean and Katherine Siva Saubel," *American Anthropologist* 75 (August 1973): 982–984; Katherine Saubel is regarded as an expert on shamanic knowledge and herbal medicines in California, see for example Professor Tad Beckman's essay "Shamanism and Ritual," Harvey Mudd College, Claremont.

5. Hotz, "The Struggle to Save Dying Languages," 1; Also see Leanne Hinton and Jocelyn Ahlers, "The Issue of 'Authenticity' in California Language Restoration," *Anthropology and Education Quarterly* 30 (March 1999): 56–67.

6. Edwin R. Bingham, *Charles R. Lummis: Editor of the Southwest* (San Marino, Ca: The Huntington Library, 2006), 111–114; Hotz, "The Struggle to Save Dying Language," 1; Hinton, "The Issue of 'Authenticity' in California Language Restoration," 56–67.

7. Hotz, "The Struggle to Save Dying Language," 1.

8. Hotz, "The Struggle to Save Dying Language," 1; Clifford Trafzer, *Earth Song, Sky Spirit, Short Stories of the Native American Experience* (New York: Doubleday, 1993), 21; Interview with Clifford Trafzer by Lisa Riggan, August 28, 2021. Author's Collection.

9. Dozier, *The Heart of Fire*, 149.

10. Katherine Siva Saubel, Newsroom, University of California, Riverside, *News*, April 25, 2002.

11. Dozier, *The Heart of Fire*, 142.

BIBLIOGRAPHY

Bean, Lowell John and Katherine Siva Saubel. *Temalpakh: Cahuilla Indian Knowledge and Usage of Plants.* Banning, Ca.: Malki Museum Press, 1972.

Bingham, Edwin R. *Charles R. Lummis: Editor of the Southwest.* San Marino, Ca.: The Huntington Library, 2006.

Dozier, Deborah. *The Heart of Fire.* Berkeley, CA: Heyday Books, 1998.

Hinton, Leanne and Jocelyn Ahlers, "The Issue of 'Authenticity' in California Language Restoration." *Anthropology and Education Quarterly* 30, March 1999.

Hotz, Robert Lee. "The Struggle to Save Dying Languages; Global Pressure Threaten Them, But More Voices Are Being Raised to Keep Them Alive." *Los Angeles Times*, January 25, 2000.

Kearney, Michael. "Review of Lowell John Bean and Katherine Siva Saubel. *Temalpakh: Cahuilla Indian Knowledge and Usage of Plants. American Anthropologist* 75. August 1973.

Podgorski, Leigh. "We Are Still Here: Katherine Siva Saubel and the Cahuilla Indians of Southern California." Malki Museum Press, 2007.

Trafzer, Clifford. *Earth Song, Sky Spirit, Short Stories of the Native American Experience.* New York: Doubleday, 1993.

Trafzer, Clifford. Interview by Lisa Riggan, August 28, 2021. Author's Collection.

FURTHER READING

Bean, Lowell John and Katherine Siva Saubel, *Temalpakh: Cahuilla Indian Knowledge and Usage of Plants.* Banning, Ca.: Malki Museum Press, 1972.

Bingham, Edwin R. *Charles R. Lummis: Editor of the Southwest.* San Marino, Ca.: The Huntington Library, 2006.

Dozier, Deborah. *The Heart of Fire.* Berkeley, Ca: Heyday Books, 1998.

Hinton, Leanne and Jocelyn Ahlers, "The Issue of 'Authenticity' in California Language Restoration." *Anthropology and Education Quarterly* 30. March 1999.

Hotz, Robert Lee. "The Struggle to Save Dying Languages; Global Pressure Threaten Them, But More Voices are being Raised to Keep Them Alive." *Los Angeles Times*, January 25, 2000.

Podgorski, Leigh. "We are Still Here: Katherine Siva Saubel and the Cahuilla Indians of Southern California." Malki Museum Press, 2007.

Trafzer, Clifford. *Earth Song, Sky Spirit, Short Stories of the Native American.*

Trafzer, Clifford E. *Fighting Invisible Enemies: Health and Medical Transitions Among Southern California Indians* (Norman: University of Oklahoma Press, 2019).

Trafzer, Clifford E. *Strong Hearts and Healing Hands: Southern California Indians and Field Nurses, 1920–1950* (Tucson: University of Arizona Press, 2020).

Chapter Twelve

Community, Educational, and Cultural Activist

Lorene Sisquoc (b. 1960–)

Kevin Whalen

Lorene Sisquoc (Fort Sill Apache/Mountain Cahuilla) was born in Riverside, California, in 1960. A direct descendant of Mangas Coloradas, the last chief of the Mimbreño Apaches, Chief Loco of the Warm Springs Apaches, and the Mountain Cahuilla leader *Net* (Chief) Manuel Largo, Sisquoc is the Cultural Traditions Leader at Sherman Indian High School (formerly Sherman Institute) and the Director of the Sherman Indian Museum. Through a lifetime of work as an activist, cultural educator, curator, historian, and archivist, she has helped to transform Sherman Indian High School from a place of assimilation into a site of cultural reclamation for Native people.

An off-reservation federal boarding school for Native American children, Sherman Institute opened in 1902. From the beginning, the school worked to rid young American Indians of their languages and cultures. Following the lead of Bureau of Indian Affairs (BIA) Supervisor of Indian Schools Estelle Reel, founding Sherman Superintendent Harwood Hall and his staff crafted a curriculum rooted in low expectations for Indian students. Industrial, agricultural, and vocational classes prepared students for lives of domestic service and menial labor. The daily rhythms of non-reservation boarding schools proved to be a shock for many young Indians. Students lived according to a tightly regimented, military-like schedule, moving from military drills to assigned work duties to classes at the factory-like sounds of bells and bugles. They wore heavy, military-style wool uniforms and cheap, government-issued boots that caused blisters. School officials forced male students to cut their hair short, and strictly forbade Native languages and spiritual practices.[1]

Even as they worked to destroy Native languages, cultures, and communities, federal Indian boarding schools such as Sherman Institute often hired Native American employees. These Native teachers, disciplinarians, cooks, seamstresses, and laborers did what they could to soften the most harmful elements of school curricula and daily routines. In Southern California and beyond, Sisquoc's ancestors became part of this larger tradition of cultural resistance and persistence among Native employees and students at federal Indian boarding schools.[2] Sisquoc's maternal grandfather, Anthony Largo (Mountain Cahuilla), and his siblings were among the early students at the Perris Indian School, the forerunner of Sherman Institute located in nearby Perris, California. In 1902, the Largo students and many others moved from Perris to Sherman Institute in Riverside. Sisquoc's grandmother, Ida Gooday-Largo (Warm Springs Apache) was born a prisoner of war at Fort Sill in 1903; her family had been imprisoned there following years of warfare against the United States government. Following the tragic and unexpected death of her mother, Ida enrolled at Chilocco Indian School, and off-reservation federal boarding school in Oklahoma. Gooday-Largo's family had struggled to care for her in the sudden absence of her mother. Like many Native families in the late nineteenth and early twentieth century, Gooday-Largo's family sought enrollment at Chilocco to provide her with food, clothing, and shelter in the midst of turbulent times.[3] Gooday-Largo later enrolled at the Phoenix Indian School, and after completing her studies there she earned a teaching certificate in 1927 from Haskell Indian School in Lawrence, Kansas (today known as Haskell Indian Nations University). She taught at schools on the Pima, Hopi, Tohono O'odham and Navajo reservations before arriving at Sherman Institute in 1951. Just as her granddaughter would, Gooday-Largo spent her career educating young Native people.[4]

As was common for employees at Sherman Institute and other off-reservation boarding schools, Gooday-Largo took residence on Sherman's campus and raised her family there. Because employees of government schools were forbidden to enroll their own children at the schools where they worked, Gooday-Largo's children attended public schools in Riverside. Even though Gooday-Largo's daughter Tonita Largo-Glover did not attend classes at Sherman, she developed close bonds with students and teachers there. As did many of the children who grew up on Sherman's campus, she became part of the "Sherman family." Following college and a brief stint working as a nurse, Largo-Glover returned to Sherman Institute in June of 1969 to work as a teaching assistant and dormitory supervisor. Largo-Glover brought her daughters, nine-year-old Lorene and two-year old Stephi, with her. Following in the footsteps of her mother, Largo-Glover raised her family on Sherman's campus.[5]

Many scholars of federal Indian boarding schools have noted that in the wake of New Deal-era reforms, schools were less harsh in their repression of Native American languages and cultures. But as Largo-Glover began her career at Sherman, she noted that while school officials did not outlaw Native languages and cultures, they certainly did not push students to embrace their identities. If students wanted to speak their languages or practice ceremony, they had to do so on their own time. The only cultural activities supported by school administrators involved painting in art class or performing Native songs and dances for campus visitors. Beyond these two activities, students had few opportunities to engage in the traditional cultural and spiritual practices of their tribes. Throughout the 1980s, Largo-Glover worked quietly to create informal spaces where students could share elements of their cultures with one another.[6]

In 1982, Sisquoc began working as a dormitory staff member at Sherman. She returned in the middle of this quiet cultural renaissance. She quickly joined in the work started by her mother, encouraging students to teach one another about their languages and cultures. Moreover, she amplified a message passed down to her by elders, encouraging students to use the spiritual and cultural traditions of their home communities as a way to resist the lures of drugs and alcohol. By the middle of the decade, the mother-daughter team had made a distinct impact on the cultural life of the campus. Each evening, students could be found singing and dancing. Native languages echoed through the dormitory hallways. A tangible marker of this progress came in 1986, when Tonita Largo-Glover co-coordinated the first ever powwow held on the Sherman campus. Sisquoc soon began working beyond Sherman Indian High School to preserve and continue Native American cultures when she founded the Mother Earth Clan with Tongva Indian scholar and activist Cindi Alvitre in 1986. Sisquoc and Alvitre used cultural programming to bring a message of Indigenous cultural revitalization to urban Native American youth in Southern California.[7]

In just a few short years, Sisquoc had become a leader in culturally centered Indigenous education. Don Sims, the principal of Sherman Indian High School, took note. He asked Sisquoc to teach a course on the cultural traditions of Native peoples in Southern California. For the first time, Sisquoc had a classroom, a budget, and time dedicated to cultural education. She had reached a milestone; Indigenous cultures had moved from the informal spaces of school dormitories into the everyday curriculum.

Later, Sisquoc offered courses in traditional Native American basketry and museum studies, along with museum and cultural programming internships to students from Sherman Indian High School and the University of California, Riverside. In 2000, Sisquoc received the official title of Cultural Traditions Leader of Sherman Indian High School. As word spread of Sisquoc's role in cultural revitalization at Sherman Indian High School, American Indian Studies programs at the University of Illinois, Urbana-Champaign, and the University of California, Riverside invited Sisquoc to share her cultural and educational expertise. She is currently a board member at the Malki Museum. Located on the Morongo Reservation in Banning, California, Malki is dedicated to the preservation of Cahuilla culture. For many years, Katherine Siva Saubel, a Cahuilla elder and inspiration to Lorene Sisquoc, managed the Malki Museum.[8]

As Sisquoc became an important leader in Indigenous cultural education at Sherman Institute and beyond, she also worked to maintain the Sherman Indian Museum, located on the school's campus. She started working at the museum in 1985 under the mentorship of Ramona K. Bradley, the museum's co-founder. Bradley trained Sisquoc in the care of the museum's archival holdings: thousands of pages of onionskin letterbooks, boxes of correspondences, and books of photographs that spanned Sherman's history. Bradley also emphasized the critical importance of maintaining and presenting to the public cultural materials representing the cultures and lifeways of the tribes represented teachers and students at Sherman. Sisquoc became curator and archivist of the museum in 1991. Even with few resources and no full-time staff at her disposal, she worked tirelessly to maintain the museum's aging archival materials and expand its cultural holdings. In her time as manager and curator, Sisquoc managed and expanded a substantial collection of Indian art. Works by activist artists such as Billy Soza Warsoldier reflected on critical themes, including tribal self-determination, control over and protection of natural resources, cultural and spiritual regeneration, and the harmful nature of the stereotypical portrayals of Indians that plague the popular culture of the United States.[9]

Informed by her deep knowledge of the campus the families who have maintained connections to it, Sisquoc has also guided countless researchers through "the vault," the small museum room that holds the archival documents and photographs so crucial to telling the Sherman story. In so doing, she has carried forward Bradley's legacy of providing access to the museum's archival materials. Sisquoc's careful and culturally informed guidance has helped historians Clifford Trafzer, Jean Keller, Leleua Loupe, Matthew Sakiestewa Gilbert, Victoria Haskins, and Bill Medina comb through the thousands of documents housed at Sherman Indian Museum. Sisquoc's guiding hand has helped to frame a growing body of scholarship on Sherman Institute. The publications that have come from archival research in the vault have shed new light on student experiences at Sherman, and on the history of federal Indian boarding schools more broadly.

In addition to facilitating continued scholarly interest in the archives, Sisquoc assisted a steady stream of visitors continues to visit the Sherman Indian Museum in their searches for information about parents, grandparents, siblings, aunts, and uncles who attended the school. Sisquoc's efforts have helped relatives and descendants of Sherman students learn about their ancestry and culture. Starting in 2016, Sisquoc collaborated with students, faculty, and librarians from the University of California, Riverside, on a three-year effort to digitize the archival holdings of Sherman Indian Museum, making them accessible to Sherman alumni and their descendants, as well as scholars who are unable to make the journey to Southern California. Just as importantly, the digitization project ensured continued preservation of aging documents. "These records of our school's history," noted Sisquoc, "are now preserved for future generations to know their story."[10]

In 1991, Sisquoc joined a longstanding effort to revitalize the Sherman school cemetery, which had fallen into disrepair in large part because of its distance from Sherman's main campus. As at all off-reservation boarding schools, close living quarters and a limited grasp of contagious diseases led to frequent illnesses and epidemics, with trachoma, tuberculosis, influenza, and typhoid fever among the most common illnesses suffered by students. Sixty-two students died at Sherman during its first two decades, many from contagious diseases. Challenges in communicating with distant family members and arranging for train travel meant that many students could not be returned home and were interred at the Sherman cemetery.

In 1904, Superintendent Harwood Hall established the school cemetery at the school farm, located five miles from the school's main campus in what would become the foothills of Corona, California. He did so to avoid negative attention from tourists and passersby at the school's main campus. When administrators sold the school farm to private developers in 1944, the plot quickly deteriorated. Hidden between the Corona foothills and tucked behind thick rows of eucalyptus trees, the site became a popular spot for alcohol-fueled parties. Teenagers kicked over the concrete headstones, and markers were stolen and deposited in downtown Corona. Dirt bikers built jumps near the edge of the plot. Discarded furniture lay strewn between remaining headstones. The cemetery had fallen into disrepair.[11]

Efforts to restore the cemetery began as early as 1964, when Riverside County officials pulled down trees so that parties would no longer be hidden from public view. In the same year, the Bureau of Indian Affairs installed a large granite headstone with the names of those interred at the site. A decade later, Sherman Institute installed a fence around the property. These efforts drew the attention of local citizens, who volunteered time to pick weeds, clean up trash, and discourage trespassers from entering the property.

In 1991 Sisquoc took up leadership of efforts to restore the cemetery. At the helm of a newly formed cemetery committee, Sisquoc led renewed efforts to clean up the cemetery; she received funding from the BIA to erect a wrought iron fence around the cemetery, and she coordinated efforts by local volunteers to build an archway over the entrance to the cemetery. Later, Sisquoc led efforts to hire a geosciences firm to conduct ground penetrating radar on the site to confirm the location of graves, and she raised funds from the Pechanga Band of Luiseño Indians to purchase new markers. Alongside historian Jean Keller, Sisquoc worked diligently to bring attention and funding to the cemetery. The pair wrote the BIA and the Department of the Interior in search of funding for improvements, and they contacted local news outlets and informed local community leaders of the importance of the site. Finally, in 2009 Sisquoc helped to arrange for a ceremony by Southern Paiute Salt Song Singers who shared songs asking the spirits of these children to move on from the cemetery and into the next world.[12] Forgotten and neglected for so many decades, the students laid to rest in the Sherman Cemetery finally received long-needed care. Because of her work at the cemetery, Sisquoc became one of only five people ever to receive the Martin Luther King, Jr. Visionary Award for community cultural awareness from the City of Riverside, which she received in 1997.[13]

In 2000, Sisquoc became a co-founder, along with Donna Largo, Rosemary Morillo and Daniel McCarthy, of *Nex'wetem*, an association of basket weavers in Southern California. All three are students and artistic descendants of Cahuilla elder and basket weaver Donna Largo. *Nex'wetem* travels throughout Southern California to gather traditional basket weaving materials and hold weaving circles. In this way, Sisquoc and her colleagues support one another and revivify the basketry traditions of southern California tribal peoples. The group also gives basketry lectures and workshops to tribal youth and community programs. They use basket weaving as a vehicle to teach about the importance of traditional foods, cultural materials, tribal language, and spiritual practices. *Nex'wetem* also stresses traditional teachings concerning the ways in which people should connect to their environment.[14]

As Sherman neared its one hundredth year of Indian education, Sisquoc took the lead in organizing centennial celebrations. She produced a documentary film on the history of the institution that centered on the voices of elders and alumni, designed a commemorative garden in honor of alumni, and coordinated an alumni gathering. That same year, she co-organized and hosted the "Boarding School Blues" symposium with Clifford Trafzer, Distinguished Professor of History and Costo Chair at the University of California, Riverside. At the symposium, some of the leading scholars working on the history of Indigenous education shared their research with Sherman students and community members; just as importantly, these scholars listened to the experiences of Sherman students and alumni who gathered for the event. Sisquoc, Keller, and Trafzer collected and edited the papers given at the symposium, which the University of Nebraska Press published as *Boarding School Blues:*

Revisiting American Indian Educational Experiences in 2006. Many of the articles included substantial input from current students at Sherman Indian High School. The United States Department of the Interior recognized Sisquoc's efforts in hosting these events with its prestigious Star Award.[15]

In fall 2007, Sisquoc collaborated with fellow cultural educator Josie Montes to reopen the Clarke Culture Center, previously the Clarke Behavioral Health Center. Named in honor of Sherman graduate Dr. Frank Clarke, the center offered information and education holistic health. Sisquoc and Montes combined Indigenous cultural teachings related to health with access to traditional herbs, medicines, foods, and sweat ceremonies. The center also provided space for students to engage with their cultures via nightly cultural programming, including arts, crafts, stories, songs, talking circles, and Indigenous language conversations.[16]

Since the first off-reservation institution opened over a century and a half ago, boarding schools have changed in profound ways. They had once stood as sites of suffering and dispossession, where stern teachers forced students to forget their Indigenous languages, spiritualities, and cultures. Despite these attempts at cultural erasure, all along, Native people like Lorene Sisquoc have embraced Indian boarding schools and worked to change their culturally harmful aspects from the inside. Today, Sherman is far from a place of cultural destruction. On the contrary, all incoming students are asked to learn and appreciate the traditions of the southern California Indians and their own peoples. Where Sherman originally sought to prove to the public that it eradicated Indian identities, the school now celebrates and proudly displays the traditional cultures of its students. Like her mother and grandmother before her, Lorene Sisquoc has stood at the center of the transformation at Sherman Indian High School and Southern California, fostering activism by Native students, scholars, and members of the community.

NOTES

1. For a broad and accessible overview of students experienced as they arrived at boarding schools, see K. Tsianina Lomawaima, Brenda Child, and Margaret Archuleta, *Away from Home: American Indian Boarding School Experiences, 1879–2000* (Phoenix: Heard Museum, 2000). On Sherman Institute, see Matthew Sakiestewa Gilbert, *Education beyond the Mesas: Hopi Students at Sherman Institute, 1902–1929* (Lincoln: University of Nebraska Press, 2012), and Kevin Whalen, *Native Students at Work: American Indian Labor and Sherman Institute's Outing Program, 1900–1945* (Seattle: University of Washington Press, 2016). For information on Estelle Reel and her influence on vocational curricula at boarding schools, see K. Tsianina Lomawaima, "Estelle Reel, Superintendent of Indian Schools, 1898-1910: Politics,

Curriculum, and Land," *Journal of American Indian Education* 35, no. 3 (Spring 1996): 5–31.

2. On Native employees in federal Indian boarding schools, see Cathleen Cahill, *Federal Fathers and Mothers: A Social History of the United States Indian Service* (Chapel Hill: University of North Carolina Press, 2011).

3. For more on how families sometimes sought to send their children to boarding schools because of difficult living conditions on reservation communities, see Brenda Child, *Boarding School Seasons: American Indian Families, 1900–1940* (Lincoln: University of Nebraska Press, 2000).

4. Tamar Laddy, "Born a Captive of Government, Oldest Tribal Survivor Endures," *Riverside Press-Enterprise*, July 10, 1993, B3.

5. For another example of a child of Sherman employees who grew up on the school's campus, see Whalen, *Native Students at Work*, 6–7.

6. Lorene Sisquoc, personal interview with the author, Sherman Indian Museum, February 1, 2010.

7. Ibid.

8. Ibid.

9. Kyle Mays and Kevin Whalen, "Decolonizing Indigenous Education in the Postwar City: Native Women's Activism from Southern California to the Motor City," in *Indigenous and Decolonizing Studies in Education: Mapping the Long View*, eds. Linda Tuhiwai Smith, Eve Tuck, and K. Wayne Yang, 116–130. New York: Routledge, 2018.

10. "Sherman Indian Museum Digitized Collection on Track to surpass 13,000 items," accessed September 15, 2021, https://library.ucr.edu/about/news/sherman-indian-museum-digitized-collection-on-track-to-surpass-13000-items

11. Clifford E. Trafzer and Jean Keller, "Unforgettable Lives and Symbolic Voices: The Sherman School Cemetery," in *The Indian School on Magnolia Avenue: Voices and Images from Sherman Institute,* eds. Clifford E. Trafzer, Matthew Sakiestewa Gilbert, and Lorene Sisquoc (Corvallis: Oregon State University Press, 2012), 159–172.

12. Ibid.

13. "Five Honored for Exemplifying King," *Riverside Press-Enterprise* January 26, 1997, B8. Accessed September 7, 2011. http://www.newsbank.com.

14. Bennet, Tina. "Weaving a Connection to the Past; Apache Woman Crafts Traditional Cahuilla Baskets, Teaches Others the Art. *Press-Enterprise* April 5, 2002, B1.

15. Clifford E. Trafzer, Jean Keller, and Lorene Sisquoc, *Boarding School Blues: Revisiting American Indian Educational Experiences* (Lincoln: University of Nebraska Press, 2006); Lorene Sisquoc, personal interview with the author, February 1, 2010.

16. Ibid.

BIBLIOGRAPHY

Adams, David Wallace. *Education for Extinction: American Indians and the Boarding School Experience, 1875–1928.* Lawrence: University Press of Kansas, 1995.

Bahr, Diana Meyers. *The Students of Sherman Indian School: Education and Native Identity Since 1892.* Norman: University of Oklahoma Press, 2014.

Bennet, Tina. "Weaving a Connection to the Past; Apache Woman Crafts Traditional Cahuilla Baskets, Teaches Others the Art. *Press-Enterprise* April 5, 2002, B1.

Cahill, Cathleen D. *Federal Fathers and Mothers: A Social History of the United States Indian Service.* Chapel Hill: University of North Carolina Press, 2011.

Child, Brenda. *Boarding School Seasons: American Indian Families, 1900–1940.* Lincoln: University of Nebraska Press, 2000.

"Five Honored for Exemplifying King." *Press-Enterprise* January 26, 1997, B8.

Interview of Lorene Sisquoc by Kevin Whalen, February 1, 2010, Sherman Indian Museum.

Keller, Jean. *Empty Beds: Indian Student Health at Sherman Institute, 1902–1922.* East Lansing: Michigan State University Press, 2002.

Laddy, Tamar. "Born a Captive of Government, Oldest Tribal Survivor Endures." *Press-Enterprise*, July 10, 1993, B3.

Lomawaima, K. Tsianina. "Estelle Reel, Superintendent of Indian Schools, 1898–1910: Politics, Curriculum, and Land," *Journal of American Indian Education* 35, no. 3 (Spring 1996): 5-31.

Lomawaima, K. Tsianina, Brenda Child, and Margaret Archuleta. *Away from Home: American Indian Boarding School Experiences, 1879–2000.* Phoenix: Heard Museum, 2000.

Mays, Kyle T. and Kevin Whalen. "Decolonizing Indigenous Education in the Postwar City: Native Women's Activism from Southern California to the Motor City," in *Indigenous and Decolonizing Studies in Education: Mapping the Long View*, eds. Linda Tuhiwai Smith, Eve Tuck, and K. Wayne Yang, 116–130. New York: Routledge, 2018.

Sakiestewa Gilbert, Matthew. *Education beyond the Mesas: Hopi Students at Sherman Institute, 1902–1929.* Lincoln: University of Nebraska Press, 2012.

Trafzer, Clifford, Jean Keller, and Lorene Sisquoc, eds. *Boarding School Blues: Revisiting American Indian Educational Experiences.* Lincoln: University of Nebraska Press, 2006.

Trafzer, Clifford, Jeffrey Smith, and Lorene Sisquoc. *Shadows of Sherman Institute: A Photographic History of the Indian School on Magnolia Avenue* (Pechanga: Great Oak Books, 2017.

Trafzer, Clifford, Matthew Sakiestewa Gilbert, and Lorene Sisquoc, eds. *The Indian School on Magnolia Avenue: Voices and Images of Sherman Institute.* Corvallis: Oregon State University Press, 2012.

University of California, Riverside. "Sherman Indian Museum Digitized Collection on Track to Surpass 13,000 Items." Accessed September 15, 2021. https://library.ucr.edu/about/news/sherman-indian-museum-digitized-collection-on-track-to-surpass-13000-items.

Whalen, Kevin. *Native Students at Work: American Indian Labor and Sherman Institute's Outing Program, 1900–1945.* Seattle: University of Washington Press, 2016.

Chapter Thirteen

Desegregating the Last Frontier

Elizabeth Wanamaker Peratrovich (1911–1958)

Benjamin T. Jenkins

Native American activist women have educated society in numerous ways. Some have done a great deal in the classroom, teaching native histories, languages, and cultural beliefs. Others perform different forms of education, such as advocating for equality in the classroom. Elizabeth Wanamaker Peratrovich, a Tlingit woman from southeastern Alaska, spent much of the mid-twentieth century educating the white population of the Last Frontier to reject anti-Native discrimination. With her husband, Roy Peratrovich, Elizabeth organized Native peoples in Juneau, the capital of Alaska, to dismantle segregated facilities across Alaska. This western activist's career culminated with her testimony in favor of an anti-discrimination bill before the territorial legislature of Alaska, where she educated legislators by offering an impassioned defense of equal rights for Native and white Alaskans. Rightly celebrated for her political and social accomplishments, Elizabeth Peratrovich offers a strong example of positive, productive activism for Indigenous peoples across the United States and the globe, as well as a model for educating society about the importance of native equality.

The Tlingit girl who eventually took the name Elizabeth Peratrovich was born in 1911 in Petersburg, in southeastern Alaska. This region was home to the Tlingit and Haida peoples, who, by the turn of the twentieth century, had survived Russian colonization and suffered depredations leveled against them by migrants and miners as their homeland came under the control of the United States. Mary and Andrew Wanamaker, a Tlingit missionary couple that shared in this heritage of endurance, adopted Elizabeth. The Wanamakers raised Elizabeth to appreciate the importance of American culture as well as her Tlingit roots and taught her to value education. Upon graduating high school, Elizabeth attended the Western College of Education in Washington State, then called Bellingham Normal. Here she met Roy Peratrovich, whom she married during her first semester of college in 1931. Together, they had three children: Roy Jr., Frank, and Loretta.

After they moved back to Alaska, Elizabeth and Roy felt dismay over the territorial government's treatment of Indigenous populations. Native peoples such as the Tlingit lived under less-than-ideal circumstances in Alaska by the early-twentieth century. To "civilize" Indians, acculturation had become a common tactic in the territory, as it had across much of the continental United States. The territory followed Nelson Act, passed in 1905, which allowed only "civilized" children to attend public schools. This murkily defined term relegated many Native children to substandard schools, where white educators forced them to abandon their traditions for western culture. Under this act, the government forced Indians to speak English, eat European food, and wear nonnative clothing. Fortunately for Elizabeth Wanamaker, because she lived with missionaries, she was able to attend Ketchikan High School. Although Elizabeth successfully avoided total acculturation through this school system, it demonstrated the zeal with which white Alaskans repressed Native peoples, and later came under fire for its role in suppressing Tlingits and other indigenous groups.

Beyond the lack of educational opportunities, Native Alaskans faced other serious inequalities in their homeland. In 1896, in its famous decision in *Plessy v. Ferguson*, the Supreme Court of the United States institutionalized the doctrine of separate but equal facilities for Caucasians and African Americans. Many white Alaskans applied this finding to Native peoples such as the Tlingit. Even after the federal government granted Indians citizenship in 1924, private entities refused to cater to them. Signs in businesses across the territory forbade dogs or Indians from entering their establishments. This left the Tlingit and other Natives no choice but to organize to protect their rights as citizens and their human dignity, crafting a movement in which Elizabeth would eventually play a critical leadership role. Over time, Elizabeth and her husband became leaders in the struggle for equal rights for the Tlingit and all Native peoples.

In response to institutionalized segregation and unequal educational opportunities, Native activists in southeastern Alaska formed the Alaska Native Brotherhood in 1912, the same year the territorial legislature came into being and one year after Elizabeth's birth. This organization educated society about the need for Native rights and equality under the law, and secured suffrage for Alaska's first peoples in 1922. In 1915, the Alaska Native Sisterhood formed to include women into this struggle. The Peratrovichs became heavily involved in these organizations. Roy, who had already shown political ability as the mayor of Klawock, achieved the position of Grand President of the Alaska Native Brotherhood. Elizabeth joined him as Grand Vice President of Alaska Native Sisterhood starting in 1941, and eventually ascended to the rank of Grand President herself. Simultaneously, to increase the impact of their political activism, in 1941 Elizabeth and Roy Peratrovich moved to Juneau, the capital of Alaska. By catapulting themselves onto this stage, the Peratrovichs laid the groundwork to expand their crusade for civil rights across the territory.

In Juneau, Elizabeth and Roy Peratrovich engaged in a struggle that would define their legacy as activists. The couple fought against businesses with signs that kept Native peoples out. The Peratrovichs shrewdly took advantage of the political circumstances of the Second World War to garner public support for their protest. Starting in December 1941, when the United States declared war on the Axis Powers and mobilized its resources to win a global conflict, Elizabeth and Roy compared the signs barring Indians from entering certain businesses to the anti-Semitic laws of Nazi Germany, America's opponent on the battlefield. Their first target was the Douglas Inn in the city of Douglas, which they noted had a sign reading "No Natives Allowed." "In the present emergency," Elizabeth and Roy maintained, "our Native boys are being called upon to defend our beloved country, just as the White boys. There is no distinction being made there, but yet when we try to patronize some business establishments, we are told in most cases that Natives are not allowed."[1] The Peratrovichs appealed to Americans' sense of patriotism and asked them to band together in wartime to end segregation. They pressured Governor Ernest Gruening, a political ally, to dismantle anti-Native segregation in Alaska.

The Peratrovichs used strong rhetoric in their quest to improve Native lives and pointed to the numerous contributions that Tlingits and others made to the war effort and everyday life in Alaska. "In view of the present emergency," they wrote in a letter to Gruening, "when unity is being stressed don't you think that [segregation] is very Un-American? We have always contended that we are entitled to every benefit that is accorded our so-called White Brothers."[2] This included the right to education. After all, the Peratrovichs pointed out, "Our Native people pay the School tax each year to educate the White children, yet they try to exclude our children from these schools." As Native peoples across Alaska gave their time, energy, and money to support the war effort, the Peratrovichs' appeal could hardly be denied. Newspapers published their letters, igniting widespread unease with segregation. The pair also mailed copies of anti-discrimination laws from across United States to Anthony J. Diamond, a representative in Alaskan Territorial House of Representatives who favored Native rights. Elizabeth and Roy's efforts to curry favor with allies later paid tremendous dividends.

Most significantly, the Peratrovichs directly entered the legislative realm in the 1940s. In 1943, Roy and Elizabeth introduced an Anti-Discrimination Bill to the Alaska Territorial Legislature. It went down in defeat, as did another draft following year. It took a major public event to transform the pair's dream of racial equality into a reality. The watershed moment that the Peratrovichs needed to propel their anti-discrimination bill through the legislature occurred in 1944. In Nome, an Eskimo woman named Alberta Schenck was arrested for sitting in a "whites only" section of a movie theater. Shortly before her ouster from the theater, Schenck had written an editorial in the *Nome Nugget* detailing the poor conditions that Eskimos and other Native peoples faced in Alaska. Elizabeth and Roy immediately capitalized on Schenck's story, which captivated people across the territory. Schenck's sympathetic case gave the Peratrovichs the political capital they needed to render discrimination illegal. When debate over another anti-discrimination bill ensued in the Alaskan territorial legislature, proponents of the bill cited Schenck's story as a reason to overturn racial discrimination.

As testimonies before the territorial legislature drew to a close, Elizabeth took the stand to share her views on Native rights, and in the process solidified her place in Tlingit and Alaskan history. She educated legislators about the need to safeguard the liberties and equality of native peoples. "I would not have expected," she remarked with caustic sarcasm, "that I, who am barely out of savagery, would have to remind gentlemen with 5,000 years of recorded civilization behind them, of our bill of rights," which segregation directly challenged.[3] She shared personal stories from her time in Juneau, detailing the discrimination against which she had led the Alaska Native Sisterhood. Peratrovich masterfully rebutted criticism from opponents of the bill. For instance, members of the Alaska senate asked Peratrovich if the law would eliminate discrimination outright. She answered that it would not, but riposted "do your laws against larceny and even murder prevent those crimes? No law will eliminate crimes, but at least you, as legislators, can assert to the world that you recognize the evil of the present situation and speak of your intent to help us overcome discrimination."[4] Elizabeth's testimony served as a powerful last word on the debate over the bill, as well as the zenith of her political career.

Through her moving speech, Elizabeth Peratrovich won support from the territorial legislature and the Alaskan public. The *Daily Alaska Empire* proudly exclaimed that Elizabeth's testimony drew applause from the floor of the Senate and the gallery. After Elizabeth finished her testimony, the anti-discrimination bill passed the senate by a vote of 11 to 5. The Anti-Discrimination Act became law in February 1945. It empowered Native peoples and limited the social and political impact of bigotry in Alaska. Elizabeth attended the signing of the bill by Governor Ernest Gruening. While no law could eliminate prejudice against Native peoples in Alaska, it did result in the removal of anti-Indian signs in businesses across the Last Frontier.

Following her victory in the territorial legislature of Alaska, Elizabeth Peratrovich maintained her activism. She worked in the office of the legislature before representing the Alaska Native Sisterhood in the National Congress of American Indians. She also actively involved herself in a number of community organizations in Juneau. With Roy and her children, Elizabeth moved to Nova Scotia and later Oklahoma, but returned to Alaska in her final years. Sadly, Elizabeth succumbed to cancer in 1958. However, her role as a Native Alaskan civil rights pioneer in Alaska guaranteed her a place in the state's history. According to Governor Gruening, without Elizabeth's constant presence in the Alaskan legislature, the anti-discrimination law would never have passed. In 1988, Governor Steve Cowper declared February 16 Elizabeth Peratrovich Day, keeping her legacy of activism alive for future generations and educating Alaskans about the importance of equality.

NOTES

1. "A Recollection of Civil Rights Leader Elizabeth Peratrovich, 1911–1958," *Alaskool.org.* http://www.alaskool.org/projects/native_gov/recollections/peratrovich/ Elizabeth_1.htm.

2. Quoted in Benson, Diane E. "Elizabeth Peratrovich: The Right to Education." Susan Imel and Gretchen T. Bersch, eds. *No Small Lives: Handbook of North American Early Women Adult Educators, 1925–1950* (Charlotte, NC: Information Age Publishing, Inc., 2015): 193–200.

3. "A Recollection of Civil Rights Leader Elizabeth Peratrovich, 1911–1958," *Alaskool.org.* http://www.alaskool.org/projects/native_gov/recollections/peratrovich/ Elizabeth_1.htm.

4. "A Recollection of Civil Rights Leader Elizabeth Peratrovich, 1911–1958," *Alaskool.org.*

BIBLIOGRAPHY

Benson, Diane E. "Elizabeth Peratrovich: The Right to Education." Susan Imel and Gretchen T. Bersch, eds., *No Small Lives: Handbook of North American Early Women Adult Educators, 1925–1950.* Charlotte, NC: Information Age Publishing, Inc., 2015.

"A Recollection of Civil Rights Leader Elizabeth Peratrovich, 1911–1958." *Alaskool. org.*

FURTHER READING

Cole, Terrence M. "Jim Crow in Alaska: The Passage of the Alaska Equal Rights Act of 1945." *Western Historical Quarterly* 23, no. 4 (November 1992): 429–449.

Huber, Tonya. "Peratrovich, Elizabeth W." Carole Barrett and Harvey Markowitz, eds., *American Indian Biographies*. Pasadena, CA: Salem Press, Inc., 2005.

Kurtz, Matthew. "Ruptures and Recuperations of a Language of Racism in Alaska's Rural/Urban Divide." *Annals of the Association of American Geographers* 96, no. 3 (September 2006): 601–621.

Oleska, Michael. "Elizabeth Peratrovich and Roy Peratrovich." Nora Marks Dauenhauer and Richard Dauenhauer, eds. *Haa Kusteeyí, Our Culture: Tlingit Life Stories*. Seattle: University of Washington Press, and Juneau: Sealaska Heritage Foundation, 1994.

Peratrovich, Roy, and Elizabeth Peratrovich. "Eliminate This Discrimination." Daniel M. Cobb, ed. *Say We Are Nations: Documents of Politics and Protest in Indigenous America since 1887*, Chapel Hill: The University of North Carolina Press, 2015.

"Super Race Theory Hit in Hearing: Native Sisterhood President Hits at 'Rights' Bill Opposition." *Daily Alaska Empire (Juneau Empire)*, February 6, 1945.

Swensen, Thomas Michael. "The Relationship between Indigenous Rights, Citizenship, and Land in Territorial Alaska: How the Past Opened the Door to the Future." In *Proceedings from the Alaska Native Studies Conference, 2015*. Fairbanks: University of Alaska, Fairbanks.

Chapter Fourteen

Preserving Indigenous Cultures and Languages

Ofelia Zepeda (b. 1952–)

Jordan Cohen

The invasion of North America led to the oppression and forced assimilation of Native American cultures. Assimilation manifested through the suppression of Indigenous languages and later social and political pressures on American Indians abandon their languages. This then led to a rapid decline in the literacy and fluency in Native languages. The United States forced Indian children to forsake their native languages, which were and are inherently tied to their cultures and identities. Ofelia Zepeda was born to the Tohono O'odham tribe, formerly known as the Papago tribe.

Like many Indigenous tribes of America, the Tohono O'odham have experienced a loss of native cultural practices, including language. The O'odham language continued until than one percent of the Tohono O'odham people could read and write their language. Zepeda is an activist for the preservation of her language and every Indigenous language. She explained that migration due to economic and social factors have contributed to her people being introduced "into a society dominated by English."[1] As a linguist and Native of the Tohono O'odham tribe, Ofelia Zepeda's work demonstrates her commitment to preserving the culture and language of her people. As a linguistics professor and poet at the University of Arizona, she has recorded and preserved the culture and language of the Tohono O'odham people. She has also brought Native American culture into the collective consciousness of the United States and beyond.

Zepeda was born near the Tohono O'odham Reservation in Stanfield, Arizona, in 1952. Ofelia cites the importance of growing up within the O'odham culture as the agent that encouraged her with her scholarly work. Although she grew up off her reservation, she was very much a part of the Native culture during her childhood. This culture would shape her personal identity and her academic career. She and her family were referred to as the "people that live in the cotton fields," referring to her family's year-round work in agriculture.[2] She knew that this agricultural work was the fate of many of her people. This motivated her to pursue education as a means of escaping agricultural work, leading her to become the first in her family to graduate from high school and attend college. In addition, she saw education as her right to pursue further knowledge and she decided to take advantage of the activism that fought for educational rights for Native people. Zepeda quickly moved through education, earning her BA in 1980, MA in 1981, and PhD in 1984 in linguistics from the University of Arizona. Significantly, she now teaches at the same university located near her people and homeland.

Zepeda initially began her academic career studying sociology. Yet, while working under Kenneth Hale, a visiting professor from the Massachusetts Institute of Technology, she began transcribing traditional Tohono O'odham stories. She became focused on the writing, grammar, and language of the Tohono O'odham people, and she found her passion. She would later refer to this time being reintroduced to her Native language. With this influence and field experience, she then switched her focus from sociology to linguistics. She became a leading activist for the preservation of Native American languages. Most notably she is known for compiling *A Papago Grammar*, the first text written to teach the Tohono O'odham language. In her foreword to her book, Zepeda writes, "The book is intended for classroom use in teaching native and non-native speakers."[3] Zepeda published this book in 1983, inspired by her own desire to learn more about her language. Moreover, she was concerned about the decline in language fluency within the Tohono O'odham community.

Zepeda's focus on creating a textbook that sought to teach people the language ran contrary to linguists interested in the study of languages. She was most concerned about the preservation and teaching of Indigenous languages. She explained the importance of language during a talk given at Arizona State University. She said language is part of a chain that holds people together, along with land and memory. By orienting her book toward teaching the language, she intended to preserve the culture and language of the O'odham people. Zepeda also addressed the importance of language in her essay, targeting the attempt in 1983 in Arizona to make English the official language "U.S. English" or "Official English" was a movement that began in 1983, formed by Senator S. I. Hayakawa and John Tanton, who promoted English as the official language of the United States.

"Official English" was eventually passed into law in Arizona in 2006 under Proposition 103. Reintroducing Native language became increasingly more important as there were more and more measures seeking to silence Spanish and Indigenous languages. In 2010, the Tucson Unified School District passed a bill banning many books by Chicano and Native American authors, including Zepeda's book of poetry, *Ocean Power: Poems from the Desert.* School officials at the district reasoned that they politicized students. This attack on Indigenous voices and languages demonstrated how important Zepeda's work had become as a means of preserving American Indian culture and identity.

Zepeda remains a leader within the Tohono O'odham community, as she holds many positions that work toward aiding the preservation of language and culture within the indigenous communities of her own tribe and many others. She has also served as the Director of the American Indian Studies Program at the University of Arizona from 1986–1991 and has been the co-director of the American Indian Language Development Institute (AILDI) from 1989 to the present. Each of these administrative roles gives her a vehicle for spreading awareness and increasing education about Native American languages, specifically the Tohono O'odham language. She has also helped maintain accuracy and proper representation of Native Americans generally by serving as a consultant on a multitude of projects, including the video "Code Talkers: The First 29." Her presence in the academic world and the importance of her keystone work, *A Papago Grammar*, is made more evident by her award of a MacArthur Fellowship Grant in 1999 and a research grant from the Endangered Language Fund in 1997.

Her teaching of her Indigenous language as a Professor at the University of Arizona is another form of activism. As a professor, Zepeda is helping to rebuild American Indian languages, which American colonialism attempted to destroy by forcing school-age children to speak English only and by denigrating their Indigenous languages and cultures. Zepeda is a linguist that emphasizes language preservation and learning. She is not a theoretical linguist interested only in research. She is an active proponent for revitalizing the language and she teaches the language as a means of reintroducing Indigenous languages to the people. Although many Tohono O'odham people speak the language, too few people can read or write it fluently, if at all. Zepeda continues to teach at the University of Arizona, and as a scholar, she focuses on the structure of Tohono O'odham language, language maintenance, and revitalization. In addition, she is the editor for Sun Tracks Publications, a series of books through the University of Arizona Press that focuses on Native American authors. Zepeda takes her work very seriously, defining what it means to be a teacher in the Native American community, saying, "It is a position of responsibility, not power . . . [a teacher] would then have the responsibility to make things happen so the tribal community could perpetuate or continue."[4] Zepeda's work to preserve the culture of her community and other Indigenous communities fulfills her own Native definition of the work she does.

While cultivating the careers of other Native American authors, Zepeda also makes her own contributions through her poetry. Zepeda is the author of three books of poetry, *Ocean Power: Poems from the Desert*, *Jewed 'I-hoi/ Earth Movements* (a book of bilingual poetry) and *Where Clouds Are Formed*. Her poetry often contains themes that connect with the Tohono O'odham language and discuss the importance of language. Zepeda's poetry also helps bring the indigenous voice into the conversation of what Native American culture means in modern society. Kenneth Hada reported, "Zepeda's poetry offers glimpses of collective identity informed by historical and cultural forces that contribute to contemporary responses within the cultural context of the Tohono O'odham people."[5] This is also evident in her use of the Tohono O'odham language within her poetry, which creates a deeper understanding of the past Native tradition and the present circumstances within her community.

By explaining her experiences using poetry and Native language, Zepeda introduces the Native way to a broad audience. Rather than just using the language, which she does in her poetry, she also connects to Native American thoughts and ideas. For example, a prominent motif is the importance of land and sacred places, as she details the meaning of certain landmarks. She recognizes the fact that these landmarks are part of what makes one feel connected to their past. Zepeda also uses this idea of a collective past as a way of re-writing Native American history. By using collective memory, Zepeda uses a voice of "ours" not "I." In this way, she draws her community closer together and helps readers know her world through the identification of their shared practices and beliefs. This use of collective memory, rather than her own individual experiences, is a common theme in Native American tradition.

Ofelia Zepeda's dedication to preserving the Tohono O'odham language is part of a much bigger work by Native American and non-Native people seeking to perpetuate Native American languages and cultures. Zepeda's activism stems from her heart and knowledge. She is committed to revitalizing and reintroducing the language through education in the local community, university, and her own poetry. Her revitalization of Native American culture and language is well-known to members of the American Indian communities and scholars interested in Indigenous languages. Zepeda is an example of one person who has made a difference in the preservation of Native American languages. Zepeda's past work has marked a changing narrative and definitive stance against the eradication of Native American languages, and she continues the work in the early twenty-first century.

NOTES

1. Ofelia Zepeda, *A Papago Grammar* (Tucson: The University of Arizona Press, 1983), xiv.

2. Ofelia Zepeda, "Legacies of the Tribal Languages of Arizona: Gifts or Responsibilities?" for the Simon Ortiz and Labriola Center Lecture on Indigenous Land, Culture, and Community, October 11, 2012, Heard Museum, YouTube video, 1:00:25, https://www.youtube.com/watch?v=sSGMna2hrfE, quote at 9:03–9:05.

3. Ofelia Zepeda, *A Papago Grammar* (Tucson: The University of Arizona Press, 1983), xiv.

4. JoAnn di Fillipo, "Ofelia Zepeda," Sharon Malinowski, ed. *Notable Native Americans* (Detroit: Gale Research Inc., 1995), 476.

5. Kenneth Hada, "One Must Know Where We Don't Want to Go: Identity in Ofelia Zepeda's Ocean Power and Where Clouds Are Formed," *Journal of the West* 51 (Fall 2012), 55.

BIBLIOGRAPHY

Hada, Kenneth. "One Must Know Where We Don't Want to Go: Identity in Ofelia Zepeda's *Ocean Power* and *Where Clouds Are Formed.*" *Journal of the West* 51. Fall 2012. 55–59.

Hill, Jane and Ofelia Zepeda. "Mrs. Patricio's Trouble: The Distribution of Responsibility in an Account of Personal Experience." In Jane Hill and Judith T. Irvine, eds. *Responsibility and Evidence in Oral Discourse.* New York: Cambridge University Press, 1993.

Zepeda, Ofelia. *A Papago Grammar.* Tucson: The University of Arizona Press, 1983.

Zepeda, Ofelia. "American Indian Language Policy." In Karen L. Adams and Daniel T. Brink, eds. *Perspectives on Official English: The Campaign for English as the Official Language of the USA.* Berlin and New York: Mouton de Gruyer, 1990.

Zepeda, Ofelia. "Afterword." In Heidi A. Orcutt-Gachirl and Tania Granadillo, eds. In *Ethnographic Contribution to the Study of Endangered Languages.* Tucson: University of Arizona Press, 2011.

Zepeda, Ofelia. "Bury Me with the Band." In *Reinventing the Enemy's Language: Contemporary Native Women's Writings of North America.* Joy Harjo and Gloria Bird, eds. New York: W. W. Norton and Company, 1997.

FURTHER READING

Hada, Kenneth. "One Must Know Where We Don't Want To Go: Identity in Ofelia Zepeda's *Ocean Power* and *Where Clouds and Formed.*" *Journal of the West* 51. Fall 2012. 55–59.

Hill, Jane and Ofelia Zepeda. "Mrs. Patricio's Trouble: The Distribution of Responsibility in an Account of Personal Experience." In Jane Hill and Judith T. Irvine, eds. *Responsibility and Evidence in Oral Discourse.* New York: Cambridge University Press, 1993.

Zepeda, Ofelia. *A Papago Grammar.* Tucson: The University of Arizona Press, 1983.

Zepeda, Ofelia. "American Indian Language Policy." In Karen L. Adams and Daniel T. Brink, eds. *Perspectives on Official English: The Campaign for English as the Official Language of the USA.* Berlin and New York, Mouton de Gruyer, 1990.

Zepeda, Ofelia. "Afterword." In Heidi A. Orcutt-Gachirl and Tania Granadillo, eds. In *Ethnographic Contribution to the Study of Endangered Languages.* Tucson: University of Arizona Press, 2011.

Zepeda, Ofelia. "Bury Me with the Band." In *Reinventing the Enemy's Language: Contemporary Native Women's Writings of North America.* Joy Harjo and Gloria Bird, eds. New York: W. W. Norton and Company, 1997.

Chapter Fifteen

Public Historian and Sustainability Activist

Roberta Conner (Sisaawipam) (b. 1955–)

Benjamin T. Jenkins

For much of her life, Native leader Roberta Conner has worked to educate Americans about the environment and of the cultures of the Umatilla, Nez Perce, and Cayuse Indians of the Pacific Northwest. As an advocate for environmentally sustainable practices and the director of the Tamástslikt Cultural Institute, Conner influenced educational and ecological undertakings to improve human balance with the environment and to perpetuate the use of Native worldviews and languages from the Columbia Plateau. Although she completed much of her work within the Confederated Tribes of the Umatilla Indian Reservation, Conner's achievements drew her into national movements and organizations, such as the National Museum of the American Indian in Washington, DC. Through her stewardship of Cayuse, Nez Perce, and Umatilla culture, Connor cemented her position in the annals as an educator, environmentalist, and leading public historian.

Roberta Conner, or Sisaawipam, was born in Pendleton, Oregon, in 1955. She completed high school and moved on to matriculate at the University of Oregon and the Atkinson Graduate School of Management at Willamette University. Upon completing her education, Conner completed a long stint with the United Indians of All Tribes Foundation, where she helped promote technical education among Native peoples. From there, she moved on to the U.S. Small Business Administration in 1984. All the while, she retained an active leadership presence on the Confederated Tribes of the Umatilla Indian Reservation. Conner descended from Cayuse, Umatilla, and Nez Perce ancestry. These peoples, who made their homes on the Columbia Plateau, perceived themselves as having originated in that country. They have no stories of migrating to that region from any previous homeland. "We have always been here," Conner once wrote with historian William L. Lang. Conner's forebears lived in what she called Cayuse country, along the Snake River.[1] They did marry with Salish and Crow peoples, though, demonstrating connectivity to the world around them. As an enrolled member of the Confederated Tribes of the Umatilla Indian Reservation, Conner has led her people through cultural and environmental activism.

The history of the Confederated Tribes of the Umatilla Indian Reservation informs Conner's work. After centuries of peace and stability where the Cayuse, Nez Perce, and Umatilla prospered in tandem with the environment around them, outsiders gradually invaded the Columbia Plateau. Meriwether Lewis and William Clark ventured through the region in 1803–1806. Lewis and Clark, sent by President Thomas Jefferson to explore the Louisiana Purchase as the heads of the Corps of Discovery, saw the land as a resource to exploit. Fur traders followed in their footsteps, taking resources from the land in unsustainable ways. The Cayuse, Umatilla, and Walla Walla watched as Americans and British settlers built forts and vied for geopolitical power in the Columbia Plateau. By the 1830s, invaders' desire to control Native peoples emerged in the form of Protestant missions meant to "civilize" Indians by teaching them how to farm and behave. As more American migrants entered the Pacific Northwest, Conner likened their numerical multiplication as increasing from a trickle to a flood. This exemplified the general American view of the United States' "manifest destiny" to expand across North America, which resulted in military conquest of large portions of Mexico and Native America throughout the nineteenth century.

American incursion into the Pacific Northwest crested with the acquisition of Native country through "treaties" with Indian leaders, such as Conner's ancestors. These included Istikus, Old Joseph, and Timothy, who participated in the Walla Walla Treaty Council of 1855. The treaty produced at this event, shaped largely by white politicians and military figures, forced the Native nations of the Columbia Plateau to cede the homelands where they had thrived for countless generations. Indians retained control of a paltry 500,000 acres. This was carved down over time, after the government surveyed lands in 1871 and passed the Allotment Act in 1885. Conner cited Christianity, white intervention, and alcohol as forces that undermined the longevity of vibrant Native cultures.

The trajectory of Roberta Conner's efforts to promote Native cultures and environmental sustainability derived directly from her roots on the Columbia Plateau. Conner's family, particularly her grandmother, instilled in her a fervent belief in sustainability. This led Conner to adopt a holistic environmental outlook, which positioned humans as a single component within nature, not its dominant force. Conner cared just as much for her horses, dogs, and the wild strawberries that grow in her homeland as she did for herself. She directly linked this worldview to health concerns, opining that people could more effectively overcome cancer or diabetes if they avoided placing toxins into nature to begin with. Physical health, then, translated to spiritual health in this mindset. To Conner, "Being instructed formally and finding answers from nature" through working with the land, fishing, and picking "are both accepted methods of obtaining knowledge."[2]

Conner's worldview revolved around maintaining balance between humans and with nature. She argued passionately in favor of a more naturalistic, and less anthropocentric, understanding of the world. This has resulted in peoples of the Confederated Tribes of the Umatilla Indian Reservation reintroducing salmon to the Northwest. This is culturally significant, since members of the Umatilla reservation believe that salmon were their ancestors' first source of food. They have also reintroduced mussels to the Umatilla River, improving nature's ability to care for itself. Beyond wildlife management, Conner cited the opening of an environmentally friendly power plant as a way to mesh Indian environmental theories with western electrical practices. She characterized these activities as a check on the ideology of manifest destiny that has shaped American politics and society. In this system, modernity and nature coexist. "Salmon and hydroelectricity," Conner once wrote, "do not have to be incompatible, any more than economic strength and cultural vitality have to cancel each other out."[3]

Conner used her environmental and social views to educate contemporary society. She rejected the idea of rigid reservation boundaries imposed by the federal government in favor of a view that included the lands of her ancestors from across the Columbia Plateau. Conner also extended the idea of her community past her immediate family to include wildlife. This stood in direct contrast to the expansionist ethic of westward moving Euro-Americans during the nineteenth century, many of whom acted greedily, Conner asserted, by taking more than what they needed from nature, settlers created an imbalance with the environment. In the traditional worldview of the Natives of the Pacific Northwest, humans should only take what they need from the environment, and do so respectfully. "If we don't use all of the parts of the animal that's hunted," Conner once elucidated, "if we just take things for trophy or sport, then we are not doing things respectfully."[4]

Roberta Conner's professional experiences allowed her to educate a large, diverse audience in this ideology. On the Umatilla Indian Reservation, she served as executive director of the Tamástslikt Cultural Institute starting in 1998. This establishment was created to share the cultural history of the reservation with others, whether they derived from Native or non-Native stock. As executive director, Conner straddled the fields of education, museum work, and public history, all while maintaining her Native identity. Conner eschewed the practice of labeling artifacts at the museum because she believed this practice detached the present from the past. In this conception of the past, history remains relevant to the present, and people must understand it as completely as possible to live more sustainably in the future.

Through the Tamástslikt Cultural Institute, Conner has shaped educational programs to educate visitors on the histories of her people from creation through the white "settlement" of the frontier. Exhibits she helped curate, such as *Many Nations Many Voices*, have toured the country. She periodically lectured and published in scholarly and popular venues on the history of Umatilla, Cayuse, and other Native nations. She served as vice president of National Council of the Lewis and Clark Bicentennial Board of Directors, exploring how the Corps of Discovery and Native peoples interacted. She joined the Lewis and Clark Bicentennial to promote Native understandings of contact with the expedition and the United States in the nineteenth century. "The tragedy for me," she once explained during an interview, "is that there's much to be learned from the Lewis and Clark story, but will we actually learn anything while we're worrying about benches and Port-a-potties and picnic tables and off-ramps and trains to locations where there's an interpretive center?" For Native peoples who participated in the bicentennial of Lewis and Clark's expedition, the event was "not a celebration. It is an observance or commemoration. We want both sides of the story told—the army expedition's and our own—and we want to tell our own story."[5]

This statement largely characterized the Tamástslikt Cultural Institute's outlook: interpreting the heritage of the Columbia Plateau in such a way that invited the public to participate. History, to Conner, represented a mechanism for Indians to reclaim culture and share it with a larger audience. Of Indian perspectives on Lewis and Clark, Conner lamented that "it is very unlikely that you have heard our story. It is not typically represented in history books or classroom lessons or cotemporary politics." She meant to "make the record complete" by telling the full story of the expedition from Native perspectives. In one chapter she authored for a history commemorating the Lewis and Clark expedition from Native perspectives, Conner excerpted portions of diaries from the Corps of Discovery and rebutted misperceptions about peoples of the Pacific Northwest with detailed explanations of tribal traditions, lore, and worldviews. "We were resident," she said of the Native nations of the Pacific Northwest, while "Lewis and Clark and all members of the expedition were transient. They saw much that they did not comprehend, even when they tried in earnest to understand."[6] It has fallen to Conner and her colleagues to explain Native cultures from Indigenous perspectives.

This task is inherently bound up with the preservation of Indian languages. To further increase the vitality of Native cultures, Conner used the Tamástslikt Cultural Institute as a vehicle to revitalize dying languages. For centuries, hundreds of Native dialects became extinct as a result of invasions such as those that the Indigenous populations of the Columbia Plateau suffered in the nineteenth century. The Cayuse language was once such dialect. As Conner remarked in 2011, the last generation of Native speakers was rapidly dying off by the turn of the twenty-first century. "Now that the Cayuse language is extinct," Conner once explained, "save about 350 documented words, most Cayuse descendants who speak a Native language speak lower or upper Nez Perce. The few persons who speak Walla Walla as a first language are all elders. Those who speak Umatilla as a first language are a handful of adults and the rest elders."[7]

To forestall further cultural loss, Conner did everything in her power to keep the languages of the Columbia Plateau alive through education. She strongly believed that Native language intertwined with Indian history. To underscore the importance of Native dialects, Conner linked the preservation of indigenous languages to a less anthropocentric understanding of the environment. Prior to Lewis and Clark's expedition, Native peoples had names for all components of the landscape. For instance, Conner once pointed out that language and Native peoples' connections to the land allowed Indians to locate condor nests that scientists could not find. Conner's people have no term that is comparable to the notion of "wilderness" because Natives of the Columbia Plateau know every part of the land; they do not artificially separate humans from it the way explorers such as Lewis and Clark did. Language and landscape blend together in Conner's worldview. Keeping such knowledge and history alive served a living purpose, Conner believed, since it helped humans understand how to live in balance with each other and with the environment, and to see themselves not as the apex of creation, but simply another component that should not dominate the rest of nature.

Conner's efforts to spread Native understandings of the world earned her acclaim in the fields of environmental science and public history. In 2007, she received the Buffett Award for Indigenous Leadership from Ecotrust for her work promoting Native concepts of sustainability. In 2008, Conner joined the Board of Trustees of the Smithsonian Institution's National Museum of the American Indian. She chaired that body for six years. Locally, she sat on boards of the Oregon Cultural Trust, Oregon Parks and Recreation Commission, and Oregon Council for the Humanities.

Much of Conner's professional life has drawn her back to her Native homeland on the Columbia Plateau. "Our people have always been from this very same landscape, 6.4-million-acre landscape, this very same part of the Columbia River drainage," she once explained.

> We have been from here for so long, and people have done horrible things—federal government policies, lots of well-intentioned desires to 'kill the Indian and save the child.' Over the course of time, the past 150 years, people have

treated Indians very badly. What I've not understood until very recently, is that we know something that nobody else seems to get: we're not leaving. We're not giving up. We're not giving in. We're here for the long-term. We're here forever.[8]

For Conner, the Columbia Plateau "is the place the Creator gave us. It is our only home. We may reside elsewhere temporarily but this is the only place we'll ever be from. It is part of us, and we are part of it." By fostering dialogue over how to perceive this environment and how to understand history from a Native perspective, as a public educator and historian, Conner has done a great deal to ensure that her people remain a vibrant part of the Columbia Plateau for generations to come.

NOTES

1. Roberta Conner and William L. Lang, "Early Contact and Incursion, 1700–1850," in *Wiyáx̣ayx̣t/Wiyáakaáawn/As Days Go By: Our History, Our Land, and Our People – The Cayuse, Umatilla, and Walla Walla* (Pendleton, OR: Tamástslikt Cultural Institute; Portland: Oregon Historical Society Press; Seattle: University of Washington Press, 2006), 24.

2. Roberta Conner, "Our People Have Always Been Here," in Alvin M. Josephy, Jr., with Marc Jaffe, eds., *Lewis and Clark through Indian Eyes* (New York, NY: Alfred A. Knopf, 2006), 103.

3. Roberta Conner, "The Lewis & Clark Bicentennial: Putting Tribes Back on the Map," in Kris Fresonke and Mark Spence, eds., *Lewis & Clark: Legacies, Memories, and New Perspectives* ed. (Berkeley: University of California Press, 2004), 273.

4. Roberta Conner, "Native Perspectives on Sustainability: Roberta Conner (Cayuse)," transcript of an oral history conducted 2007 by D. E. Hall. Native Perspectives on Sustainability, 3.

5. Roberta Conner, "The Lewis & Clark Bicentennial: Putting Tribes Back on the Map," in Kris Fresonke and Mark Spence, eds., *Lewis & Clark: Legacies, Memories, and New Perspectives* ed. (Berkeley: University of California Press, 2004), 266.

6. Roberta Conner, "Our People Have Always Been Here," in Alvin M. Josephy, Jr., with Marc Jaffe, eds., *Lewis and Clark through Indian Eyes* (New York, NY: Alfred A. Knopf, 2006), 101.

7. Roberta Conner, "The Lewis & Clark Bicentennial: Putting Tribes Back on the Map," in Kris Fresonke and Mark Spence, eds., *Lewis & Clark: Legacies, Memories, and New Perspectives* ed. (Berkeley: University of California Press, 2004), 266.

8. Roberta Conner, "Native Perspectives on Sustainability: Roberta Conner (Cayuse)," transcript of an oral history conducted 2007 by D. E. Hall. Native Perspectives on Sustainability, 15.

BIBLIOGRAPHY

Conner, Roberta. "The Lewis & Clark Bicentennial: Putting Tribes Back on the Map." In *Lewis & Clark: Legacies, Memories, and New Perspectives*, edited by Kris Fresonke and Mark Spence, 265–273. Berkeley: University of California Press, 2004.

Conner, Roberta. "Our People Have Always Been Here." In *Lewis and Clark through Indian Eyes*, edited by Alvin M. Josephy, Jr., with Marc Jaffe, 85–119. New York, NY: Alfred A. Knopf, 2006.

Conner, Roberta. "Native Perspectives on Sustainability: Roberta Conner (Cayuse)." Transcript of an oral history conducted 2007 by D. E. Hall. Native Perspectives on Sustainability.

Conner, Roberta, and William L. Lang. "Early Contact and Incursion, 1700–1850." In *Wiyáx̣ayx̣t/Wiyáakaàawn/As Days Go By: Our History, Our Land, and Our People – The Cayuse, Umatilla, and Walla Walla*, 23–57. Pendleton, OR: Tamástslikt Cultural Institute; Portland: Oregon Historical Society Press; Seattle: University of Washington Press, 2006.

FURTHER READING

"2007 Ecotrust Indigenous Leadership Award: Awardee: Roberta (Bobbie) Conner." *Ecotrust*.

Abbott, Carl, Roberta Conner, William L. Lang, and Christopher Zinn. "Epilogue: A Conversation on the History of Lewis & Clark & the Bicentennial Commemoration of 2005." In *Two Centuries of Lewis and Clark: Reflections on the Voyage of Discovery*, ed. William L. Lang and Carl Abbott, 105–133. Portland: Oregon Historical Society Press, 2004.

Baer, April. "Stories Hidden from History: Roberta Conner." *State of Wonder*. Portland: Oregon Public Broadcasting, July 14, 2015.

Conner, Roberta. "TEDxPortland 2011 – Roberta Conner." YouTube video. Posted by TEDx Talks, June 30, 2011.

Contemporary Voices along the Lewis and Clark Trail. Directed by Sally Thompson. Big Sky Pictures, LLC, 2014

Hiers, Rebecca H. "Leadership from the Heart: One Tribe's Example." *Journal of Law and Religion* 26, no. 2 (2010–2011): 541–583.

Karson, Jennifer Marie. "Bringing It Home: Instituting Culture, Claiming History, and Managing Change in a Plateau Tribal Museum." PhD dissertation, University of Texas at Austin, 2007.

Korengel, Kathy. "Tamástslikt Director Wins Indigenous Leadership Prize." *Walla Walla Union-Bulletin*, September 27, 2007, A11.

Wandschneideer, Rich. "Bobbie Conner New Board Chair at NMAI." *Alvin M. and Betty Josephy Library of Western History and Culture*. Josephy Center for Arts and Culture. February 6, 2012.

Chapter Sixteen

Public Health Reformer

Susan La Flesche (b. 1865–d. 1915)

Robert D. Miller

Susan La Flesche, born in 1865 on the Omaha Reservation in Nebraska, was the daughter of Joseph La Flesche and Mary Gale. Joseph was the son of Joseph La Flesche, Sr., a French-Canadian fur trader and *Wa-tun-na*, a Ponca or an Omaha. Mary Gale was the daughter of Dr. John Gale and an Omaha woman named *Nicomi*. In 1853, Chief Young Elk held a public ceremony and adopted Joseph, naming him the heir to the chieftainship of the Elk Clan. Joseph La Flesche set a model that his daughter followed by supporting the adoption of "civilization" in order to preserve the Omaha community. He encouraged the Omaha to adopt Euro-American homes and agriculture while promoting education. Joseph ensured that his children received schooling to help them acquire the training they needed to be successful in a world dominated by settlers. Susan first attended a Presbyterian mission boarding school but once it closed, she transferred to a nearby Quaker day school. Susan La Flesche and her sister, Marguerite started attending the Elizabeth Institute for Young Ladies in Elizabeth, New Jersey, in September 1879—the same time in which Carlisle Indian Industrial School opened. After completing their studies in 1882, the two sisters returned home where Susan La Flesche found work teaching young children at the mission school.[1]

In 1884, Susan and Marguerite La Flesche traveled eastward to continue their education at the Hampton Normal and Agricultural Institute in Hampton, Virginia. General Samuel C. Armstrong had founded the Hampton Institute in 1868 in order to provide education to former slaves. In 1878, Hampton Institute expanded its focus to include American Indians after Lt. Richard Pratt brought twenty young men to the school. Though Pratt established a separate school for American Indians at Carlisle Barracks, Pennsylvania, the following year, Native students continued to attend Hampton Institute. Supporters of the school hoped that the presence of Native students might diminish white southerners' antipathy for the black students. Though off-reservation boarding schools typically prepared students for careers involving manual labor, both the school physician, Dr. Martha Waldron, and General Armstrong supported La Flesche's desire to pursue her academic education and acquire a medical degree. In May 1886, Susan La Flesche graduated from Hampton Institute as salutatorian.[2]

Dr. Waldron wrote a letter to her own alma mater, the Women's Medical College of Pennsylvania, to request admission and a scholarship for Susan. Though the school could not provide any funding for 1886, Sara Thompson Kinney, the President of the Connecticut Indian Association, helped finance Susan's education by convincing the organization to provide support for three years. Kinney secured government funding to help defray the cost as the federal government paid $167 per year for each American Indian attending boarding school. Kinney sought the same support for Susan and secured the endorsement of Commissioner of Indian Affairs John D. C. Atkins. Susan La Flesche spent the next three years at the Women's Medical College of Pennsylvania. While still a student, Susan provided medical advice to members of her family through the letters she sent home. Following her second year at the Women's Medical College, Susan returned to the Omaha Reservation for the summer to assist her ailing parents. During her stay, Susan tended to the field work, the management of the household, and provided medical care to members of her tribe. The Omahas greatly needed her services as a measles epidemic struck the reservation that summer. Limited access to medical care found on the Omaha Reservation—and most other reservations in the closing years of the nineteenth century—exacerbated the situation. Providing care to the members of her tribe helped to convince Susan of the need Indigenous people had for her medical services and her ability to teach them about health and hygiene.

In March 1889, Susan La Flesche graduated at the top of her class from the Women's Medical College and became the first American Indian woman to earn a medical degree in the United States. In June 1889, she wrote to the Commissioner of Indian Affairs to request appointment as the government physician for the Omaha Agency Indian School. Susan explained that her cultural background would benefit her as she could communicate in Omaha, and she understood the customs of her people. She began her work at the school in August of 1889 and by the end of the year, her work expanded to include the adults on the Omaha reservation. This appointment was important for the Omaha as the closest government physician maintained an office on the Winnebago Reservation, ten miles distant from the Omaha Reservation. La Flesche played an important role in extending healthcare to American Indian women as many of them were apprehensive about meeting with male Euro-

American doctors. As the Indian Service paid scant attention to the medical care available to American Indians, La Flesche drew upon her connections with eastern philanthropists to secure necessary supplies. At times, the dearth of medicine led her to gather local plants and herbs.[3]

Susan La Flesche spent the next four years serving her people as the government physician. She spent much of her time traveling over unimproved roads of the Omaha Reservation to aid tribal members. Her workload increased when epidemics spread through the reservation. For example, Susan visited over 130 patients in September 1891 during an influenza epidemic. The Omaha continued to suffer through the spring of 1892, prompting Susan to travel across the reservation in sub-zero temperatures. Through her laborious care for the sick, death rates remained low. For example, despite the freezing weather in December 1891, only a single patient succumbed to influenza.

In addition to her medical responsibilities, Susan assisted her sister, Marguerite, who taught at the government school. Though La Flesche labeled the children under her care as "backward," she simultaneously defended Native cultures by highlighting their positive attributes. For example, she informed the Connecticut Indian Association of the respect American Indians showed for their elders. La Flesche framed her arguments to appeal to the Victorian sensibilities of her Euro-American supporters. She furthered these arguments by emphasizing that many Omahas owned machinery or farming implements. She explained that few Omahas lived in tepees or wore traditional clothing and pointed to the work that educated Omahas found as farm hands or store clerks. Susan La Flesche knew that these jobs paid low wages and provided little room for advancement. However, her goal was to demonstrate that American Indians merited the respect and assistance of Euro-Americans. Such efforts were essential in the 1890s after the Wounded Knee Massacre demonstrated the destructive consequences of Euro-American fear of Native peoples. Consequently, La Flesche's familiarity with Euro-American cultural norms helped her to cast her community in a way that would garner their support.[4]

Susan's exhausting schedule took a toll on her health, prompting her to resign as the government physician for the Omaha in October 1893. Her medical problems dated back to her years in college, and she would suffer from maladies that caused her pain in the back of her neck for the rest of her life. She also contended with impaired hearing that would eventually result in deafness. In 1894 Susan married Henry Picotte from the Yankton Agency. Susan gave birth to two sons, Caryl and Pierre, and continued to practice medicine despite her ongoing health problems. Susan La Flesche helped to establish the Thurston County Medical Association and served on the Walthill

Health Board on several occasions. She was chairman of the State Health Committee of the Nebraska Federation of Women's Clubs for three years and devoted her time to urging the Nebraska legislature to pass bills relating to public health. She led efforts to raise public awareness about the housefly, tuberculosis, and the sharing of drinking cups.

One of La Flesche's main objectives was to reduce the deleterious impact of tuberculosis on her community. The "white plague" posed a threat to the Omaha as it left many tribal members weak and unable to fend off influenza or other ailments. The Indian Office made few efforts to limit the spread of tuberculosis until the end of the first decade of the twentieth century. Though medical discoveries from the early 1880s linked the cause of tuberculosis to a pathogen, public opinion continued to view tuberculosis as a hereditary condition. Commissioner William Jones shared the earlier understanding of the disease, thereby hindering efforts to limit the spread of tuberculosis on reservations. It was not until 1904 that an Office of Indian Affairs study convinced government officials of the pathology of tuberculosis. Furthermore, the government did not implement definitive policies to combat tuberculosis until Commissioner Robert Valentine designated Joseph Murphy as the first medical supervisor of the Indian Service during the presidency of William Howard Taft. Susan La Flesche's struggles to improve public health mirrored similar efforts undertaken across the United States during the Progressive Era. For example, the widespread acceptance of the validity of the germ theory promoted efforts to reduce sources of bacteria. Susan gave speeches explaining how individuals could limit the spread of tuberculosis by disposing of bodily discharges properly to limit the contamination of other individuals while eschewing the use of the common drinking cup. She also explained the dangers of the housefly and identified it as a major vector responsible for the spread of the tubercle bacillus.[5]

La Flesche's most significant medical accomplishment was the construction of a reservation hospital to serve the needs of her tribe. As La Flesche had grown skeptical of the federal government and realized she would receive little aid from it, she focused on raising private support for the project. In 1910, Susan approached the Presbyterian Home Mission Board and urged them to help fund the construction of the hospital in order to reduce high infant mortality rate on the reservation. She once more drew upon her knowledge of middle-class, Euro-American sentimentalities in order to frame the project in a manner that they would find appealing. Through the Presbyterian Home Mission Board, nearby churches, and local Omahas and Euro-Americans, Susan secured the necessary funds. Though the workers completed the structure of the building on schedule, Susan's poor health delayed the opening of the hospital.[6]

Throughout her life Susan La Flesche supported the temperance movement. Susan may have acquired her initial opposition to alcohol from her father who worked to suppress its usage after he became chief. Only after his death in 1888 did alcohol once again pose a significant problem for the Omaha. During her years in college, La Flesche attended lectures from prominent opponents of alcohol. She started to give speeches favoring temperance in 1891. La Flesche attacked alcoholism for bringing about the destruction of Omaha families and linked liquor to the economic hardships that her tribe faced on the reservation. La Flesche contended that men used the money they earned from leasing their land to purchase liquor rather than investing in tools or their homes. La Flesche also had a personal reason to support the temperance movement as a combination of tuberculosis and heavy drinking led to her husband's early death in 1905.

Le Flesche also opposed the usage of peyote as she saw it as detrimental to the health of her people upon its appearance on the Omaha reservation at the end of 1906 and the start of 1907. She urged the United States government to restrict the importation of peyote from Mexico. Despite her misgivings, La Flesche acknowledged the experiences of Omahas who credited peyote with curbing their usage of alcohol. Though La Flesche never publicly discussed the role of peyote in reviving Omaha customs, she increasingly focused on its usage to help her people remain sober. La Flesche's description of peyote as a tool to combat alcoholism continued her practice of framing her arguments in ways that would appeal to the broader public.

When La Flesche discussed alcoholism with Euro-American reformers, she emphasized the intransigence of liquor traders and explained that the Omahas had yet to learn all of the tricks that whites employed to cheat them. Susan thereby placed the blame for alcoholism on Euro-Americans, particularly saloon owners, while portraying American Indians as victims who desired sobriety. She chastised Euro-Americans who defended the right of American Indians to drink as citizens of the United States and emphasized the role that outsiders played in promoting drinking among American Indians. La Flesche's framing of the issue was important as she sought to counter arguments that linked Native health issues to notions of their supposed inferiority. Though Susan's stance on the prohibition of alcohol made her unpopular with members of her tribe, La Flesche's efforts derived from her desire to prevent the abuse of the Omahas and improve their health. Yet, Susan's opposition to alcohol extended beyond a desire for better health, for she also identified alcohol as a tool that Euro-Americans used to defraud American Indians of their land.[7]

Susan La Flesche did not limit her activism to the improvement of public health on the Omaha Reservation, for she also promoted greater economic independence for her people. Following the death of her husband, Susan encountered difficulties when attempting to assume control over Henry Picotte's allotment in South Dakota. The problems that La Flesche encountered raised questions about the benevolence of the federal government. As the federal government still held Henry Picotte's allotment in trust at the time of his death, assuming control of the land proved complicated. Even after the sale of the land, Susan encountered additional difficulties when she attempted to collect the money owed to herself and her children. She encountered further delays when she attempted to gain approval for the lease of her land parcels in Nebraska. Her experiences led her to realize that allotment, like alcohol, was another aspect of Euro-American society that brought harm to Native communities.

Susan La Flesche learned that she was not the only American Indian who faced such obstacles to securing inheritances or proceeds from the leasing or sale of allotment. The passage of the Omaha Allotment Act of 1882 created conditions that led to the dispossession of her people and restricted their economic choices. Proponents of allotment believed the policy would "Americanize" native populations by dividing up communal land holdings to promote individualism. The act included a provision which stipulated that the allotted lands would remain inalienable for a period of twenty-five years. The trust period would have ended in 1910 but the federal government unilaterally extended it for an additional ten years. The federal government justified its actions by arguing that American Indians lacked education and required the protection of the government.

Susan La Flesche countered these assertions by noting that the Omahas possessed a high literacy rate and explained that her people were capable of managing their own affairs. La Flesche cited cases where Omahas wanted to draw upon their money in order to pay for necessary medical treatments. The bureaucratic delays resulted in the deaths of tribal members before they received the necessary funds. She explained that the rejection of legitimate claims drove her people to turn to Euro-American moneylenders for the necessary funds. These individuals took advantage of the Omahas' condition and charged usurious rates. Easing restrictions on the leasing and sale of Indian lands would permit the Omahas to achieve greater financial security and limit the opportunities for Euro-Americans to take advantage of them.

Susan La Flesche took an active role in helping her people prove their competency by writing letters on their behalf. Susan also aided Omahas in their confrontations with Euro-American lessees who failed or refused to pay the rent they owed. The Omahas unanimously selected Susan as one of their delegates to present their objection to the extension of the trust period to the Secretary of the Interior and the United States Attorney General. Though

Susan expressed misgivings about taking the job due to her poor health, she met with the Secretary of the Interior on February 7, 1910. Susan's testimony helped to secure the necessary authorization to permit most of the Omahas to lease their lands and receive their payments.[8]

Her efforts had little to do with promoting assimilation but centered on her desire to defend the autonomy, sovereignty, and freedom of her people to manage their land as they saw fit. Unfortunately, the result of the policies she advocated deprived the Omahas of their land but this was not Susan La Flesche's goal. She wanted the Omaha to have the liberty to manage their own property so that they could procure the funds necessary to start businesses, build homes, pay bills, and educate their children. The federal government's inability to defend Native interests left La Flesche little reason to continue to place faith in its promises or claims regarding its benevolent paternalism. In addition, La Flesche realized that the designation of American Indians as incompetent bolstered notions of racial inferiority. Disposing of the federal government's paternalistic policies would indicate that the Omaha were just as capable and deserving of independence as Euro-Americans. La Flesche's decision to support the removal of restrictions on allotments reflected the difficult circumstances that American Indians faced during the early years of the twentieth century. Susan had to find a way to protect members of her tribe from fraud while simultaneously reducing the detrimental presence of the federal government.

In Susan La Flesche's final years, her declining health led her to refuse requests for medical care from Euro-Americans so that she could save her strength to help members of her tribe. In 1915, La Flesche passed away due to bone cancer. Her career focused on improving public health on the Omaha Reservation and providing her tribe with better access to medical care. Though she counseled the Omahas to assimilate into American society, she also worked to educate Euro-Americans about positive aspects of Omaha culture while countering popular views of American Indians as backwards. Through her usage of the rhetoric of "civilization," Susan La Flesche attempted to demonstrate the accomplishments of her people on terms that her Euro-American contemporaries could understand. Susan La Flesche was thereby able to use her education and her assimilation of Euro-American norms in order to benefit the lives of the Omaha.

NOTES

1. Sarah Pripas-Kapit, "'We Have Lived on Broken Promises': Charles A. Eastman, Susan La Flesche Picotte, and the Politics of American Indian Assimilation during the Progressive Era," *Great Plains Quarterly* 35, no. 1 (Winter 2015): 55–56;

Valerie Sherer Mathes, "Susan LaFlesche Picotte, M.D.: Nineteenth-Century Physician and Reformer" *Great Plains Quarterly* 13, no. 3 (Summer 1993): 172–173.

2. Joe Starita, *A Warrior of the People: How Susan La Flesche Overcame Racial
and Gender Inequality to Become America's First Indian Doctor* (New York: St.
Martin's Griffin, 2018), 84–107.

3. Mathes, 177; Starita 158–189; Benson Tong, *Susan La Flesche Picotte, M.D.:
Omaha Indian Leader and Reformer* (Norman: University of Oklahoma Press, 1999),
87–103.

4. Malea D. Powell, "Down by the River, or How Susan La Flesche Picotte Can
Teach Us about Alliance as a Practice of Survivance," *College English* 67, no. 1 (Sept.
2004): 55.

5. Mathes, 179–181; Pripas-Kapit 69–73.

6. Pripas-Kapit, 71–73; Starita, 261–266

7. Pripas-Kapit, 66–69; Starita, 190–223; Tong, 106–146.

8. Mathes, 18–181; Powell 56; Pripas-Kapti, 67–69; Tong, 159–173.

BIBLIOGRAPHY

Mathes, Valerie. "Susan LaFlesche Picotte, M.D.: Nineteenth Century Physician and
    Reformer." *Great Plains Quarterly* 13. No. 13 (Summer 1993): 172–186.
Powell, Malea. "Down by the River, or How Susan La Flesche Picotte Can Teach Us
    about Alliance as a Practice of Survivance." *College English* 67, no. 1 (September
    2004): 38–60.
Pripras-Kapit, Sarah. "'We Have Lived on Broken Promises': Charles Eastman, Su-
    san La Flesche Picotte, and the Politics of American Indian Assimilation during the
    Progressive Era." *Great Plains Quarterly* 35, no. 1 (Winter 2015): 51–78.
Starita, Joe. *A Warrior of the People: How Susan La Flesche Overcame Racial and
    Gender Inequality to Become America's First Indian Doctor*. New York: St. Mar-
    tin's Griffin, 2018.
Tong, Benson. *Susan La Flesche Picotte, M.D.: Omaha Indian Leader and Reformer*.
    Norman: University of Oklahoma Press, 1999.

FURTHER READING

Mathes, Valerie. "Susan LaFlesche Picotte, M.D.: Nineteenth Century Physician and
    Reformer." *Great Plains Quarterly* 13. No. 13 (Summer 1993): 172–186.
Mathes, Valerie. "Dr. Susan LaFlesche Picotte: The Reformed and the Reformer."
    *Indian Lives: Essays on Nineteenth- and Twentieth-Century Native American
    Leaders*, eds. L.G. Moses and Raymond Wilson. Albuquerque: University of New
    Mexico Press, 1985.
Powell, Malea. "Down by the River, or How Susan La Flesche Picotte Can Teach Us
    about Alliance as a Practice of Survivance." *College English* 67, no. 1 (September
    2004): 38–60.

Pripras-Kapit, Sarah. "'We Have Lived on Broken Promises': Charles Eastman, Susan La Flesche Picotte, and the Politics of American Indian Assimilation during the Progressive Era." *Great Plains Quarterly* 35, no. 1 (Winter 2015): 51–78.

Starita, Joe. *A Warrior of the People: How Susan La Flesche Overcame Racial and Gender Inequality to Become America's First Indian Doctor.* New York: St. Martin's Griffin, 2018.

Tong, Benson. *Susan La Flesche Picotte, M.D.: Omaha Indian Leader and Reformer.* Norman: University of Oklahoma Press, 1999.

Chapter Seventeen

Navajo Health Activist and Educator

Annie Dodge Wauneka (b. 1910–d. 1997)

Brendan Lindsay

On April 11, 1910, the woman some would later call the "Legendary Mother of the Navajo Nation" was born.[1] In her lifetime, Annie Dodge Wauneka was a vital, sometimes intimidating force for saving and improving the lives of the Navajo people. A true activist, she was involved in everything to do with the health, welfare, and sovereignty of her people, approaching the problems of the Navajo people as ones inescapably interrelated. Her impressive record of achievement was one founded upon a commitment to education. She approached all problems from an assumed position of ignorance, then engaged in intense study, research, and community dialogues to find answers for these problems, subsequently implementing these solutions in public campaigns to educate her people and offer them workable resolutions in a way that remained consistent with the Navajo worldview. Her methods developed during her youth, as she lived with and observed her prominent father in action.

Annie Dodge was born in a Navajo hogan to the third wife of Henry Chee Dodge on the Navajo Reservation. After living nearly a year away from him, she was moved to live with her father at the age of eight months.[2] Henry Chee Dodge was a prominent leader of the *Diné*, the People, as the Navajo call themselves. Henry Chee Dodge was the last head chief and first elected tribal chairman of the Navajo, the possessor of great wealth in the form of land and herd animals, a famous former interpreter for the United States Army, and a veteran of the Long Walk. Annie Dodge's early experiences with her father and his home helped shape her activism and mission on behalf of the Navajo for the rest of her life.[3]

In her father's household, Annie Dodge became schooled in the workings of two worlds blended together: the traditional Navajo way and the ways of whites that were well known to her father. As befitted custom, she was a sheepherder from an early age and responsible for caring for part of her father's herds. But she also experienced the workings of tribal politics while living within the walls of a clapboard-sided multistory home, rather than in a traditional Navajo log-built hogan. Henry Chee Dodge spoke both English and the Navajo language, and his daughter picked up both languages with facility. Perhaps because Henry Chee Dodge had no formal education and because of his intimate knowledge of the challenges of Indian-white relations, he valued schooling greatly, and saw to it that his daughter went away to a government boarding school at Fort Defiance at the age of eight years. She would build upon her basic knowledge of English in school and develop a talent with the spoken word, in both English and her native tongue. And she developed new skills, as well, ones gained through grim experiences that would shape her mission in life.[4]

While in grade school, young Annie Dodge first experienced the terrible problems associated with the diseases that increasingly afflicted her people. In 1918, the Great Influenza Epidemic struck her boarding school and the Navajo reservation, claiming the lives of thousands of her people, including many of her classmates. After recovering from a mild case of the disease, Annie Dodge began nursing her sick schoolmates in support of the single, overwhelmed government nurse assigned to the school. She helped by feeding, bathing, and tending her ill classmates, some of whom died. Not long after the influenza epidemic subsided, a trachoma outbreak struck the school, adding more lessons to her grim practical education of disease. Unbeknownst to the young Annie Dodge, these horrible experiences would be the foundation of her life's work and service to her people.[5]

Following completion of the eleventh grade, Annie Dodge left school to work in her father's household. But her practical education did not cease. Given her fine command of English, she often accompanied her father to important tribal gatherings and meetings with government officials from the Bureau of Indian Affairs. She worked informally as a translator in support of her father and her people. She became well-versed in many of the pressing issues that confronted Navajo people, both on and off the reservation. Henry Chee Dodge often reiterated to his daughter that her mission should be one of service to the community of her people. Her father made decisions that affected the lives of thousands of people, and she learned much by his example. She learned that what was right and what was popular were not always of a piece.[6]

In particular, Henry Chee Dodge's backing of the federal government's mandatory stock reductions of Navajo herds must have made a lasting impression. Thousands of animals were slaughtered by federal officials to prevent an overgrazing disaster on the reservation. But many Navajo resented this mightily, not understanding the larger ecological implications or the reasoning behind the reductions. Henry Chee Dodge worked to explain the stock reductions in ways that his fellow Navajo could understand them. He supported the policy, despite its unpopularity. Annie Dodge aided her father by helping translate not simply words, but concepts related to the reductions—to make sense of ideas and concepts that were completely foreign to the worldviews of the Navajo. Even after marrying George Wauneka, Annie Dodge Wauneka continued in her role of translator, eventually going in new directions, directions in which she could serve her people best.[7]

As Carolyn Niethammer has argued, Annie Dodge Wauneka's great value to her people was as an interpreter of language, culture, and ideas, a cultural bridge between diverse peoples and worldviews. This bridge had the foundations of its span in two worlds.[8] On one side, the Navajo Nation was in the violent throes of life in a twentieth century dominated by primarily white neighbors and their state and federal government, holding sway over them as wards or domestic, dependent nations. Although Navajo people had the largest population of the Native American tribes of North America and housed within the ostensibly safe boundaries of the massive Navajo reservation, the wounds of the nineteenth century remained unhealed and many threats existed, old and new.[9]

Some of these threats were only being fully realized in the twentieth century, particularly the problems of a shrunken land base and problems attendant to the encroachment of non-Indians on the lands of the Southwest. Many of these problems were totally alien to the Navajo, as evidenced by the absence in the Navajo language of words even to describe them. On the other side, white United States government officials struggled to implement paternalistic policies to preserve what remained of Native American peoples after the bloody nineteenth century.[10] Many well-meaning federal officials made policies they hoped would save Indians, only to meet frustration born of ineffectiveness, ineptitude, ignorance, or apathy. Many of these solutions made perfect sense to the officials, and were born of a clear, concise logic, and seemed to present surefire answers to the problems of Indian affairs. Yet, many policies failed, and great harm often ensued. Many officials could not make sense of these failures. Annie Dodge Wauneka's entrance into Navajo political life in 1951 would help bridge this gap and elevate the level of understanding between Navajo and non-Navajo over the next three decades.[11] But it was often a mission strewn with obstacles and setbacks, one that bucked tradition and trespassed on the feelings, egos, and self-interests of others.

Navajo tradition did not include women as political leaders of the people. Women had important roles including caretakers of the land and families, and in ownership of herds and hogans. But men dominated tribal leadership. In her 1951 election to the Navajo Tribal Council, Annie Dodge Wauneka became the only woman on the council. She refused to be silenced or intimidated by the male-dominated body.[12] Her initial path in Navajo politics was chosen for her when she was appointed to head the Health Committee for the council. Wauneka was not chosen because of her early experiences with nursing or epidemics, but because she was female; women bear much of the burden for caring for the sick in Navajo culture. Nonetheless, a better match between person and purpose could not have been made, given her experiences as a girl and her now-deceased father's wishes for her to serve her people.[13]

Wauneka's informal training as a nurse helped her confront one of the great challenges to Navajo existence in the twentieth century, tuberculosis. Tuberculosis is an airborne bacterial infection that typically attacks the lungs of a victim, although some strains can attack the skin, organs, or other systems in the body. Tuberculosis did not exist among the Navajo prior to the arrival of Euro-Americans in the Southwest; the Navajo had no antibodies to tuberculosis in their immune systems and traditional Navajo medicine had no treatments that effectively dealt with the disease. Indeed, the Navajo, like other Native Americans, had no conception of microorganisms such as bacteria in their worldview, and no words or concepts for germs or microorganisms in their language and culture. Wauneka explained the disease to the Navajo in ways that made sense to them, culturally. This was not an easy process, however. Traditionally, medicine people are responsible for treating the ailments of the Navajo, and many people were reluctant to adopt Western medicine in place of their own, especially the medicine people. Wauneka worked to bridge the gap between these two medicine ways. In this she succeeded where many non-Navajo outsiders had failed previously.[14]

Wauneka founded her campaign on education, beginning with herself. In a strategy she would frequently repeat, she approached tuberculosis by first educating herself as thoroughly as possible. With the help of federal government doctors and nurses, Wauneka familiarized herself with tuberculosis, its causes and cure. She learned about the disease from the standpoint of Western medical doctors.[15]

Wauneka understood that traditional Navajo medicine was holistic in its approach. It treated mind, body, and spirit. Wauneka worked to convince her people that Navajo medicine was ineffective in dealing with that part of the disease that afflicted the body. She educated her people about germs, bacteria, and the transmission and symptoms of tuberculosis. Her main argument to convince her people to change was that tuberculosis was not a Navajo disease, but one that came from the outside world and in need of treatments from that world as well. She proposed a blending of indigenous medicine and Western medicine to treat the sickness, a solution that allowed preservation of Navajo medicine rather than its marginalization. Wauneka engaged the assistance of traditional Navajo medicine men in her campaign. She convinced them that patients needed both the help of Navajo medicine men and medical doctors to beat the disease. She got Navajo medicine men to refer patients for treatment by medical doctors, in conjunction with their own treatments. This was particularly important in admitting the sick into hospitals; many Navajo feared hospitals as places where one went to die. She brought white doctors together with the medicine men. Using her observations of their dialogue, and her education at the hands of public health officials, she created a Navajo-English, English-Navajo medical dictionary to help caregivers and patients communicate. In many cases, Wauneka created words and phrases in Navajo to describe symptoms, treatments, and other medical terminologies heretofore unknown in the Navajo language.[16]

Wauneka also worked directly to aid in getting patients into hospitals and treated. She traveled widely on the reservation, giving talks, meeting with the sick and their families, and encouraging Navajo to get tested for tuberculosis or seek treatment when ill. Wauneka traveled extensively on the reservation, talking to her people about proper hygienic and sanitary practices in the hogan. Hogans had dirt floors, no indoor plumbing, no electricity, no heating or refrigeration units, and poor ventilation. These conditions contributed to the prevalence of tuberculosis and other diseases among Navajo living in hogans. She attempted to instruct her people on how to change their everyday lifestyles to prevent conditions conducive to diseases. She had to be careful in her instruction: how one lives is an extremely personal matter, and she had to be careful not to give offense. Indeed, some did not care for her advice or her opinions of their living arrangements.[17]

Wauneka also helped bring doctors onto the reservation, expand public health services, and work to increase public health screening exams. She even starred in two films, government-funded productions on Indian health, created to disseminate information about health and disease. Wauneka used radio broadcasts in Navajo to reach the people of the massive reservation, hosting a weekly Sunday morning radio program for over two years focused on issues related to health. Wauneka described the show in an interview: "I talked about everything under the sun about health that pertains to my People. I went with the cycle of the weather . . . in the winter I'd be talking about pneumonia: how to take care of yourself, how you must be dressed; and then when the spring came, I'd talk about flies and diarrhea."[18] Her instruction included proper techniques to promote good health: boiling water to ensure potability, dishwashing, bathing, and food safety were among numerous topics covered. She encouraged her people to take an interest in serving the health needs of their communities, a message that many took to heart; at the height of her popularity and influence in the early 1970s, almost 75 percent of nursing staffs at Indian Health Service hospitals on the reservation were Navajo. She also helped establish a "health visitor" program that sent trained public health workers out to Navajo homesteads on the reservation to check for disease and provide counsel about living conditions.[19] Her efforts produced dramatic results.

Rates of tuberculosis began to decline on the reservation, as did infant mortality rates (children often dying of the tubercle bacteria). She had managed to convince over 20,000 Navajo to obtain tuberculosis screening X-rays to identify those infected; approximately 10 percent of those screened had to be immediately hospitalized.[20] And more and more pregnant women sought prenatal care and birthed their babies in hospital, helping to reduce complications and deaths associated with childbirth and reducing infant mortality. Not satisfied, she sought tribal funding to retrofit hogans with hard floors to increase the health of the occupants. This was controversial, and initially rejected by the tribal government. Eventually, she convinced the tribe to establish a small fund to subsidize retrofits, although some critics charged that it was unnecessary.

In what would eventually become dozens of trips to Washington, DC, she lobbied Congress, met with officials, and sought aid and funding from the federal government to help her people. The Indian Health Service and the federal government began to fund free clinics and hospitals on the reservation, increasing the likelihood of Navajos seeking out non-traditional medicine for illnesses. This made free healthcare available to all Navajo on the reservation. Despite these and later successes, she met frequent opposition, and tuberculosis and other prevalent maladies were not overcome at once. She had to battle tradition: the traditional role of women that she challenged in her efforts and ideas, the traditions of Navajo medicine that she sought to augment with Western medicine, and the everyday traditions of Navajo life. Indeed, despite the decline in rates of tuberculosis, 50 percent of those diagnosed with the disease still refused treatment. In an extremely unpopular and controversial move, Wauneka called for involuntary treatments of those refusing aid voluntarily. Although initially resisted, the Navajo Tribal Council eventually relented, leading to even greater declines in the disease.[21]

Wauneka's successful efforts in reducing the instances, mortality, and misery of tuberculosis among the Navajo drew national recognition, including her selection to receive the Presidential Medal of Freedom, the highest peacetime award a civilian may receive. Selected by President John F. Kennedy prior to his assassination, she received the medal from President Lyndon B. Johnson on December 6, 1963, in recognition of "her long crusade for improved health programs [through which] she has helped dramatically to lessen the menace of disease among her people and to improve their way of life." As the citation for her award suggests, Wauneka's crusade to improve the health of her people extended far beyond tuberculosis. She mounted campaigns to improve prenatal and infant health, fight alcoholism, and prevent the spread of other diseases, such as trachoma and dysentery among the Navajo—all problems that had severe, sometimes mortal consequences for members of the tribe. Many of these campaigns again led her in unpopular directions for some of the Navajo.[22]

The rates of alcoholism on the reservation were high and posed a major problem for the Navajo. Again, Wauneka approached the problem by first educating herself on alcoholism. As with tuberculosis and other diseases on the reservation, Wauneka had some personal experiences to build upon, including several family members who had struggled with drinking problems. Still, what she learned dismayed her. She learned that the high rate of alcoholism on the reservation had many factors underlying it, including social and economic causes. The consequences were also far-ranging: significant numbers of auto accidents, child abuse cases, and instances of violence were alcohol related. By 1962, she was fighting to educate her people about alcoholism as a disease. As with the causes of tuberculosis, eradicating alcoholism was not simply limited to fighting the disease itself, but also wiping out those root causes that led to heavy drinking, and sometimes addiction. As alcohol consumption and alcoholism can be intensely personal matters, Wauneka found many opponents for her views. Drinking by council members was not uncommon, including being intoxicated during council sessions, even though sale and consumption of alcohol were illegal on the reservation. Many members resented her chastisements of drinkers and her teetotaling. Nonetheless, the council appointed her to head the tribe's committee on alcoholism. Wauneka discovered that many Navajo thought drunkenness was not a serious issue. She implored the council to recognize the complexity of the problem and to fund and promote educational and treatment campaigns. Unlike tuberculosis, though, alcoholism continued to be a problem on the reservation despite her best efforts. In 1975, Wauneka noted with frustration that alcoholism was the foremost killer on the Navajo Reservation. Even after her passing, significant problems with drinking and alcoholism persisted on the reservation and still exist today.[23]

Wauneka also campaigned against the legalization of peyote on the reservation beginning in 1963. Peyote had been banned on the reservation for decades, but some on the reservation called for legalization. This put her into conflict with many on the reservation, including the newly elected tribal chairman, Raymond Nakai, who had been elected on a platform promoting the legal use of peyote. A psychotropic drug created from a cactus species of the Southwest, peyote was not traditionally used by the Navajo. It was introduced among them in the twentieth century, especially in conjunction with the spread of the Native American Church onto the Navajo Reservation. In her anti-drug position, Wauneka was typical of traditionalists on the reservation known as the Old Guard. They resisted the introduction of the mind-altering and potentially dangerous drug by non-traditionalists like Nakai and his supporters. The debate created a serious rift between Wauneka and Nakai, who refused to reappoint Wauneka to the Health Committee despite her prominence and effectiveness. Still, she managed to prevent the legalization of peyote on the reservation.[24]

By the 1960s, her mission to educate her people about their health and welfare, perhaps logically, morphed into activism related to education policy itself. Wauneka helped found the Navajo Area School Board Association in 1969 and Navajo Community College (Diné College). The goal of Wauneka and the association was to promote Navajo control of educational programs for Navajo children. True to her previous methods, she investigated the problems of education closely. She visited schools, talked with students, and evaluated for herself the needs of the schools and children. Wauneka learned that many children lived in such poverty that they lacked the proper clothing to even attend school. She worked successfully to get the Tribal Council to appropriate funds to help children buy proper clothing. She was also an early advocate of preschools and the Head Start program. Although educated at boarding schools in her youth, Wauneka fought for a transition to day schools for Navajo children, rather than the boarding schools that had been traditional for decades. This kept families together, and children in school.[25]

Wauneka also led by example, finishing out her own schooling by attending the University of Arizona and earning a bachelor's degree in public health. Perhaps most important in her crusade to improve Navajo education was her impact on the young people she met in her travels and investigations. Many prominent tribal leaders have credited Wauneka with having an early, positive impact on their lives and the paths they chose, specifically her demand that Navajo young people properly educate themselves. She insisted that children do their best, stay in school, and serve their people. For Wauneka, the future of the Navajo depended upon education. Without proper schooling, she believed, the Navajo's ability to "communicate with the outside world" would be diminished, the economy would continue to deteriorate, and the tribe would suffer. With proper education, the Navajo could do more for themselves, avoid outside interference, and recover their independence.[26] Despite the apathy of many Navajo regarding formal education for their children, Wauneka worked diligently to convince her people that in the two worlds the Navajo existed in, Western-style education was paramount to preserving Navajo Nation and tradition.[27] For her work, she was appointed to the Board of Trustees for Navajo Community College, today known as Diné College.

Like many American women in the 1970s, Wauneka was active in the women's rights movement, both on and off the reservation. She believed that the link between tribal sovereignty and self-determination and the rights of women were inextricably connected. Her perspective was one informed by decades of work within tribal government and life on the reservation and refined in meetings she held to investigate the issues of Navajo women. She learned from these meetings that housing, health problems (especially alcoholism), and lack of job opportunities for women were the key concerns of Navajo women. When she presented her findings to the Tribal Council, she found some Navajo men critical and unsympathetic to her findings. Some men suggested that she should know her proper place and leave well enough alone. Wauneka believed such attitudes were, at heart, a product of the troubles for her entire people: the influence of non-Indian culture, economics, and politics. She argued that Indian-white relations had introduced a more male-dominated view of gender relations to the Navajo, one that made Navajo women "second-class citizens" where they had not been before. Wauneka, in an address to the Southwest Indian Women's Conference in 1975, urged Native American women to "become more active in politics and become aware of the educational opportunities open to Native American women" in order to regain their proper places in their communities. However, she counseled Indian women to seek in a way that was sensitive and true to their cultures: "Basic beliefs must remain unchanged," she said, arguing for women to regain their traditional places rather than complete equality that some women were seeking in the 1970s. In this, Wauneka echoed the complexity of the question of identity confronting Native American women throughout the United States in the late twentieth century.[28]

Her battles with the tribal council extended beyond the issues of policy regarding health, education, and the role of women, to attacking the corruption on the tribal council that became prevalent in the 1970s. This, too, drew national attention. In 1976, Wauneka published a report as part of her service on a national committee on women. The report, republished in an abridged form in a nationally circulated Native American newspaper, focused on the continued progress of Indian peoples gaining tribal self-determination. Nothing could more easily derail Navajo self-determination and sovereignty than corruption. Wauneka and likeminded Navajo protesters marched in protest of corruption on the Navajo Tribal Council, particularly the crimes of Chairman Peter MacDonald. On May 18, 1976, Wauneka and hundreds of other protesters staged a demonstration outside the tribal council chambers and sent in a delegation with demands for investigation and reform. Although MacDonald dismissed the protesters as "vigilantes" and denied their allegations, he and others were federally indicted and convicted for their corruption. While the accusations of the protesters proved true, in the short-term, Wauneka lost her seat on the tribal council in 1978. By this time, Wauneka was the most prominent woman on the reservation, well-known in the halls of federal and state governments, and criticized by many, especially prior to MacDonald's conviction. Clearly, her prominence, forthright manner, and media attention had generated resentment among some of the tribe. Following her defeat, she did not seek elected office again, although she worked to help elect other candidates and serve in an advisory role to the tribal government.[29]

Despite the controversies she had involved herself in the 1960s and 1970s, during the 1980s, many Navajo recognized her with honors in retirement. In 1984, on "Annie Wauneka Day," she received the Navajo Medal of Honor for her life's work on behalf of her people, the tribe's highest award and the honor she cherished above all others. The tribe also created a scholarship in her name. Many regional and national awards followed.[30]

In 1997, Annie Dodge Wauneka died at the age of 87 from Alzheimer's disease. Her death drew national attention, including coverage in the *Los Angeles Times* and *New York Times*.[31] Her example of activism and service founded upon education was a powerful one, cited by many Navajo as being prominent in their own decision to serve their people. Kelsey Begaye, Speaker of the Navajo National Council, encouraged young people to study Annie Dodge Wauneka's life and emulate her example of service to her people. "Because of her work and dedication to the Navajo people," Begaye stated, "we have a better way of life here on the Navajo nation."[32] Her legacy to her people was better health, founded on a commitment to education and predicated on the idea that all issues for her people were interrelated ones needing resolution, first and foremost, by the Navajo themselves. As Begaye put it, "We can proudly call her our Mother because for so many years, she took care of us."

In 2000, the National Women's Hall of Fame at Seneca Falls, New York, inducted Annie Dodge Wauneka into its illustrious ranks for her achievements in science and public health; an honor which the Navajo Nation celebrated as a sign of respect for both Wauneka, as an individual, and the Nation, as a whole.[33]

NOTES

1. Cynthia R. Kasee, "Annie Dodge Wauneka," in Sharon Malinowski, ed., *Notable Native Americans* (Detroit: Gale Research, Inc., 1995), 453.

2. Kasee, "Annie Dodge Wauneka," in Sharon Malinowski, ed., *Notable Native Americans* (Detroit: Gale Research, Inc., 1995), 453.

3. Catherine A. Clay, "Henry Chee Dodge," in Sharon Malinowski, ed., *Notable Native Americans* (Detroit: Gale Research, Inc., 1995), 127–129.

4. Clay, "Henry Chee Dodge," in Sharon Malinowski, ed., *Notable Native Americans* (Detroit: Gale Research, Inc., 1995), 127–129; Kasee, "Annie Dodge Wauneka," in Sharon Malinowski, ed., *Notable Native Americans* (Detroit: Gale Research, Inc., 1995), 453–454.

5. Helen M. Bannan, "Wauneka, Annie Dodge," in Donald L. Fixico, ed., *Treaties with American Indians: An Encyclopedia of Rights, Conflicts, and Sovereignty* (New York: ABC-CLIO, 2007), 912, ProQuest Ebook Central; Carolyn Niethammer, *I'll Go and Do More: Annie Dodge Wauneka, Navajo Leader and Activist* (Lincoln: University of Nebraska Press, 2001), 27–32; Kasee, "Annie Dodge Wauneka," in Sharon Malinowski, ed., *Notable Native Americans* (Detroit: Gale Research, Inc., 1995), 453.

6. Niethammer, *I'll Go and Do More: Annie Dodge Wauneka, Navajo Leader and Activist* (Lincoln: University of Nebraska Press, 2001), 53–62.

7. Kasee, "Annie Dodge Wauneka," in Sharon Malinowski, ed., *Notable Native Americans* (Detroit: Gale Research, Inc., 1995), 453; Niethammer, *"I'll Go and Do More": Annie Dodge Wauneka, Navajo Leader and Activist"* (Lincoln: University of Nebraska Press, 2001), 46–68.

8. For a discussion of Wauneka serving as a cultural bridge, see Niethammer, *I'll Go and Do More: Annie Dodge Wauneka, Navajo Leader and Activist* (Lincoln: University of Nebraska Press, 2001); Mary Carroll Nelson, *Annie Wauneka: The Story of an American Indian* (Minneapolis: Dillon Press, 1972); and Sally Zanjani, *Two Native Daughters of Substance: Sarah Winnemucca and Annie Dodge Wauneka* (Lincoln: University of Nebraska Press, 2001).

9. Cynthia Kasee, "Wauneka, Annie Dodge," in Gretchen M. Bataillie, ed., *Native American Women: A Biographical Dictionary* (New York: Garland, 1993), 274–275.

10. Clifford E. Trafzer, *The Kit Carson Campaign: The Last Great Navajo War* (Norman: University of Oklahoma Press, 1982), 198–223. See the testimony of Diné people in the first-person accounts of the Long Walk and its aftermath in Ruth Roessel, *Navajo Stories of the Long Walk Period* (Tsaile: Navajo Community College Press, 1973).

11. Niethammer, *I'll Go and Do More: Annie Dodge Wauneka, Navajo Leader and Activist* (Lincoln: University of Nebraska Press, 2001), xi–xii, xxiii, 75–77.

12. There is some debate concerning whether Annie Dodge Wauneka was the first woman elected to the tribal council. According to Wauneka's biographer, Carolyn Niethammer, it is often written that Annie Dodge Wauneka was the first woman elected to the Navajo Tribal Council, however, that distinction belongs to Lily J. Neil; see Niethammer, *I'll Go and Do More: Annie Dodge Wauneka, Navajo Leader and Activist* (Lincoln: University of Nebraska Press, 2001), 76. Yet, even today, many Navajo believe it was Wauneka; see, for example, stories in the *Navajo Times*, dating from the 1970s to the 2010s.

13. Kasee, "Wauneka, Annie Dodge," in Gretchen M. Bataillie, ed., *Native American Women: A Biographical Dictionary* (New York: Garland, 1993), 274; Kasee, "Annie Dodge Wauneka," in Sharon Malinowski, ed., *Notable Native Americans* (Detroit: Gale Research, Inc., 1995), 454.

14. Robert A. Trennert, *White Man's Medicine: Government Doctors and the Navajo, 1863–1955* (Albuquerque: University of New Mexico Press, 1998), 213–217.

15. Niethammer, *I'll Go and Do More: Annie Dodge Wauneka, Navajo Leader and Activist* (Lincoln: University of Nebraska Press, 2001), 80–85, 90–96, 98–102, 116–119.

16. Robert T. Bergman, "Navajo Health Services and Projects," in Alfonso Ortiz, ed., *Handbook of North American Indians: Southwest* 10 (Washington, DC: Smithsonian Institution Press, 1983), 634, 676–768.

17. Bergman, "Navajo Health Services and Projects," in Alfonso Ortiz, ed., *Handbook of North American Indians: Southwest* 10 (Washington, DC: Smithsonian Institution Press, 1983), 634, 676–678.

18. Liz Sonneborn, *A to Z of American Indian Women*, Revised Edition (New York: Infobase, 2007), 266.

19. Niethammer, *I'll Go and Do More: Annie Dodge Wauneka, Navajo Leader and Activist* (Lincoln: University of Nebraska Press, 2001), 108, 104–122.

20. Sonneborn, *A to Z of American Indian Women*, Revised Edition (New York: Infobase, 2007), 265–266.

21. Kasee, "Annie Dodge Wauneka," in Sharon Malinowski, ed., *Notable Native Americans* (Detroit: Gale Research, Inc., 1995), 454; Trennert, *White Man's Medicine: Government Doctors and the Navajo, 1863–1955* (Albuquerque: University of New Mexico Press, 1998), 213–217.

22. Kasee, "Annie Dodge Wauneka," in Sharon Malinowski, ed., *Notable Native Americans* (Detroit: Gale Research, Inc., 1995), 454.

23. Kasee, "Annie Dodge Wauneka," in Sharon Malinowski, ed., *Notable Native Americans* (Detroit: Gale Research, Inc., 1995), 454; Niethammer, *I'll Go and Do More: Annie Dodge Wauneka, Navajo Leader and Activist* (Lincoln: University of Nebraska Press, 2001), 125–127.

24. Niethammer, *"I'll Go and Do More": Annie Dodge Wauneka, Navajo Leader and Activist"* (Lincoln: University of Nebraska Press, 2001), 128–130, 153, 210, 247.

25. Kasee, "Annie Dodge Wauneka," in Sharon Malinowski, ed., *Notable Native Americans* (Detroit: Gale Research, Inc., 1995), 454; Niethammer, *"I'll Go and Do More": Annie Dodge Wauneka, Navajo Leader and Activist"* (Lincoln: University of Nebraska Press, 2001), 163–166.

26. An Interview with Dr. Annie Dodge Wauneka, in National Commission on the Observance of International Women's Year, *". . . to Form a More Perfect Union . . .": Justice for American Women: Report of the National Commission on the Observance of International Women's Year* (Washington, D.C.: U.S. Department of State, 1976), 74–77.

27. Niethammer, *"I'll Go and Do More": Annie Dodge Wauneka, Navajo Leader and Activist"* (Lincoln: University of Nebraska Press, 2001), 78, 161–63, 168, 213, 230–31, 237, 246.

28. Shirley Hill Witt, "An Interview with Dr. Annie Dodge Wauneka," *Frontiers: A Journal of Women's Studies* 6, no. 3 (Autumn 1981): 66–67; Niethammer, *"I'll Go and Do More": Annie Dodge Wauneka, Navajo Leader and Activist* (Lincoln: University of Nebraska Press, 2001), 206-208, 245.

29. Niethammer, *I'll Go and Do More: Annie Dodge Wauneka, Navajo Leader and Activist* (Lincoln: University of Nebraska Press, 2001), 205–206, 238–240, 247.

30. Niethammer, *I'll Go and Do More: Annie Dodge Wauneka, Navajo Leader and Activist* (Lincoln: University of Nebraska Press, 2001), 209–210, 215, 247–248.

31. "Annie Dodge Wauneka; Navajo Leader Won Freedom Medal," *Los Angeles Times*, November 12, 1997; Wolfgang Saxon, "Annie D. Wauneka, Dies; Navajo Medical Crusader," *New York Times*, November 16, 1997.

32. Kelsey A. Begaye, "Be Proud of Your 'Mother,'" *Navajo Times*, July 13, 1997. Begaye later became President of the Navajo Nation.

33. National Women's Hall of Fame, "Annie Dodge Wauneka," accessed September 28, 2021, https://www.womenofthehall.org/inductee/annie-dodge-wauneka/; Kelsey A. Begaye, "During the Holidays, the Nation Has Much to Be Proud Of," *Navajo Times*, December 21, 2000.

BIBLIOGRAPHY

Bergman, Robert T. "Navajo Health Services and Projects." In Alfonso Ortiz, ed., *Handbook of North American Indians: Southwest* 10. Washington, DC: Smithsonian Institution Press, 1983.

Clay, Catherine A. "Henry Chee Dodge." In Sharon Malinowski, ed., *Notable Native Americans*. Detroit: Gale Research, Inc., 1995.

Fixico, Donald L., ed. *Treaties with American Indians: An Encyclopedia of Rights, Conflicts, and Sovereignty*. New York: ABC-CLIO, 2007. ProQuest Ebook Central.

Kasee, Cynthia R. "Annie Dodge Wauneka," In Sharon Malinowski, ed., *Notable Native Americans*. Detroit: Gale Research, Inc., 1995.

———. "Wauneka, Annie Dodge." In Gretchen M. Bataillie, ed., *Native American Women: A Biographical Dictionary*. New York: Garland, 1993.

Gridley, Marion Eleanor. *American Indian Women*. New York: Hawthorn Books, 1974.

National Commission on the Observance of International Women's Year. *". . . to Form a More Perfect Union . . .": Justice for American Women: Report of the National Commission on the Observance of International Women's Year*. Washington, DC: U.S. Department of State, 1976.

Nelson, Mary Carroll. *Annie Wauneka: The Story of an American Indian*. Minneapolis: Dillon Press, 1972.

Niethammer, Carolyn. *I'll Go and Do More: Annie Dodge Wauneka, Navajo Leader and Activist*. Lincoln: University of Nebraska Press, 2001.

———. *Keeping the Rope Straight: Annie Dodge Wauneka's Life of Service to the Navajo*. Flagstaff: Salina Bookshelf, 2006.

Roessel, Ruth. *Navajo Stories of the Long Walk Period*. Tsaile: Navajo Community College Press, 1973.

Sonneborn, Liz. *A to Z of American Indian Women*. Revised Edition. New York: Infobase Publishing, 2007.

Trafzer, Clifford E. *The Kit Carson Campaign: The Last Great Navajo War*. Norman: University of Oklahoma Press, 1982.

Trennert, Robert A. *White Man's Medicine: Government Doctors and the Navajo, 1863–1955*. Albuquerque: University of New Mexico Press, 1998.

Witt, Shirley Hill. "An Interview with Dr. Annie Dodge Wauneka." *Frontiers: A Journal of Women's Studies* 6, no. 3 (Autumn 1981): 64–67.

Zanjani, Sally. *Two Native Daughters of Substance: Sarah Winnemucca and Annie Dodge Wauneka*. Lincoln: University of Nebraska Press, 2001.

FURTHER READING

Bergman, Robert T. "Navajo Health Services and Projects." In Alfonso Ortiz, ed., *Handbook of North American Indians: Southwest* 10. Washington, DC: Smithsonian Institution Press, 1983.

Clay, Catherine A. "Henry Chee Dodge." In Sharon Malinowski, ed. *Notable Native Americans*. Detroit: Gale Research, Inc., 1995.

Kasee, Cynthia R. "Annie Dodge Wauneka," In Sharon Malinowski, ed. *Notable Native Americans.* Detroit: Gale Research, Inc., 1995.

Kasee, Cynthia. "Wauneka, Annie Dodge." In Gretchen M. Bataillie, ed. *Native American Women: A Biographical Dictionary*. New York: Garland, 1993.

Gridley, Marion Eleanor. *American Indian Women*. New York: Hawthorn Books, 1974.

Nelson, Mary Carroll. *Annie Wauneka: The Story of an American Indian*. Minneapolis: Dillon Press, 1972.

Niethammer, Carolyn. *I'll Go and Do More: Annie Dodge Wauneka, Navajo Leader and Activist*. Lincoln: University of Nebraska Press, 2001.

———. *Keeping the Rope Straight: Annie Dodge Wauneka's Life of Service to the Navajo*. Flagstaff: Salina Bookshelf, 2006.

Roessel, Ruth. *Navajo Stories of the Long Walk Period*. Tsaile: Navajo Community College Press, 1973.

Trafzer, Clifford E. *The Kit Carson Campaign: The Last Great Navajo War*. Norman: University of Oklahoma Press, 1982.

Trennert, Robert A. *White Man's Medicine: Government Doctors and the Navajo, 1863–1955*. Albuquerque: University of New Mexico Press, 1998.

Zanjani, Sally. *Two Native Daughters of Substance: Sarah Winnemucca and Annie Dodge Wauneka*. Lincoln: University of Nebraska Press, 2001.

Chapter Eighteen

Activism through Medicine

Lori Alvord (b. 1958–)

Jeffrey Allen Smith

The first Navajo woman surgeon, Lori Arviso Alvord, incorporates Native and non-Native knowledge to treat patients in a revolutionary holistic manner. Guided by her belief in Navajo traditional lifeways, Alvord uses innovative Western medical technology to heal patients. Raised on the Navajo Reservation, Alvord left the Native world she loved for educational opportunities at Dartmouth and Stanford, ultimately returning to New Mexico determined to help her people. Alvord deftly balances the Native and non-Native world, striving to "walk in beauty," the ideal form of life according to the Navajo.

Navajo refer to themselves as *Diné*, which translates into English as "the People." Traditionally, Navajo believed creative forces gave them their lands in Arizona, New Mexico, Colorado, and Utah. Four sacred mountains lie within Navajo Country, including *Tsoodzil* (Mount Taylor), *Doko'oosliid* (San Francisco Peak), *Tsisnaasjini'* (Mount Blanca), and *Dibé Nitsaa* or Mount Hesperus. Today the Navajo Reservation includes 26,000 square miles of lands in northeastern Arizona, southeastern Utah, and northwestern New Mexico. The Navajo Reservation constitutes a land area roughly the size of West Virginia.

In traditional Navajo culture, *hataałii*, or medicine men, are entrusted with the healing of individuals. They use their medicinal and spiritual understanding to treat the whole patient, which includes the person's mind, body, and spirit in addition to the patient's communal and ecological environment.[1] Everything must function in a natural harmony in order for the person to maintain good health. This form of Native healing is naturally multifaceted and the pathway that allows Navajos to *hózhó* or *hózhóni* or "walk in beauty." This Navajo belief system intertwines traditional religion and medicine to view sickness as a result of a life that has fallen out of balance or strayed off the *hózhó* path. Thus, the only way to become truly healthy is to regain a state of balance and once again "walk in beauty."[2]

One of the most powerful and continually used medical treatments by Navajo is that of song. Navajo sing specific healing songs, often referred to as chantways, to treat a broad spectrum of illnesses and disorders. Focused on nature, individualized chantways address precise problems. While some western doctors may disagree over the medical effectiveness of such songs, physicians do not dispute the hope chantways provide Navajo patients and the resulting increase in positive outcomes as a direct result. It is ideas such as "walking in beauty" and the power of the chantway that Lori Arviso Alvord incorporates into her healing process as the first Navajo woman surgeon.

Alvord is a half *Diné* and half *bilagáana*, or white person, the daughter of her full-blooded Navajo father, Robert Cupp, and a mother of European descent, Rita Colgan. Navajo describe this genealogical makeup as a person who is in half, or '*ahní*. Born in a military hospital in Tacoma, Washington, Alvord grew up on the Navajo Reservation community of Crownpoint in a family devoid of economic or political privilege. However, this was not uncommon in Crownpoint, the northwestern New Mexico area of the Navajo Reservation where most people's first language was Navajo. Most people herded sheep as their ancestors had done before them. Many lived in hogans (houses) that did not have electricity or running water. Alvord learned the history and lifeways of her people through the teachings of Grace Cupp, her Navajo grandmother or *Shínálí*. Education was important in Alvord's family, and while neither her father nor mother held a college degree, they always encouraged and supported her academic endeavors, as well as those of her two younger sisters. In grade school, Alvord believed that she, "might someday hold a college degree, [but] resisted any larger dreams, for fear they could not come true."[3]

Alvord planned to attend a college near the Navajo Reservation, but after talking to a Navajo student attending Princeton, she decided to apply to an Ivy League school despite not fully understanding the significance of her decision. At the age of sixteen, Alvord received an early acceptance letter from Dartmouth, a college founded in 1769 in Hanover, New Hampshire, to acculturate and Christianize local area Native Americans. Attending Dartmouth meant Alvord had to leave Crownpoint, New Mexico, a home from which she had never significantly traveled. In addition, Navajo tradition dictates that leaving the lands protected by the four secret mountains welcomes imbalance and may prevent one from "walking in beauty."

Alvord's matriculation at Dartmouth was not easy. She double majored in psychology and sociology, with an emphasis in Native American Studies. Alvord was unfamiliar with the social customs and morays of the mostly affluent non-Native student body. To further compound matters, professors interpreted Alvord's Navajo upbringing, which had emphasized humility and silence, as disinterest and aloofness. However, she took solace in the few things that reminded her of home, such as the stray dogs that roamed the campus and being a member of the Native American community at Dartmouth. Alvord graduated cum laude from Dartmouth in 1979, returning to her reservation to put her newly acquired degree and skill sets to work.[4]

Back in Crownpoint, Alvord quickly came to the realization that the economic recession of the early 1980s had all but destroyed the reservation job market. Determined to find employment, she believed that Albuquerque, New Mexico, the closest metropolitan area, would yield better results. It was while searching through the *Albuquerque Journal* classifieds, that she found a position working as a brain physiology research assistant at the University of New Mexico under Gary Rosenberg, M.D. In between the preparation of chemicals, labeling of specimens, and general cleaning of the lab, Dr. Rosenberg posed a fateful question to Alvord, "Lori, have you ever thought about going to medical school?"[5]

Initially demure and unpersuaded, only a few weeks after Rosenberg's query, Alvord started taking premedical courses at the University of New Mexico. Prompted by her success in her studies, Alvord quit her position as a research assistant to become a full-time student with the goal of entering medical school. Her perseverance paid off, when Alvord was accepted into Stanford Medical School.

Stanford Medical School proved challenging for Alvord, despite having her sister Karen attending the same institution. Unfortunately, the same misinterpretations of Alvord's quietness and humility that had dogged her at Dartmouth plagued her in medical school, amplified by the interpersonal nature of this professional training. The hardest part of medical school for most students is the cadaver, which proved exponentially more difficult for Alvord given her Navajo beliefs. Navajo teachings hold that one should never touch a deceased person under any circumstances, for the dead hold *ch'įįndis*, or evil spirits. According to the Navajo belief system, when a person dies, the "good" portion of that person leaves the earthly body, thus only the "bad" remains associated with the corpse. However, as Alvord progressed though her medical classes, she felt a certain sense of separation from her Navajo teachings, that occasionally manifested themselves in thoughts of cultural uncertainty. Eventually, Alvord was able to balance her Navajo beliefs with her aspirations to become a doctor because of her desire to heal and help her people. Alvord naturally gravitated toward surgery, despite the obvious obstacles the specialty presented. At the time Alvord was in medical school, only about four percent of the practicing surgeons were women, and of the hand full of Native American surgeons, none were women. Alvord credits her much of her success in this field to Dr. Ron Lujan, Alvord's mentor at Acoma-Cañoncito-Laguna Hospital (ACL) close to the Navajo Reservation.

Lujan and the Navajo patients at ACL educated Alvord in the art of a different, more culturally sensitive type of medicine not taught in medical schools at this time. During Alvord's periodic rotations at ACL, she saw patients primarily from Navajo communities. Yet, due to her detached western medical education, Alvord felt uncomfortable asking probing questions and struggled to gain the trust of her Navajo patients. It was only through the guidance of Lujan that Alvord was able to relax and find her own identity. This change resulted in more enjoyable doctor-patient relationships. In the operating room of Cibola General Hospital in Grants, New Mexico, twenty miles west of ACL, Lujan provided Alvord the advantage and opportunity to work with him as his first assistant. This form of hands-on training coupled with Lujan's desire to steel Alvord to the stressors and toll of surgery though assigning her the most difficult patients put Alvord ahead of her fellow Stanford medical students. When she returned to Stanford, Alvord utilized all that she learned from Lujan and the Navajo patients at ACL to earn high marks and impress her professors.

While from the outside everything appeared to be going great for Alvord, unknowingly her life had strayed off the path of beauty. During her medical rotations at Santa Clara Valley, Alvord regularly worked sixteen-hour days and occasionally worked up to thirty-six hours straight when on call. The demanding workload took a toll on Alvord's physical, mental, and emotional wellbeing. In January 1987, Alvord was diagnosed with pleural effusion on her right side, the fluid filling in the pleural cavity and constricting breathing.[6] This eventually formed an empyema, or a collection of pus. Alvord found herself surrounded by her family, fighting for to stay alive. Alvord ultimately spent three weeks in the hospital and another three weeks on bed rest. However, Alvord credits this experience with teaching her about the frustrations and failures of the medical system from the patient's perspective. Once recovered, Alvord returned to her medical education at Stanford successfully completing medical school in 1991.

After graduation, Alvord persuasively argued with the federal Indian Health Services (IHS) to assign her a position as a surgeon at the Gallup Indian Medical Center (GIMC). Located in western New Mexico, GIMC is an IHS hospital located in the town of Gallup. It primarily serves Navajo patients with some Zuni, Apache, and others. Alvord finally had her dream job; she was using her medical training to help her people. In recognition for her work with Navajo, in 1992, New Mexico's governor selected Alvord for the Governor's Award for Outstanding Women. A year later, she was appointed to a National Institute of Health Task Force on the Recruitment and Retention of Women in Clinical Research.

At GIMC, Alvord routinely performed laparoscopic surgery, also called minimally invasive surgery, a revolutionary procedure in which a surgeon performs abdominal surgery through small "keyhole" incisions in the abdomen. Usually, Alvord employed this procedure to remove a patient's infected gallbladder. Most doctors attribute the increased rate of infected gallbladders in the Navajo population to the influence of a western diet and lifestyle that is high in fats and sugars, and low in physical activity. Alvord recognized that these as well as other issues facing the Navajo community also came from not "walking in beauty." During her time at GIMC, Alvord endeavored to incorporate traditional Navajo belief systems into her professional and personal life.

In 1993 Alvord met Jon Alvord, a blond, blue eyed Army Special Forces medic training at GIMC.[7] Although she was thirty-four and he twenty-three at the time, Alvord decided to casually see the serviceman. After a year courtship, the couple married in the summer of 1994 in a pair of weddings. The first wedding was a traditional western wedding in Salt Lake City, while the second was conducted in a Hogan at Churchrock on the Navajo Reservation. The couple have two children together, Kodiak and Kaitlyn. With a fulfilling career, loving marriage, and burgeoning family, Alvord was "walking in beauty." However, unbeknownst to Alvord, she still had another step along her long path to improve the health of Native peoples.

Unexpectedly, Dartmouth alumnus and chairman of the board of overseers for the Dartmouth Medical School, Gordon Russell called Alvord to ask her to apply for the position of associate dean of student affairs at Dartmouth Medical School. After much soul searching and contemplation Alvord accepted the position. In 1997, again, she would move outside the protection and familiarity of the four sacred mountains, but this time with her family. They moved to New Hampshire, where Alvord became the Dartmouth Medical School associate dean of student affairs, minority affairs, and assistant professor of surgery. During her tenure at Dartmouth, Alvord's expertise and reputation in the medical resulted in several other appointments including in 2003, when she served as an associate faculty member of the Center of American Indian Health at the Johns Hopkins School of Public Health and later in 2008, as a member of the National Center for Complementary and Alternative Medicine, one of the centers that makes up the National Institutes of Health. In 2010, Alvord left Dartmouth for the opportunity to aid in developing a new medical school and serve as the associate dean and professor of surgery at the Central Michigan University School of Medicine. Two years later, in 2012, Alvord became the associate dean of students and admissions at the University of Arizona College of Medicine.[8] As recognition for lifetime of achievement and advocacy, in 2013 the National Indian Health Board and National Congress of American Indians endorsed Alvord as a candidate for U.S. Surgeon General.[9] In 2018, Alvord joined Astria Health in Washington state in a continued effort to provide medical and surgical services to Native populations, and was also honored by the Stanford Medicine Alumni Association with their prestigious J. E. Wallace Sterling Lifetime Achievement Award in Medicine.[10] Over the course of her career, in addition to her administrative, academic, and surgical duties at hospitals and medical schools across the U.S., Alvord has received invitations to speak on her implementation of Navajo concepts of health and healing at numerous universities and was featured in the 2016 PBS documentary Medicine Woman. For Alvord, "It's all interconnected and Native people speak of it that way. It's the western world that needs to catch up."[11] The non-Native world has grown increasingly interested in the Navajo idea of "walking in beauty," with articles about her research and ideas reaching an even broader audience though countless newspaper articles and press interviews.

According to Alvord, "I wanted to make a difference in the lives of my people."[12] Through her tireless work in the medical field, she continues to accomplish this goal. Her holistic approach to medicine is gradually gaining favor with doctors and patients alike. While Alvord may have set out to help her people, her work transcends cultural boundaries. Alvord's patients bear this out with her, "seeing many fewer complications"[13] and living happier. Alvord stresses the interconnectivity of life, from the macro to the micro; all must be in balance if one wants to "walk in beauty."

NOTES

1. National Library of Medicine, "Dr. Lori Arviso Alvord," Changing the Face of Medicine, http://www.nlm.nih.gov.

2. Edna Francisco, "Bridging the Cultural Divide in Medicine," *Science*, last modified December 3, 2004, https://www.sciencemag.org/careers/2004/12/bridging-cultural-divide-medicine.

3. Lori Arviso Alvord and Elizabeth Cohen Van Pelt, *The Scalpel and the Silver Bear* (New York: Bantam Books, 1999), 13.

4. Kristin Maffei, "Culturally Competent Care: Three Questions for Lori Arviso Alvord '79," Dartmouth, last modified July 30 , 2018, https://alumni.dartmouth.edu/content/culturally-competent-care-three-questions-lori-arviso-alvord-79.

5. Lori Arviso Alvord and Elizabeth Cohen Van Pelt, *The Scalpel and the Silver Bear* (New York: Bantam Books, 1999), 36.

6. Lori Arviso Alvord and Elizabeth Cohen Van Pelt, *The Scalpel and the Silver Bear* (New York: Bantam Books, 1999), 54.

7. Lori Arviso Alvord and Elizabeth Cohen Van Pelt, *The Scalpel and the Silver Bear* (New York: Bantam Books, 1999), 129.

8. "Associate Dean Lori Arviso Alvord, MD, Sees Priorities for Medical Admissions and Student Affairs," *The University of Arizona College of Medicine,* December 1, 2012.

9. Alastair Lee Bitsoi, "Leaving It Up to the Universe," *Navajo Times*, July 25, 2013.

10. "Stanford University Honors Astria Health General Surgeon, Lori Arviso Alvord, MD," *Astria Health*, December 3, 2018.

11. "Medicine Woman," *NetNebraska.org*, http://netnebraska.org/basic-page/television/medicine-woman

12. Lori Arviso Alvord and Elizabeth Cohen Van Pelt, *The Scalpel and the Silver Bear* (New York: Bantam Books, 1999), 13.

13. Alvord, Lori Arviso and Elizabeth Cohen Van Pelt, *The Scalpel and the Silver Bear* (New York: Bantam Books, 1999), 189.

BIBLIOGRAPHY

Alvord, Lori Arviso and Elizabeth Cohen Van Pelt. *The Scalpel and the Silver Bear*. New York: Bantam Books, 1999.

Dartmouth News. "Lori Arviso Alvord, First Navajo Woman Surgeon, to Open Dartmouth's Academic Year." (September 1999).

Focus on Complementary and Alternative Medicine, volume XIV, number3. (Summer 2007). http://www.nccam.nih.org.

Lori Arviso Alvord." *Winds of Change*. (Spring 2000). http://www.wocmag.org.

National Library of Medicine. "Dr. Lori Arviso Alvord." *Changing the Face of Medicine*. http://www.nlm.nih.gov.

National Institute of Health. "Perspective: Dr. Lori Arviso Alvord." *CAM at the HIH:* [Au: please complete citation]

Ostic, Kathryn. "Navajo Surgeon Describes Mix between Medicine, Cultural Beliefs." *Los Alamos National Laboratory News*. (July 2003). http://www.lanl.gov.

Westberg, Jane. "The Scalpel and the Silver Bear, First Navajo Woman Surgeon: Dr. [Au: please complete citation]

FURTHER READING

Garrod, Andrew, et al., editors. *First Person, First Peoples: Native American College Graduates Tell Their Stories*. Ithaca, NY: Cornell University Press, 1994.

Iverson, Peter. *Diné: A History of the Navajos*. Albuquerque, NM: University of New Mexico Press, 2002.

O'Brian, Aileen. *Navajo Indian Myths*. New York: Dover, 1994.
Robert McPherson, *Dinéjí Na`nitin: Navajo Traditional Teachings and History*. Boulder, CO: University Press of Colorado, 2012.
Trafzer, Clifford E. *American Indian Medicine Ways: Spiritual Power, Prophets, and Healing*. Tucson, AZ: University of Arizona Press, 2017.

Chapter Nineteen

Remembering What We Always Knew

Kahnawake Community-Based Activist Terry Maresca, M.D. (b. 1958–)

Sarah Wolk FitzGerald

Terry Maresca is a family care physician, a medical educator, a member of the Kahnawake Band of Mohawk tribe, and an activist. She supervises medical residents at the Seattle Indian Health Board and is a professor at the University of Washington School of Medicine. She is also Director of the Native American Center of Excellence at the University of Washington School of Medicine and works with the Puyallup tribal clinic's residency program. Maresca is active in the Association of Indian Physicians and served as president from 1994–1995. Maresca uses her medical training and knowledge of traditional healing practices to serve Native communities.[1]

As an educator, Maresca teaches medical students how to combine western medical approaches with herbal and plant-based medicine. She also shares this knowledge with others in Indigenous communities because she feels it is important for individuals to make informed decisions about their medical care and be responsible for their own health. Ever since Maresca was a child, she has valued the role of advocacy. Even when she did not necessarily understand the term, she knew it was important to speak for those who did not have a voice. She explains that everyone has the capacity to be an advocate; it is just a matter of how one uses that capacity and depends upon the resources and opportunities one has at their disposal.[2]

For Terry Maresca, the resources and opportunities she uses to serve as an advocate originate from her youth. She explains that the training she works to provide medical students with, which combines western and Native medical practices, educational knowledge that was not available to her when she went to school. Her education in Indigenous medicine began during her childhood. According to Maresca, she received the tribal teachings of original instructions and laws. These were ways to act and be in the world, and her tribe has a set of instructions and creation narratives that were shared with her when she was a child. These included an emphasis on respecting the natural world as a Mohawk person, an understanding that heavily influences Maresca's approach to medicine and healing today. She explains that Mohawk instructions were different from other tribes but included some commonalities. These commonalities have helped her work with other Native communities as a medical professional.

As a child she learned that she was responsible for the health and well-being of herself, of others around her, and for the health of plants and animals. She loved the outdoors and developed a respect for the natural world, but this respect was not developed without making some mistakes along the way. When she was young, she wanted to sell dirt. She thought the dirt was beautiful and that everyone should have it. Her maternal grandmother corrected this notion. She helped young Terry to redirect this energy by teaching her about the plant world and its connection to humans. Her family felt she needed this education because her adventures in the natural world could go awry with the curiosity she exhibited. Maresca learned to garden, she was taught about the basic care of families, and about plant medicine. She learned that everyone should have these skills and that was how elders presented these concepts to her during her childhood. Unfortunately, this is no longer the case, according to Maresca. It is clear she is trying to address this more recent lack of knowledge through her role as an educator and community advocate.[3]

Another experience that shaped Maresca's professional approach was her family's interaction with a non-Native doctor when she was a young girl. She remembers the physician being very rude to her mother and felt he hated her large family. She did not know much about racism at the time, but she recalls wondering, "Why doesn't he like us?" She remembers thinking that people deserve better, not just Native people, but all people. Maresca identifies this memory as a turning point when she became interested in social justice in addition to science.

Maresca's father was also a major influence in her life, and she identifies his lessons as another source of her activism. Her father was an ironworker who built bridges and skyscrapers, including the Twin Towers. He was one of the Mohawk ironworkers famous for braving great heights to build bridges and high-rise buildings. He was not very well educated in Western-style education, but he held great knowledgeable of treaty rights. According to Maresca, he was an activist when it came to Indigenous rights and their impact on borders. He cited the Jay Treaty of 1794, which allowed for free passage of Haudenosaunee (Iroquois people) across the Canadian-United States border. He regularly crossed the border from New York into Canada and explained that he did not recognize the national border but did recognize rights of passage, commerce, hunting, trading, and other Native American practices that the national border disrupted. Maresca asserts that her father was an activist about the issue of treaty rights. Her father taught her that these are things they need to defend, because people died for that treaty. She identifies this as the point when she realized people have rights, including her community and other people.

The stories and traditions Maresca grew up with also influenced her understanding of activism and advocacy. She gives the example of the cornhusk dolls she played with as a child. The dolls had no face. They were presented with a story that taught children not to focus on themselves and their appearance. They learned that they needed to serve their family and society, or they would lose their path. These stories taught her about her inherent responsibility to the earth and to others, especially those with no voice. Maresca explains that she was not given a different message than others were, but she spent more time with the elders in her community who were able to impress these lessons upon her.[4]

Maresca began her medical education with plans to be an environmental and occupational health professional. This was largely influenced by the fact that her three brothers, along with her father, were ironworkers. This was a common profession for the Mohawk people and work-related injuries were widespread. She worked to address contamination, including the polychlorinated biphenyls (PCB) controversy that took place in upstate New York where aluminum plants along the rivers contaminated water.[5] She also worked on a sister reservation while she was in school with at-risk infants and mothers who were impacted by the aluminum contamination. She then worked with the United Auto Workers Union to address worker conditions and chemical exposure, which most people were unaware of at the time. Maresca eventually deviated from this realm of medicine because she could not find a program to work in as a physician. Regardless, she still maintained strong feelings about these issues. These feelings continue to impact her approach to medicine and patient advocacy by providing her with a unified way of thinking of health and its relationship with living systems. This was bigger than thinking on an individual or family level for health and continued to expand her approach to medicine and healing. It is part of her community-based approach to health, medicine, and well-being.[6]

Maresca works to unite Western medicine with traditional Native healing practices, but this does not come without challenges. She has confronted resistance from medical professionals who view Indigenous medicine with suspicion. Many of her non-Native colleagues have questioned Native practices because they are resistant to incorporating approaches that connect the mind and body and that are inclusive of the environment. They are suspicious because these approaches are not what they learned in school and do not fit the model they are trained in. She has shared the message of Native organizations with her colleagues, the explanation that these healing practices are a right of the tribal people and that it does not necessarily matter if Western physicians understand them. She feels these physicians would benefit and more effectively be able to treat Native patients if they worked with their systems and acknowledged their medical approaches. However, she explains the limits of how much Indigenous people are willing to share with Western physicians and complications involved with combining Native and Western medical practices. [7]

Confusion has emerged about how insurance companies would be able to cover Native healing ceremonies, consultations, herbal medicines, and other healing practices. Dr. Maresca refers to a controversy when the Veterans Administration provided insurance coverage for Native healing ceremonies but wanted to know more about the ceremonies than the Native community wanted to share. This is a common issue when combining Native and Western medicine. Native communities are often hesitant about sharing information because they worry that non-Natives might exploited or misuse Native medicine ways. As Maresca explained, there are steps physicians need to take to develop trust with Indigenous communities and they need to learn how to properly incorporate Native medicine ways with Western practices. Maresca states that decisions regarding this level of sharing "need to go to community wisdom, to the people who have ownership of that knowledge. It is for the community to decide how much they want to share or not."[8]

Maresca respects the wisdom, autonomy, and sovereignty of Native people she treats. She shares the story of when she was working with Lakota people early in her medical career. She recalls a baby falling ill with meningitis shortly before the community's Sundance ceremony. Maresca was scared and wanted to take aggressive action to treat the child, including spinal tap tests. The family refused to do so before consulting their community elder, who was already at the Sundance grounds. She knew they did not have much time to wait, but the family would not allow an IV or any medical intervention until the elder came. It is Maresca's policy to respect people's views and decisions regarding their medical care. However, the people have ownership of the consequences. She supported their decision and waited with the family until the elder arrived. The Lakota elder was joined by many others from their community. He agreed to medical treatment for the child but said that the family and community would be there for support. They all prayed in the emergency room for the child's health and recovery. Although Maresca's community does not hold Sundance ceremonies, she was familiar with the work they were doing. This was not something she learned about in school, but rather something she had background in from working with Native communities and experiencing treatments firsthand.[9]

Maresca empowers the Indigenous communities she works with and has done so since her early days of studying and practicing medicine. As a senior medical student, she worked in Navajo Nation with a Mohawk mentor. This exposed her to patients using traditional Navajo medicine, which used different approaches and a different setting from what she had previously worked with. While working with the Navajo people, she treated an old woman with a bad fever. She ordered a test and gave her medication. After a day went by she learned the woman had a major urinary tract infection (UTI). The woman later returned to see Maresca, and she was much better. She asked the woman how she got better, and the woman shared the Navajo point of view, disclosing that she went and got doctored by a healer in her community. Maresca asked herself, "What do I do with that? Do I still treat the UTI?"[10] Instead she collaborated with the woman and asked her how she wanted to be treated.

Maresca was impacted by this experience, and it shaped the way she approaches patient care. She understood the magnitude of the patient trusting her and sharing information about her own approach to healing. Maresca asserts that information shared with someone caring for you is powerful, and this allows for patient centered and culturally appropriate care. This does not mean the physician needs to adopt the beliefs of their patients, but they do need to acknowledge these beliefs and understood them as truths, incorporating them into her treatment plans. She respects her patients and tells them she needs to hear how they care for and heal themselves. She assures them that it is okay to say they do not know, and in the end she asks what they need. Dr. Maresca also defers to cultural norms with Native communities, especially when working with elders. She explains to these patients, "I can't tell you what to do." She tells them what options they have, makes suggestions, and treads lightly to respect their autonomy, medical sovereignty, and self-determination. The ultimate goal for Dr. Maresca is for her patients to advocate for themselves and be empowered. She prioritizes trust in her medical approaches.[11]

Dr. Maresca bluntly assures her patients, "I don't care which way you go, just get results. Your way is just as powerful as my way."[12] She reminds them that their approaches for medical treatment are up to them and based on individual decisions. Everyone is an expert on their own body, she explains. Maresca started practicing medicine at the young age of twenty-four. She worked with an elder in her community and has always advocated for younger people who may not have an elder they can turn to. She often uses relational terms in patient interactions because of the importance of family and community she places to individual health. She will often warn young patients, "If you were my little sister, I'd be worried." She'll ask a patient, "who do you trust? You don't have to take my word for it, but who do you trust? Don't make decisions alone."[13]

It is important to Maresca to help people find their own answers because, as she reasons, no one likes being dictated to and we are all responsible for our own health. She knows she usually will not change her patients' ways of thinking, but instead asks them, "what do you want to know?" She provides resources and information, while asking patients what will work for them. She supports her patients in their decision-making while respecting their methods and beliefs. She asserts that this is not a passive philosophy of medical care. Rather, she wants her patients to make sure that whatever happens, they have choices, and they are ready for what comes. She urges them to not give their power away and she builds on their strength and methods of prevention. These are found in their traditional ways of life, which are shared in storytelling. She asks patients, "what resonates with you for how to care for yourself, to respect yourself?"[14]

Part of what influences Maresca's approach is her realization that Indigenous communities have lost a lot but have also retained a lot in terms of traditional healing knowledge. She explains that people do not always remember traditional and Native ways of caring for themselves, and so she provides gentle reminders to help people get back on track. She thinks a lot of Native communities have lost this and as a result, have given up some of their autonomy. One of the primary ways she addresses this loss is through plant medicine. She educates medical professionals as well as Native people about plant medicine, which they use to treat and monitor medical issues and chronic ailments. She uses plant medicine to stimulate ways for Native people to care for themselves without always relying on prescriptions. She also grows and uses traditional foods for this reason. [15]

Maresca has her own seed bank, which she shares with others. She often sees Native people becoming sick from deviating from Indigenous ways of eating and living in an era of Genetically Modified Organisms (GMO) foods. In her grassroots community work, she shares seeds with people who will love and respect them and their healing powers. Maresca asserts that it is part of their healing to work with these seeds and that this is medicine, too. This hands-on work gives her joy. As she teaches physicians and other medical providers about plant medicine and traditional healing practices, she asserts that this is really the wisdom they have always had. The information she shares resonates with Native healers and causes them to ask, "How do I know that?" Dr. Terry Maresca explains that Native healers are "remembering what we always knew."[16]

NOTES

1. "Maresca leads Native American Center of Excellent," *UW News*, August 2, 2007.

2. "Maresca leads Native American Center of Excellent," *UW News*, August 2, 2007; Terry Maresca, "Strengthening Our Roots: One Region's Experience with Traditional Medicine and Health Care Settings." Indian Health Service, Eleventh Annual Advances in Indian Healthcare Conference. Clifford Trafzer's Collection, University of California, Riverside.

3. Telephone Interview of Terry Maresca by Sarah Wolk FitzGerald, October 9, 2015. Author's Collection.

4. Telephone Interview of Terry Maresca by Sarah Wolk FitzGerald, October 9, 2015. Author's Collection.

5. Polychlorinated biphenyls (PCBs) are highly toxic industrial compounds that can pose serious health risks.

6. Terry Maresca, "Strengthening Our Roots: One Region's Experience with Traditional Medicine and Health Care Settings." Indian Health Service, Eleventh Annual Advances in Indian Healthcare Conference. Clifford Trafzer's Collection, University of California, Riverside.

7. Diversity/Community Engagement Committee and Community Report. University of Washington School of Medicine, Seattle, Washington.

8. Telephone Interview of Terry Maresca by Sarah Wolk FitzGerald, October 9, 2015. Author's Collection.

9. Terry Maresca, "Strengthening Our Roots: One Region's Experience with Traditional Medicine and Health Care Settings." Indian Health Service, Eleventh Annual Advances in Indian Healthcare Conference. Clifford Trafzer's Collection, University of California, Riverside.

10. Telephone Interview of Terry Maresca by Sarah Wolk FitzGerald, October 9, 2015. Author's Collection.

11. Telephone Interview of Terry Maresca by Sarah Wolk FitzGerald, October 9, 2015. Author's Collection; Terry Maresca, "Strengthening Our Roots: One Region's Experience with Traditional Medicine and Health Care Settings." Indian Health Service, Eleventh Annual Advances in Indian Healthcare Conference. Clifford Trafzer's Collection, University of California, Riverside.

12. Telephone Interview of Terry Maresca by Sarah Wolk FitzGerald, October 9, 2015. Author's Collection.

13. Telephone Interview of Terry Maresca by Sarah Wolk FitzGerald, October 9, 2015. Author's Collection.

14. Telephone Interview of Terry Maresca by Sarah Wolk FitzGerald, October 9, 2015. Author's Collection.

15. Telephone Interview of Terry Maresca by Sarah Wolk FitzGerald, October 9, 2015. Author's Collection; Terry Maresca, "Strengthening Our Roots: One Region's Experience with Traditional Medicine and Health Care Settings." Indian Health Service, Eleventh Annual Advances in Indian Healthcare Conference. Clifford Trafzer's Collection, University of California, Riverside; Terry Maresca, "Strengthening Our Roots: One Region's Experience with Traditional Medicine and Health Care Settings." Indian Health Service, Eleventh Annual Advances in Indian Healthcare Conference. Clifford Trafzer's Collection, University of California, Riverside; Diversity/Community Engagement Committee and Community Report. University of

Washington School of Medicine, Seattle, Washington; Gary Holt, "With Herb Garden, Tribal Doctor Meshes Old Ways and New," *Seattle Post-Intellinger*, July 18, 2003.

16. Telephone Interview of Terry Maresca by Sarah Wolk FitzGerald, October 9, 2015. Author's Collection.

BIBLIOGRAPHY

Diversity/Community Engagement Committee and Community Report. University of Washington School of Medicine, Seattle, Washington.

Holt, Gary. "With Herb Garden, Tribal Doctor Meshes Old Ways and New." *Seattle Post-Intellinger,* July 18, 2003.

"Maresca Leads Native American Center of Excellent," *UW News*, August 2, 2007.

Maresca, Terry. "Strengthening Our Roots: One Region's Experience with Traditional Medicine and Health Care Settings." Indian Health Service, Eleventh Annual Advances in Indian Healthcare Conference. Clifford Trafzer's Collection, University of California, Riverside.

Telephone Interview of Terry Maresca by Sarah Wolk FitzGerald, October 9, 2015. Author's Collection.

FURTHER READING

Holt, Gary. "With herb garden, tribal doctor meshes old ways and new." *Seattle Post-Intellinger,* July 18, 2003.

"Maresca leads Native American Center of Excellent," *UW News*, August 2, 2007.

Chapter Twenty

Activist Centered Healthcare

Beverly Patchell (b. 1951–)

Robert D. Miller

Beverly Patchell, an enrolled member of the Cherokee Nation, grew up near Six Killer Lake and the Cherokee capital of Tahlequah, Oklahoma. Her childhood included an upbringing in traditional Cherokee and Creek ceremonies, storytelling, and Native medicine. At a young age, Patchell wore turtle rattles on her small legs and danced the Stomp Dance to awaken the earth. Many healers with diverse specialties lived within her community, including members of her family. Patchell supplemented this knowledge of traditional healing practices with her professional work as an employee with tribes and nations in the continental United States, Hawaii, and Alaska. Following her marriage and the birth of her two sons, Patchell decided to return to school. Heeding the advice of her family, she spoke with Martha Primeux, a Cherokee who served as the assistant dean at the University of Oklahoma's School of Nursing. As Patchell found her earlier experience as a nurse's aide rewarding, she followed Primeux's suggestion to pursue a career in nursing. Patchell subsequently received her Bachelor of Science in Nursing in 1978 from the University of Oklahoma College of Nursing. Beverly Patchell has been an activist in the field of medicine, serving as a traditional healer and a nurse trained in Western medicine. She has used both to serve American Indian people and to heal maladies of all varieties.

As Patchell neared the end of her nursing school education, she desired the opportunity to serve children and youth facing mental health issues. Consequently, following her completion of her Bachelor of Science in Nursing, Patchell found employment with a psychiatric unit for adults and adolescents at St. Anthony Hospital in Oklahoma City. Her work gave her the opportunity to provide care to children to bring about change in their lives as well as that of their families. During Patchell's work on her Master of Science in Psychiatric and Mental Health Nursing—completed in 1988 at the University of Oklahoma's School of Nursing—she found employment at Willow View Hospital in Oklahoma City where she later served as the clinical director of the inpatient children's unit from 1987 through 1991. In 1991, Patchell received certification as a Clinical Nurse Specialist in Psychiatric/Mental Health Nursing of Adolescents and Children. She continued her focus on children and adolescents when she opened a private practice, believing she could do greater good by working more directly with children, mothers, and families. Also in 1991, Patchell aided the children of military personnel deployed overseas during Operation Desert Storm.

Patchell identified a key moment in life when her family returned to Tahlequah in the Cherokee Nation. In 1991 she began work as a family therapist at the Jack Brown Center, at Sequoyah Boarding School located near Tahlequah. The Center, named after Sequoyah Boarding School superintendent, Jack Brown, received funding from the Indian Health Service, and Patchell eagerly joined the staff to work closely with Cherokee children. The Cherokee National Health Service administered the Center, which provided guidance to American Indian youth struggling with substance abuse. The Center aimed to treat both the chemical aspects of dependency and provide treatment for any mental health issues that patients might face. Due in part to Patchell's involvement, the Center currently employs doodling, photography, pottery, and sculpture to promote communication with those students unwilling to express their thoughts verbally. These forms of art therapy reflect Patchell's own observations about providing mental health therapy to American Indians as well as her advocacy on behalf of native patients. She is also cognizant of the diverse nature of American Indian communities. For example, she became involved in an effort to lower teen substance abuse rates for Plains Indians from Oklahoma. She recognized how the heterogenous nature of tribal groups required a reworking of the Cherokee Self-Reliance Model into the Native Self-Reliance Model. Rather than having individuals focus inward first before recognizing the connections with others, as the Cherokee Self-Reliance Model instructed, the reworked model incorporated Plains Indian beliefs about acknowledging the spirit within others and the world before recognizing that same spirit within themselves. Patchell further understood that any efforts to make care more culturally relevant requires the active participation of tribal leaders and community members.[1]

In 1992, Patchell became the program director for the Native American Adolescent Treatment Center at the Jack Brown Center where she oversaw the care of American Indians from across the United States. During the course of this work, Patchell identified a gap between her training and the requirements of American Indian patients. Patchell noted that talk therapy did not aid American Indians as many thought that speaking about a particular subject gave it power. Several Native American patients believed that discussing issues such as anger, fear, despair, or pain would give these problems greater influence in their lives. Though members of Patchell's own family had previously expressed similar viewpoints, she had not yet considered how these concerns reflected the beliefs of many within the American Indian community. Patchell's respect for the personal convictions of her patients encouraged her to incorporate storytelling into her therapy sessions as a new approach better suited to the cultural needs of American Indians. The usage of storytelling enabled patients to articulate their viewpoints indirectly by speaking about animals, trees, or objects. Patchell found this approach worked well in larger groups, although she still faced challenges when working with a single individual reluctant to speak. Patchell introduced art, dancing, drumming, and visits to nature to help troubled individuals and groups. [2] Patchell's efforts to address American Indian mental health issues in a culturally sensitive way represented a willingness to expand the standard understandings of healing in order to accommodate individual differences and backgrounds. She was able to recognize the ways in which Western therapies failed American Indian patients and advocate treatments with greater cultural relevance.

During the mid-1990s, Patchell worked for the Cherokee Nation training all of its employees. During her work, she traveled throughout the Cherokee Nation and contributed to a project designed to keep people out of nursing homes. Her journeys convinced her of the importance of forming relationships with Indigenous medicine people in order to learn from their wisdom and knowledge. Patchell's experiences also drove her to work as an activist promoting organizations seeking to improve health care for American Indians and Alaska Natives to help offset continued health disparities that impaired wellness. Her efforts are relevant as American Indians and Alaska Natives continue to have life spans similar to those found in developing nations while suffering higher levels of chronic disease and disability than the general population of the United States. Higher rates of unemployment coupled with generally lower income levels have exacerbated the situation by limiting access to quality health care. In addition, American Indians and Alaska Natives face inequalities in education that have perpetuated the disparity in health issues. American Indians, she found, suffered severely from the lack of access to education and from health care disparities that put Indian people at risk for disease, accidents, and deaths.

Patchell's goals encouraged her involvement with programs such as Bridges to the Future Doctoral Program. This program, founded by the National Institute of Health in 1992, facilitated the training of additional biomedical scientists from underrepresented minorities, including American Indians and Alaska Natives. Bridges to the Future Doctoral Program sought to improve the capacity of universities to train American Indian and Alaska Native students and ease their transition to other institutions. The program involved students transferring to four-year institutions with an associate degree as well as individuals pursuing a doctoral degree after receiving their Master of Science. The program would create partnerships between at least two institutions. One of the institutions offered the Master of Science as its terminal degree, while the second school provided students with the opportunity to obtain a doctoral degree in a scientific field associated with the National Institute of Health. As the Site Coordinator at the University of Oklahoma, Patchell took part in the program by leading students toward doctoral studies at the University of Minnesota. The program focused on nurses, as these health care professionals provided the primary workforce of the Indian Health Service in its service to 1.5 million Native American people. Consequently, Bridges to the Future Doctoral Program worked to increase the number of American Indian and Alaska Natives holding PhDs in nursing from the twelve individuals who possessed this degree in 2001. The Bridges program sought to double this number by 2011 and train a cadre of students to work as scientists, conducting innovative and practical research that addressed the unique cultural needs of American Indian communities.[3]

The program included tribal elders and healers so that nursing students would have the benefit of drawing on their knowledge. The students met with these elders who generously shared their wisdom through stories. These gatherings helped reconcile a cultural gap that challenged American Indian students at the time and continues to do so today. In contrast to oral cultures, which place value on the wisdom of elders, medical science emphasizes research, the creation of new knowledge, and the knowledge of health care providers. Integrating elders into the Bridges to the Future Doctoral Program allowed students to pursue new research while remaining connected to traditional healing practices. The elders themselves had their own goals for engaging doctoral students at the University of Minnesota. The elders wanted to meet potential students and faculty members, expand cultural awareness among the PhD students, and give the students advice about pursuing their research in American Indian communities. The students and faculty involved in the program appreciated the insights of knowledgeable tribal elders about cultural issues that permitted students to complete important research into areas such as American Indian views of organ transplantation, cancer causation, diabetes, and obesity.[4]

In 2001, the AIAN MS-to-PhD Nursing Science Bridge received funding from the National Institute of General Medical Sciences to help educate American Indian and Alaska Native nurses. Nurses with PhD degrees could conduct research and share their findings in professional ways that would contribute to the elimination of inequalities in health issues. The program fit within the United States commitment to Healthy People 2010, a series of health-related objectives that the United States pursued during the first decade of the twenty-first century. One of these goals involved the improvement of minority health care in six areas including cancer screening and management, diabetes, cardiovascular disease, infant mortality, HIV and AIDs, and immunization.

Patchell's work fostered cooperation between Indigenous healing practices and modern medicine. Patchell's activism garnered greater attention for the traditional medical knowledge held by Native American cultures and resulted in the application of traditional and cultural knowledge to advance the quality of care available to patients. The growing interest in American Indian traditional healing practices has encouraged scientists to conduct studies of Indigenous forms of medicine, even though many medical specialists remain skeptical of Indigenous healers. Newer studies can help dispel the negative assessments of American Indian medicine that earlier scholars made regarding indigenous healing practices during the nineteenth and early twentieth centuries. In the past, historians and anthropologists have evaluated Indigenous healing practices using their own religious and cultural viewpoints. These preconceptions prompted earlier researchers to dismiss Native healing practices and Indian healers for not conforming to Western notions of medicine. Indian agents and missionaries wanted to eliminate native medicinal and religious practices as they viewed these traditional beliefs as an obstacle to the "progress" of American Indians on the path to "civilization." Settlers, in turn, pushed for the erasure of Native cultural practices to speed the assimilation of Native Americans to open additional land to white farmers. This rejection of native knowledge discouraged the serious investigation of Indigenous healing practices. Traditional healers kept their medical knowledge to themselves, sharing them only with other Indians. They wished to avoid the ridicule of themselves and their patients by hostile observers who might label their practices as backward. Fostering greater respect for American Indian traditions and individuals is also a critical part of improving outcomes for patients. One research study Beverly Patchell participated in sought to uncover American Indian experiences with cancer in Oklahoma. The study demonstrated a need for better support for American Indians to help them navigate the health care system. However, the study also revealed that physicians could help improve trust and acceptance by their American Indian patients if they demonstrated respect for their spiritual needs and perspectives.[5]

Prior to the Indian Religious Freedom Act of 1978, Native American concerns centered on the illegality of some healing practices. After the passage of the bill, Indigenous healers could practice their traditional forms of medicine more openly—but carefully. Healers worried about the abuse or misuse of their knowledge and frequently identified healing as something that needed to remain private due to its sacred nature. Many healers transmitted their knowledge orally, thereby limiting the number of written accounts available about their work and success. Last, scientists viewed traditional healers skeptically given their perceived lack of formal training in an academic setting. Rather than attending postgraduate schools to acquire their knowledge, traditional healers received their training from other healers, inherited the skills from ancestors, or responded to their selection by the community by quietly healing others. The scientific definition of medicine left little room for the consideration of the metaphysical elements of traditional healing practices. The spiritual focus of Indigenous healing thereby fell outside the boundaries established by scientific medicine. Beverly Patchell is one woman that has bridged the great divide between American Indian medicine and Western medicine as she has received training in both methods and has integrated both into her own practice. Through her advocacy, Patchell has argued for a greater respect for Native medicine on the part of the scientific community. Patchell's activism thereby stimulates greater scholarly respect for Native healing practices and communities while simultaneously drawing upon Indigenous knowledge to improve modern medicine.

Beverly Patchell's work and writings expanded the definitions of medicine and healing by integrating traditional healing practices with modern medicine. For example, native healing practices took a more holistic approach to medicine that considered the patient's spiritual, mental, and emotional wellbeing, rather than focusing on the body alone. This tendency remained fairly consistent among healers from different tribes and nations, for though these individuals relied upon different plants and other objects to bring about healing, they shared a holistic approach. Traditional healing practices eschewed the secular focus of modern medicine through an acknowledgment of mystical elements that transcend physical explanations for illness and curing. Patchell's efforts to draw from both modern medicine and traditional healing practices involved the employment of two different approaches to healing. Patchell's writings helped to draw a distinction between traditional healing practices and modern medicine in that Indigenous techniques were not merely a precursor of modern methods but a different form of healing. Portraying traditional healing practices as an earlier stage of Western medicine gave a false impression of linear progression. Such a conception hindered the evaluation American Indian medicine by continuing to cast it as "primitive." Patchell realized that Native American healing practices did not represent an earlier stage of Western medicine for Western medicine centered on a materialistic worldview. In contrast, Native healing practices remained rooted in spirituality. Patchell recognized that both traditional healing and Western medicine have their own unique uses that can complement each other to the benefit of the patient.

Patchell learned from tribal elders among many tribes that Native American medicine often differs from Western medicine because American Indian healers have a greater understanding of the mind-body connection. In dealing with the world of Western medicine, Patchell uses this in-depth knowledge to work her medicine on the "whole" person and their families. She often advises patients that their state of mind is significant to their recovery, and she helps them with techniques drawn from Native American cultures and her own experiences as a nurse. Patchell believes that healing can occur more effectively, efficiently, and timely if the patient is in a "positive" and "healing" state of mind, and she actively trains patients in simple methods that help them manage their state of mind in the healing process. Patchell also uses such native techniques to take the initiative in being positive and pro-active in their health. In these and other ways, Patchell is an activist in the field of medicine.

Patchell's work identifies positive elements found within traditional healing that exceed aspects of modern healing. For example, Indigenous healing methods focus on teaching the patient to achieve wellness. Indian doctors empower their patients to take an active role in their healing by providing them with a sense of control. Involving the patient in the healing process provides individuals with knowledge on how to improve their health. In contrast, modern medicine leaves the patient reliant upon medical doctors and the Western system of medicine. Western medicine places the responsibility for healing with doctors while relegating patients to a passive role that can exacerbate their feelings of powerlessness. An article that Patchell coauthored explained that modern medicine eliminated the more creative elements of healing while placing an almost-exclusive focus on the business side of the medical industry by treating medical care as a commodity. Healing remains centered on the care provider rather than the patient. Lastly, the health care industry tends to focus upon alleviating the symptoms of illness rather than attempting to restore the patient to wellness.[6] Patchell has made significant strides in combining the knowledge of Western medicine with the greater patient participation found in traditional medicine within her own practice. She has also trained others in the combination of these two styles of medical care by helping Native American students pursue advanced degrees in medicine and scientific research.

Beverly Patchell mentored American Indians interested in joining the medical profession. Patchell's work as the project director for the American Indian Nursing Student Success Program at the University of Oklahoma College of Nursing exemplified her desire to exhibit cultural sensitivity to American Indian concerns about demonstrating respect for elders and ancestors. In particular, many tribal elders worried about the growing apathy of younger American Indians for ancient wisdom as this sentiment limited the ability of communities to remain cohesive. Consequently, tribal elders identified a stark choice between having children that possess higher levels of formal education and children that remain tied to their traditions. Patchell's mentoring therefore included discussions with families of prospective students to demonstrate respect for their concerns and reveal that students do not have to make the choice between either respecting their culture or pursuing a formal education. Patchell's actions indicated a respect for American Indian beliefs that center on the communal impact of decisions. Patchell noted the Cherokee belief that one must evaluate the potential impact of a decision over seven generations and found that other tribes and nations held similar beliefs. Patchell's activism enabled her to achieve her goal of increasing the number of American Indians within the medical field while also assuaging the concerns of Native communities. The interviews also provided Patchell with the opportunity to assess how well the University of Oklahoma could meet the educational needs of the student.[7]

Patchell's work also centered on finding ways to help American Indian students adapt to the requirements and stresses present within the required academic coursework found in nursing school. She experimented with different methods of alleviating the nervousness of American Indians to enhance their ability to earn high grades on tests. These considerations led her to implement the HeartMath program at the University of Oklahoma. Patchell explained that the program enabled her to demonstrate to the families of nursing students how these prospective health care workers could maintain their own well-being. The information that Patchell collected also met the evidentiary requirements necessary to introduce the program within a university. Heart-Math research revealed that the heart did more than pump blood through the body as it also operated as a sensory organ, a hormonal gland, and a means of processing information. The HeartMath program introduced students to breathing techniques and positive thinking that enabled students to calm themselves and diminish the impact of nervousness. Patchell's advocacy on behalf of native students was significant as she realized the successful training of American Indian nurses required her to help students manage anxiety and the pressure of nursing school.

Patchell supplemented the HeartMath program with a focus on Tony Buzan's Mind Mapping to help students cope with the extensive amounts of memorization and reading required for nursing school. As nursing programs require students to analyze information and think critically, rote memorization remained ineffective. Mind mapping relies upon a 10-step process that employs colors, images, and key words to help nursing students to recall, analyze, and conceptualize information. The technique, developed in the late 1960s, relies upon multiple forms of thinking such as imagery, logic, color, verbal, and spatial awareness in order to improve retention. Patchell's introduction of these techniques significantly improved the success rate of American Indian nursing students. In addition to these forms of academic assistance, Patchell worked to enhance the health and well-being of nursing students as many returned to their communities with chronic illnesses with roots in their family history or the stress of nursing school. These conditions shortened careers of these nurses while simultaneously reducing their quality of life. Though a lack of data prohibits an analysis of the efficacy of the equipment installed in the student study room, the devices such as a reflexology machine and a Chi machine for oxygenation of the body represented attempts to provide students with accessible means of improving and maintaining their health. As a follow-up measure, the Health Sciences Center Campus established a Healing Community Wellness Center. [8]

Beverly Patchell was a faculty member at the University of Oklahoma School of Nursing while serving as Project Director for the American Indian Nursing Student Success Program and the co-director of the Center for Cultural Competency and Healthcare Excellence. As the site coordinator for the Bridges to the Doctorate Program, Patchell continued to offer courses in alternative medicine, culture, and spirituality to instruct new health care professionals about the importance of exhibiting cultural sensitivity for all of their patients. In addition, Beverly Patchell works as a consultant for the National Library of Medicine and the Smithsonian's National Museum of the American Indian on matters relating to traditional and contemporary American Indian medicine. She gives many talks across the nation about her work and the importance of considering the benefits of Indigenous healing practices in order to counteract lingering prejudice against American Indian cultures and beliefs. She is also a well-known native healer who combines her knowledge of Western medicine with Native American healing ways. She is a member of the Native American Healing Community international organization that seeks to heal the wounds of people, no matter their creed, color, or religious preference. Beverly Patchell is an activist in the world of American Indian health and well-being, a unique woman who gives of herself for the benefit of people, particularly American Indian people.

NOTES

1. Beverly Patchell, et al., "The Effect of a Culturally Tailored Substance Abuse Prevention Intervention with Plains Indian Adolescents," *Journal of Cultural Diversity* 22, no. 1 (Spring 2015): 3–5.

2. "Beverly Patchell: Blending Traditional and Western Medicine," American Indians and Alaska Natives in Health Careers, October 8, 2011, http://aianhealthcareers.org/page2/page46/page48/page48.html. Please note that this webpage has been removed and is no longer available online. The author of this chapter retains a printed copy of the webpage in his research notes.

3. Susan Henly et al., "Research Careers for American Indian/Alaska Native Nurses: Pathway to Elimination of Health Disparities," *American Journal of Public Health* 94, no. 4 (April 2006): 606–611.

4. Margaret Moss et al., "Strengthening American Indian Nurse Scientist Training Through Tradition: Partnering with Elders," *Journal of Cultural Diversity* 12, no. 2 (Summer 2005): 50–55.

5. Melissa Craft et al., "The Experience of Cancer in American Indians Living in Oklahoma," *Journal of Transcultural Nursing* 28, no. 3 (2017): 259–267.

6. Wayne Nickens and Beverly Patchell, "Creating a Healing Community," *Journal of Cultural Diversity* 12, no. 2 (Summer 2005): 59–61.

7. Beverly Patchell, "Mentoring in Multiple Dimensions," *Journal of Cultural Diversity* 12, no. 2 (Summer 2005): 56–59.

8. Beverly Patchell, "Mentoring in Multiple Dimensions." *Journal of Cultural Diversity* 12, no. 2 (Summer 2005): 57–59.

BIBLIOGRAPHY

"Beverly Patchell: Blending Traditional and Western Medicine." American Indians and Alaska Natives in Health Careers http://aianhealthcareers.org/page2/page46/page48/page48.html (accessed October 8, 2011).

Craft, Melissa, Beverly Patchell, Jack Friedman, Lancer Stephens, and Kathy Dwyer. "The Experience of Cancer in American Indians Living in Oklahoma." *Journal of Transcultural Nursing* 28, no. 3 (2017): 259–268.

Henly, Susan, Roxanne Struthers, Barbara Dahlen, Bette Ide, Beverly Patchell, and Barbara J. Holtzclaw. "Research Careers for American Indian/Alaska Native Nurses: Pathway to Elimination of Health Disparities." *American Journal of Public Health* 94, no. 4 (April 2006): 606–611.

Moss, Margaret, Lorayne Tibbets, Susan Henly, Barbara Dahlen, Beverly Patchell, and Roxanne Struthers. "Strengthening American Indian Nurse Scientist Training Through Tradition: Partnering with Elders." *Journal of Cultural Diversity* 12, no. 2 (Summer 2005): 50–55.

Nickens, Wayne and Beverly Patchell. "Creating a Healing Community." *Journal of Cultural Diversity* 12, no. 2 (Summer 2005): 59–61.

Patchell, Beverly. "Mentoring in Multiple Dimensions." *Journal of Cultural Diversity* 12, no. 2 (Summer 2005): 56–59.

Patchell, Beverly, Leslie Robbins, John Lowe, and Mary Hoke. "The Effect of a Culturally Tailored Substance Abuse Prevention Intervention with Plains Indian Adolescents." *Journal of Cultural Diversity* 22, no. 1 (Spring 2015): 3–8.

Struthers, Roxanne, Valerie Eschiti, and Beverly Patchell. "Traditional Indigenous Healing: Part I." *Complementary Therapies in Nursing and Midwifery* 10 (2004): 141–149.

FURTHER READING

Clifford E. Trafzer, Beverly Sourjohn Patchell, and Ronald Ray Cooper, *Comanche Medicine Man: Kenneth Coosewoon's Great Vision, Blue Medicine, and Sweatlodge Healings* (Camano Island: Coyote Hill Press, 2015).

Craft, Melissa, Beverly Patchell, Jack Friedman, Lancer Stephens, and Kathy Dwyer. "The Experience of Cancer in American Indians Living in Oklahoma." *Journal of Transcultural Nursing* 28, no. 3 (2017): 259–268.

Henly, Susan, Roxanne Struthers, Barbara Dahlen, Bette Ide, Beverly Patchell, and Barbara J. Holtzclaw. "Research Careers for American Indian/Alaska Native Nurses: Pathway to Elimination of Health Disparities." *American Journal of Public Health* 94, no. 4 (April 2006): 606–611.

Moss, Margaret, Lorayne Tibbets, Susan Henly, Barbara Dahlen, Beverly Patchell, and Roxanne Struthers. "Strengthening American Indian Nurse Scientist Training Through Tradition: Partnering with Elders." *Journal of Cultural Diversity* 12, no. 2 (Summer 2005): 50–55.

Nickens, Wayne and Beverly Patchell. "Creating a Healing Community." *Journal of Cultural Diversity* 12, no. 2 (Summer 2005): 59–61.

Patchell, Beverly. "Mentoring in Multiple Dimensions." *Journal of Cultural Diversity* 12, no. 2 (Summer 2005): 56–59.

Patchell, Beverly, Leslie Robbins, John Lowe, and Mary Hoke. "The Effect of a Culturally Tailored Substance Abuse Prevention Intervention with Plains Indian Adolescents." *Journal of Cultural Diversity* 22, no. 1 (Spring 2015): 3–8.

Struthers, Roxanne, Valerie Eschiti, and Beverly Patchell. "Traditional Indigenous Healing: Part I." *Complementary Therapies in Nursing and Midwifery* 10 (2004): 141–149.

Index

About the Editors

Clifford E. Trazer is Distinguished Professor of History and Rupert Costo Chair in American Indian Affairs at the University of California, Riverside. His most recent books include *Strong Hearts and Healing Hands: Southern California Indians and Field Nurses* and *Fighting Invisible Enemies*: *Health and Medical Transitions Among Southern California Indians*. Most recently, with Donna L. Akers and Amanda K. Wixon, he co-edited *Indigenous Activism: Profile of Native American Women* with Lexington Books.

Donna L. Akers (Choctaw) is a professor at the University of Texas, Arlington, where she is Chair of Ethnic Studies and Native American Studies. She has been a professor at California State University, Northridge, University of Indianapolis, and University of Nebraska. She is the author of several articles and *Living in the Land of Death: The Choctaw Nation, 1830–1860.* In 2021, Lexington Books released her co-edited book, *Indigenous Activism: Profile of Native American Women.*

Amanda K. Wixon (Chickasaw) and is a Ph.D. Candidate in History at the University of California, Riverside. For the past five years, Wixon has served as an Assistant Curator and Researcher at the Sherman Indian School Museum and the Gene Autry Western Center. She is currently writing a book-length manuscript on Sherman Institute as a site of Native American incarceration. In 2021, Lexington Books released her co-edited book, *Indigenous Activism: Profile of Native American Women.*

About the Contributors

Jordan N. Cohen is a current PhD student at the University of California, Riverside. Her work focuses on the history of medicine and science in the ancient Mediterranean, researching marginalized peoples and epistemologies.

Christie Time Firtha holds a PhD and is a professor of English and Ethnic Studies at Barstow College. Her writing focuses on Native American Literary History. Her favorite place to write is sitting next to her son in her home in the San Bernardino Mountains.

Sarah Wolk FitzGerald holds a PhD in History, and she is assistant professor in the Department of History at Valdosta State University in southern Georgia. Her work focuses on public history and the Civil Rights Movement.

Kimberly Norris Guerrero (Colville, Salish-Kootenai) is an actor, producer, writer, and director who centers her practice-based research around righting the misrepresentation and under-representation of Native Americans in mainstream media. Guerrero has worked extensively with Native youth using filmmaking as a tool for empowerment, and is a founding member of The StyleHorse Collective—an award-winning group of Indigenous artists who work with tribes to create educational film, online media, and music projects. Guerrero's lengthy acting resume includes appearances in *The Wilds*, *The Glorias*, and *Rutherford Falls*, though she's most often recognized as Jerry's Indian girlfriend on *Seinfeld*. She also originated the role of "Johnna" in Tracy Letts' Tony Award winning play, *August: Osage County*, which she performed in Chicago, on Broadway and in London. Guerrero received a BA from UCLA, and garnered an MFA in Creative Writing and Writing for Performing Arts from UCR, where she went on to join the faculty and currently serves as the Artistic Director in the department of Theatre, Film, and Digital Production.

Harlan Hoffman is a professor of history at Mount San Antonio College in Walnut, California. He holds a PhD in History from the University of California, Riverside.

Benjamin T. Jenkins is an assistant professor of history and University Archivist at the University of La Verne, where he directs the Public History Program. He received his PhD in Public History at the University of California, Riverside. His current research focuses on the connections between citrus agriculture and railroad transportation in Southern California. He has worked at Public History institutions such as the Richard M. Nixon Presidential Library and the Huntington Library. He is currently completing a book manuscript titled, "Octopus's Garden: Railroads, Citrus Agriculture, and the Emergence of Southern California."

Brendan Lindsay holds a PhD in History, and he is an associate professor of history at Sacramento State University, specializing in California History, Native American History, and Genocide Studies. He is best known for his groundbreaking book, *Murder State: California's Native American Genocide, 1846-1863* published by the University of Nebraska Press, 2012.

Michelle Lorimer holds a PhD in History. She is a historian and lecturer at California State University, San Bernardino where she focuses on the history of California, the United States, public history, and teaching history methods. She is the author of *Resurrecting the Past: The California Mission Myth.* She is also actively engaged with local and statewide organizations to enhance History-Social Science education in California schools.

Robert D. Miller received his PhD in history from UC Riverside in 2011. He currently teaches at California State University, San Marcos, San Diego Mesa College, and Saddleback College. His research interests focus on American Indians at the turn of the twentieth century and exploring how Native peoples understood and challenged U.S. empire, both at home and abroad.

Emily Molesworth-Teipe, Professor Emerita Fullerton College and recipient of the Teacher of the Year Award focuses her research on Colonial America and the history of Women in the United States. Her published works include *America's First Veteran and the Revolutionary War Pensions, Different Voices: Women in United States History, A Feminist Primer*, and the upcoming *Our Beloved Friend, the Life and Writings of Anne Emlen Mifflin*, the latter coedited with Professor Gary B. Nash.

Daisy Ocampo (Caxcan, or Caz' Ahmo, Indigenous Nation of Zacatecas, Mexico) holds a PhD in History, and she is an assistant professor of history at CSU San Bernardino. Her research in Native and Public History informs her work with museum exhibits, historical preservation projects, and community-based archives. Her research integrates critical race theory, decolonial praxis of tribal sovereignty, and community traditions to create a new direction of inclusivity in Public History that recognizes Indigenous people, voices, and community narratives.

Lisa Riggin is a professor and holds a PhD in History from the University of California, Riverside. She is the author of *San Francisco's Queen of Vice: The Strange Career of Abortionist Inez Brown Burns,* University of Nebraska Press (2017). Her research and writing testify to her ability to produce well-researched, accurate, and complex tales of vice, crime, backroom deals, and the vigorous fight for justice involving complicated and controversial figures. Riggin teaches history at California State University, Fullerton, and has done extensive research at the University of California, Berkeley, Bancroft Special Collections Library. Her recent research and writing won the coveted Andrew W. Mellon Foundation Research Fellowship granted by The Huntington Library, San Marino, California.

Meranda Roberts is a citizen of the Yerington Paiute Tribe and Chicana. In 2018, she earned her PhD from the University of California, Riverside. She is currently the Education Manager at the Museum of Us in San Diego, California, where she is working on creating programs/curriculum dedicated to anti-racism and decolonization.

Jeffrey Allen Smith is an associate professor and Chair of the History Department at the University of Hawai'i at Hilo. He holds a MA and PhD in American History.

Amanda K. Wixon is completing a PhD in History at the University of California, Riverside. She is assistant curator and researcher at Sherman Indian School Museum. She is an assistant curator at the Gene Autry Western Center. She is a member of the Chickasaw Nation.

Kevin Whalen holds a PhD in American History and he is associate professor of history and Native American and Indigenous studies at the University of Minnesota, Morris. He is the author of *Native Students at Work: American Indian Labor and Sherman Institute's Outing Program, 1900–1945.*

www.ingramcontent.com/pod-product-compliance
Lightning Source LLC
Chambersburg PA
CBHW022312280326
41932CB00010B/1073